THE NATIONAL TRUST

EXPLORING
UNSPOILT BRITAIN
AND NORTHERN IRELAND

THE NATIONAL TRUST

EXPLORING
UNSPOILT BRITAIN
AND NORTHERN IRELAND

EDITED BY DERRIK MERCER

OCTOPUS BOOKS

DEDICATION
To the memory of *Robin Wright*,
Managing Editor of the National Trust,
whose help and guidance were invaluable
in preparing this book.

Photograph on previous page:
Derwentwater, the Lake District

First published in 1985 by
Octopus Books Limited
59 Grosvenor Street
London W1X 9DA

© 1985 Octopus Books Limited

ISBN 0 7064 2237 6

Phototypeset by Tradespools Ltd, Frome, Somerset

Printed in Spain

CONTENTS

Introduction 6 · Map of the British Isles 7

SEASIDE

WATERSIDE

HILLSIDE

WOODSIDE

INTRODUCTION

The British Isles are not given to extremes. The mountains are not particularly high, the rivers notable neither for their length nor their ferocity. There are no deltas or deserts, no canyons or coral reefs. Yet in few other countries can such diversity of scenery be found – certainly not within any country of comparable size, and certainly not so readily accessible.

Nobody in Britain lives more than 92 miles from tidal water and few more than an hour's drive from the fretwork of fields, woods and hills that make up the British landscape. Rivers and moorland are on industrial doorsteps, lakes and mountains rarely more than half a day's travel. However, ease of access is only one aspect of 59 million people being squeezed onto two relatively small islands: no country in the world has more footpaths per square mile than the United Kingdom. It is this unrivalled network of footpaths that holds the key to exploring the coastal and countryside areas featured in this book.

There are magnificent drives to be undertaken within Britain and it is the motor car that has enabled most people to reach the more remote areas. However, it is only on foot that you can appreciate to the full the sights, sounds and scents of the unspoilt countryside. It is also on foot that you can escape the crowds which clog the roads and, worse, shatter the very tranquillity that draws people to the countryside.

The National Trust: Exploring Unspoilt Britain and Northern Ireland is designed for people willing to leave their vehicles in the car park and take to their feet. This need not be a daunting physical challenge. Indeed, it is remarkable how swiftly crowds thin out: a quarter of a mile from a car park and you are often on your own. It is on this basis that many of the areas featured in this book have been selected. Strictly speaking, there are no unexplored areas near conurbations such as London or Birmingham. And places such as Ben Lomond, 25 miles from Glasgow, and Seven Sisters, with 750,000 people living within 20 miles, are scarcely unvisited. Yet these areas are large enough to accommodate many visitors, with little threat to the beauty or wildlife.

Not all the places featured in this book are well known, however, but what they have in common, large or small, are Britain's two National Trust organisations. For many people the Trusts have become associated with grand country houses, magnificent gardens and historic sites. Yet the preservation of natural beauty has always been just as important and today the Trusts are the largest private landowners in Britain. Their coastal and inland properties amply reflect the diversity which is the hallmark of the British countryside. Woods and fenland, moors and cliffs, waterfalls and nature reserves, mountains and lakes – all are featured in *The National Trust: Exploring Unspoilt Britain and Northern Ireland.*

The 44 areas described in the book cover most parts of the country as well as most types of scenery. However, in some areas the Trusts own much more than they do in others. As a result of this disparity some regions are more strongly represented than others. Similarly, some of the areas featured in this book are totally owned by the Trust while others contain only an element of Trust land. In all cases, however, the presence of one or other of the Trusts will ensure that the beauty captured in these pages will be protected.

The areas have also been chosen in consultation with the Trusts to ensure that they can cope with additional visitors without jeopardizing their intrinsic appeal. All have footpaths which will enable people to devise walks to match their own energy and experience. This is not a book directed primarily at experienced ramblers however; it is more for the individual or family with modest ambitions and a less exacting definition of remoteness. This book provides an introduction to areas which may be unfamiliar and which can be explored without involving specific equipment or conspicuous energy. Walks in the mountains of Scotland, Wales and the Lake District do require energy, so in these and other upland areas low-level or valley strolls have been suggested.

Yet it is the relative wildness of the hills and moors that have such appeal to the urban heart. Who of the pioneers who risked imprisonment to establish long-distance footpaths would have foreseen the explosion of interest in the countryside that has occurred during the past 20 years? The National Trust of England, Wales and Northern Ireland, for instance, has grown from fewer than 10,000 members in 1945 to more than a million in the 1980s. Long-distance footpaths, national and country parks, nature and forest trails are all postwar phenomena; but familiarity should breed respect. Anyone tempted to explore the uplands should remember the first rule of rambling: never overestimate your capabilities, never underestimate the elements.

For many of us, this warning will be unneces-sary; a day by the sea or in the countryside is a day for relaxing rather than exertion. And this book should be as helpful to the picnicker as it is to the walker. However, it aims to help people not only to get away from crowds but also to interpret and understand what they see. In the natural world knowledge enhances appreciation. Thus you will find explanations of how particular features came to be formed along with drawings of the wildlife you might encounter. You will discover how former sea beds were transformed into ranges of hills. You can learn to recognize how earlier generations shaped the landscape as they cleared the forests, reclaimed the fens and created lakes. Or you could ignore all this and simply revel in the glory of the countryside.

John Fowles, the novelist, once wrote:

'Never be brainwashed into thinking that the countryside is some fiendish identification test, which you will fail if you cannot name everything you meet. Seeing and feeling are just as important, and too many names act like blinkers: they narrow vision.' The countryside exerts its magic whether or not you recognize a single birdsong or identify a solitary flower.

The emphasis of the book is on the less familiar properties owned by the two National Trusts or, at least, the less familiar corners of the better-known areas. Each area includes a section detailing other nearby attractions to visit; these are mostly, but not always, National Trust properties. At the end of the book there are telephone numbers of National Trust and tourist board offices for each of 44 areas featured. There is also a section giving advice on what to wear if tempted by more serious walking and explaining how to get the best out of maps. For if footpaths are the key to getting away from the crowds, then maps are the means to their discovery. Luckily, in the Ordnance Survey, Britain has a map-maker to match the richness of its footpaths. An appendix lists the wildlife shown in the book, along with the pages where the illustrations can be found. Finally, there is information about the two National Trust organisations without whom this book – and, to an important degree, the countryside it describes – would not exist.

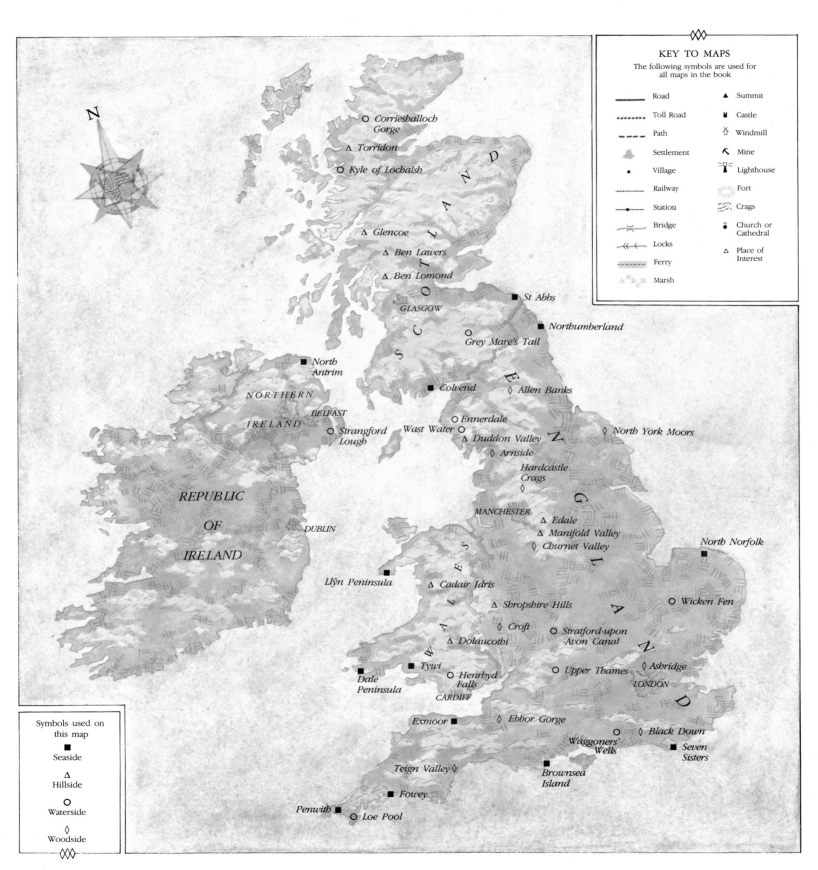

N

KEY TO MAPS

The following symbols are used for all maps in the book

———	Road	▲	Summit
••••••	Toll Road	⛫	Castle
– – –	Path	☘	Windmill
🏠	Settlement	⛏	Mine
•	Village	🗼	Lighthouse
┼┼┼┼	Railway	⚙	Fort
┼●┼	Station	⛰	Crags
⌒	Bridge	✚	Church or Cathedral
⋘	Locks	△	Place of Interest
– – –	Ferry		
⚘	Marsh		

SCOTLAND

○ Corrieshalloch Gorge

△ Torridon

○ Kyle of Lochalsh

△ Glencoe

△ Ben Lawers

△ Ben Lomond

GLASGOW

■ St Abbs

■ Northumberland

○ Grey Mare's Tail

◇ Allen Banks

■ North Antrim

NORTHERN IRELAND

BELFAST

○ Strangford Lough

○ Ennerdale

Wast Water ○

△ Duddon Valley

◇ Arnside

■ Colvend

◇ North York Moors

Hardcastle Crags

REPUBLIC OF IRELAND

DUBLIN

MANCHESTER

△ Edale

△ Manifold Valley

◇ Churnet Valley

■ North Norfolk

E N G L A N D

Llŷn Peninsula ■

△ Cadair Idris

△ Shropshire Hills

○ Wicken Fen

W A L E S

◇ Croft

○ Stratford-upon-Avon Canal

△ Dolaucothi

■ Tywi

○ Henrhyd Falls

○ Upper Thames

◇ Ashridge

LONDON

Dale Peninsula ■

CARDIFF

Exmoor ■

◇ Ebbor Gorge

◇ Black Down

Waggoners' Wells

■ Seven Sisters

Teign Valley ◇

■ Brownsea Island

■ Fowey

Penwith ■

○ Loe Pool

Symbols used on this map

■ Seaside

△ Hillside

○ Waterside

◇ Woodside

7

SEASIDE

No country in the world of comparable size has a more varied coastline than that of the United Kingdom. Its length alone is remarkable—6,000 miles or the equivalent of a return trip between London and New York. And that total excludes Northern Ireland. Few people are more than a couple of hour's drive from the coast.

It is a sinuous coastline of startling contrasts. Rugged granite cliffs are pounded by Atlantic rollers barely a dozen miles from where sedate waves lap the banks of a sleepy, wooded estuary creek. Rock stacks and caves, silvery beaches and salt marshes—'seaside' seems blandly inadequate for so majestic a coastline.

Yet the timeless quality of the shore is deceptive. Nature's margins, where land and sea meet, are never static. The shore is under constant attack from the erosive power of the sea. In places the rocks are so tough that change will be immeasurable in a human lifetime. But there are coastlines where cliffs are crumbling under the onslaught and retreating at several feet a year. About 30 villages have disappeared under the sea off the fragile Holderness coast of Yorkshire, the most rapidly eroding coastline in Europe. Sea levels also change, turning river valleys into tidal estuaries such as at Fowey or Falmouth. Elsewhere, the shore nudges out into the sea as tidal action builds up sand bars or shingle spits behind which marshland develops; this, in time, can be reclaimed as farmland.

Human activity has also contributed to the distinctive shoreline, for Britain's history has been shaped by its ability to defend its island fortress. This legacy can still be seen today—from Iron Age hill forts to Martello Towers, from the Roman forts of the Saxon shore to the medieval castles of Edward I in Wales. The sea has also been a means of earning a living, as well as a barrier against attack, so that the coastline is dotted with harbours. Some are great ports, for Britain has always been a trading nation; others are picturesque fishing villages.

The sea has been a place of recreation for barely two centuries. It was the coming of the railway that first encouraged large numbers of people to discover the seaside. In particular, the railway opened up the West Country which became the most popular of all British holiday areas. The motor age was in some ways less beneficent, spawning a profusion of caravan camps and car parks to litter the coastline. Yet cars can also enable discriminating tourists to elude the crowds which clog the quaint harbours and the transistor radios polluting quiet bays. The National Trusts have led the way in preserving the best of the unspoilt coastline. The Countryside Commissions are also actively protecting stretches of 'heritage coast' and turning old coastguard tracks into long-distance footpaths. Much still remains to be done, but anyone willing to venture beyond the car parks can now rejoice in a beauty happily protected for future generations.

The sea has shaped the history of the British Isles both as a means of defence and exploration. It continues to be a dominant force in many people's lives, either as a place of work or play.

Clockwise from below: Solva in Dyfed provides a sheltered harbour once used for trade — legal and illegal — but now mainly used for sailing; majestic Bamburgh Castle crowns a rocky throne which was once the seat of Northumbrian kings; the Valley of the Rocks in North Devon towers 800 feet above the sea; seabirds such as the puffin are very much at home on Skomer Island, a national nature reserve; Porth Ysgo is a tiny unspoilt bay in Llŷn, northwest Wales, where the waves splashing around the rocks retreat at low tide to reveal a sand-and-shingle beach.

Penwith

Map OS map SW 33/43 in 1:25000 series is best for walkers

West Penwith is the toe of England. The peninsula culminates in Land's End where walkers on the long-distance footpath are joined by day-trippers who come to gaze out across 3,000 miles of the Atlantic. The peninsula includes such tourist honeypots as St Ives and Mousehole, yet the northern shore contains some of the wildest coastlines in England.

Paths once used by smugglers lead down to coves at Portheras and Portmeor but this is essentially a coast for walking rather than bathing. Unless, that is, you want to test your skills against rock faces used for training by Royal Marine commandos. A footpath winds a sinuous course above these sheer cliffs and remote coves between rugged headlands such as Gurnard's and Zennor Heads. So winding is the coastline that the seven miles between Carn Naun Point to Pendeen Watch Lighthouse — as the crow flies — is half as much again on foot or along the B3306 which tracks the coastline a short distance inland.

Inland the landscape is equally wild with the road effectively separating a narrow shelf of farmland from a craggy succession of granite hills. Few trees grow here in the face of the Atlantic gales and most of the highest land has remained untamed. Yet this very remoteness and wildness has helped to ensure the survival of some remarkable species of Celtic Britain: nowhere else' in the country has so many antiquities in so small an area. Even the tiny stone-walled fields date back 2,000 years or more. The lack of trees meant that local granite had to be used as a building material not only for walls but even for the stiles between the fields. Narrow shafts of stone were laid horizontally to form 'stile grids' many of which still remain along the paths around the hamlets of Zennor and Morvah.

Agricultural reclamation, aided by development grants, poses a continuing threat to the unspoilt moorland, ancient field systems and other antiquities, but much of the coastline is now owned — and protected — by the National Trust. Although there is a long history of settlement on Penwith, it is now sparse and scattered, with small-scale dairy farming the prime occupation. Here and there, though, isolated chimneys and ruined buildings stand as broken memorials of a once-thriving tin industry. Several were worked into the 20th century but now only one remains — at Geevor, west of Pendeen.

Tin mine

Above Gurnard's Head epitomizes the rugged north Cornwall coast. Remnants of an Iron Age hill fort and a 19th-century tin mine recall man's past attempts to tame this bleak craggy headland. Now only the birds remain. ◇

Above Tin has been mined since pre-Roman times in Cornwall. Many inland paths in southern England, now happily trod by walkers, were old mining tracks developed as a result of the tin trade. Most of the mines were forced to close, however, when newly discovered—and cheap— tin from Malaya took control of the market in the 1870's. Scattered across the countryside, the ruins of the chimneys and engine houses can still be seen—such as this one at Bosigran—mute testimony to the struggle of miners against water. ◇

Herring Gull

Above Herring gulls nest along cliffs in early summer but in winter often scavenge for food in fishing ports. ◇

Below Chysauster is an astonishing survival of an Iron Age village. Nine houses remain, each with a labyrinth of rooms opening on to a central courtyard. ◇

Exploring the coast

Old coastguard tracks along the clifftops form the South-West Peninsula Coast long-distance footpath. Clearly waymarked, it runs roughly parallel to the B3306. In summer a bus service plies this road, enabling walkers to return to their starting point; details are available from local tourist offices. Although nothing can match the grandeur of the cliffs and coves, there are inland paths which can enable shorter circuits to be devised—notably the Church Path near Zennor and one from Treveal to Mussel Point on the coast. ◇

Lanyon Quoit

Prehistoric Penwith

Why should Penwith be so rich in prehistoric remains? One reason is its location: too remote for large-scale development, too unsuitable for intensive agriculture. And since the lack of woodland forced the inhabitants to build in stone, the buildings have survived the erosion of the centuries.

Cornwall was also a place of some importance in prehistoric times. It had tin, discovered during the Bronze Age, and its position made it a port of call for sea adventurers from Brittany and Wales.

The combination of these factors has produced a rich array of remains from stone circles to hill

Men-an-tol

forts, burial mounds to a complete village. The oldest are the *cromlechs* or *quoits* — stones which were once the skeleton of grass-covered burial mounds. Lanyon Quoit is easiest to reach but Chun Quoit is the best preserved. There are several stone circles, all presumed to have religious origins as is Men-an-tol — the monument with a hole. Iron-Age settlements of Chun Castle and Chysauster both survived into Roman times. ◇

Discovering the wildlife

Late spring and late summer are the most colourful times around Penwith. In spring, thrift adds waves of pink blooms to cliffs while a purple swathe of heather marks the end of summer.

Gorse, too, is everywhere, sometimes blanketed by the red tendrils of that strange parasitic plant, the dodder. The Bosigran area is probably the most rewarding spot for anyone interested in flora, since here is a range of natural vegetation uninterrupted by farmland from sea level to the granite summit

of Carn Galver. Small streams further diversify the flora and in the summer hedges and walls are enlivened by campion and pennywort. But Penwith is virtually treeless; few survive the battering Atlantic gales.

Seabirds nest on the coast, although not in great numbers. The cliffs of Bosigran provide the ledges favoured for breeding by kittiwakes and auks. Fulmars have colonized a few sites, but you are as likely to see land-based birds — ravens, jackdaws, meadow pipits and kestrels. Gulls are everywhere.

Seals often cluster on the Carracks, or the Seal Islands as the St Ives boatmen craftily advertize them. Could the legendary mermaid of Zennor — immortalized in the parish church — owe her origins to a seal? ◇

Worth a detour
St Michael's Mount Famous castle linked by causeway to mainland at low tide. At Marazion S of A393. NT.
The Mines Restored engines at Pool, S of Camborne, and winding houses at Bosigran SW of St Ives on B3306. NT.
Trengwainton Large shrub garden with many plants which seldom grow outdoors elsewhere in England. 2 miles NW of Penzance. NT.

Fowey

Daphne du Maurier

Above Novelist Daphne du Maurier has lived around Fowey for most of her life. Menabilly, one former home south of The Gribbin, was used as Manderley in *Rebecca* while Polruan is the setting for *The Loving Spirit* and Polkerris for *The House on the Strand*. Pont Pill vies with Frenchman's Pill off Helford River as the inspiration for *Frenchman's Creek.*
The eponymous Jamaica Inn still stands on Bodmin moor, but souvenir shops are more in evidence than desperate smugglers. ◇

Right Rock samphire produces narrow, fleshy leaves which can be pickled and eaten. It flowers in late summer. ◇

Rock Samphire

Cornwall and the sea are inseparable. No English county has a longer coastline: even in the heart of Bodmin Moor you are barely 15 miles from the shore. More people holiday in the southwest than in any other region and many are no doubt lured by romantic images of Atlantic waves breaking endlessly over beaches of golden sand.

But this image of rugged coasts, as epitomized by Penwith, is only one face of Cornwall. There is also a softer south where wide river estuaries have carved deeply into the rocky plateau of Cornwall and Devon and where trees stretch down to the waterline of placid creeks. Whereas the northern coast has only one major estuary — at Padstow — the south has Helford, Fowey and Falmouth in Cornwall alone.

These estuaries were formed when sea levels rose after the last Ice Age to turn what were once river valleys into tidal estuaries; the rivers that flow north in Cornwall and Devon follow shorter and steeper courses which accordingly lack the size and depth to produce an estuary. Fowey is typical of these drowned river valleys, or *rias*, and since Roman times its natural harbour has been used for commercial traffic, with china clay today replacing tin as the staple product of trade. Two tiny ferries shuttle across the busy harbour, threading their way between the ubiquitous dinghies of modern sailing.

Fowey itself is a town of narrow streets, barely wide enough for a single car, which offers magnificent views over the harbour. It becomes quite crowded in the summer but still manages to avoid the commercialization rampant in Polperro some eight miles to the east. Yet for those who seek it, tranquillity is rarely more than a short walk or ferry ride away. Pont Pill, for instance, is a wooded creek that can be explored only by foot or boat; east and west of Fowey the cliffs are softened by coves such as Polridmouth and Lantic Bay which, again, are the preserve of walkers rather than motorists. The cliffs themselves are largely owned by the National Trust and are crossed by the long-distance path which follows the 268 miles of Cornwall's contrasting coastlines.

Robin

Left Polridmouth Bay is typical of many coves along the gentler southern coast of Cornwall: small, safe and secluded. Polridmouth (which is pronounced *Pridmouth*) is rarely crowded as it can be reached only by a half-mile walk from either of the National Trust car parks at Menabilly Barton or Lankelly Lane. Behind the cove, at the foot of the valley, a dam has formed a freshwater lake. ◇

Left The robin, easily the most recognizable bird in Britain. Both sexes have red breasts and defend their own territories. ◇

Below Bodinnick is just a ferry ride away from Fowey. Follow the lane which climbs the hill for an excellent view of Fowey and the estuary. ◇

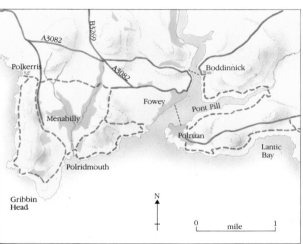

Discovering the wildlife
The headlands around Fowey are neither so high nor so rugged as those of the north coast. But the cliffs are still breezy enough to restrict trees to a few stunted ash and blackthorn. Pont Pill is much richer with oak, ash, hazel, chestnut, sycamore and beech along the slopes. Birds attracted here include the wren, chaffinch and robin, while on the open grassland kestrel, skylark, meadow pipit, wheatear, stonechat and the occasional buzzard can be seen. Animal life is limited, as well as elusive, with weasel, stoat, badger, rabbit and the grey squirrel the most common. On the clifftops cornflower, field pansy, field speedwell and tormentil are found with tree mallow and rock samphire on the cliff faces and sea spurge on the shoreline. ◇

Exploring the coast
The Fowey area offers good and varied walking, both around the sheltered waters of the estuary and along the clifftop paths.
Hall Walk There is a ferry (and a pub) at the beginning and end of this circular four-mile walk around the wooded creek of Pont Pill opposite Fowey. Start from either Bodinnick ferry (from where a sign, a short distance past the inn, says 'Hall Walk') or from Polruan ferry (from where the sign at the crossroads says 'To the Hills'). Either way it offers magnificent views across the harbour. It is mostly easy walking with only two steep climbs and a good picnic place at the creek head.
The Gribbin Longer walks can be devised by using sections of the coastal footpath. One circuit leads via the sandy cove of Polridmouth and The Gribbin to the tiny harbour of Polkerris. The Gribbin headland is topped by a red-and-white 'day mark'

erected in 1832 to warn ships. There are stupendous views from the headland but the old coastguard track includes some steep climbs. Fowey to Polkerris via the coastal path is 5½ miles but other paths offer short cuts, and can also lead to the beach at Polridmouth. ◇

Worth a detour
Lanhydrock   17th-century house largely rebuilt in the 19th century with formal gardens and woods. 2½ miles SE of Bodmin. NT.
Cotehele Medieval house with garden, pond, watermill and quay with shipping museum. On W bank of Tamar 8 miles SW of Tavistock. NT.
Antony House 18th-century house surrounded by extensive grounds, also on W banks of Tamar. 2 miles NW of Torpoint. NT.

Exmoor

Map OS Tourist Map of Exmoor

The cliffs of the Exmoor coast are rarely craggy, but they lack neither height nor drama. In places, the moorland plateau of 1,000 feet falls to the sea in barely half a mile of thickly wooded slopes; Countisbury Hill, for instance, reaches 991 feet within a quarter of a mile from the shore. Moorland streams tumble energetically to the sea, carving steep clefts into the convex cliffs. Only at Lynmouth, where two rivers meet, is there a valley large enough to contain a modest-sized coastal village: a location which was to prove tragic in 1952 when floods swept through its houses. Elsewhere, until the Vale of Porlock marks the eastern boundary of true Exmoor, this is a coastline where neither settlement nor road touches the shore. The steepness of the cliffs also means that there are few beaches, even for those willing to clamber down (and up) precipitous paths to the shore. It is, above all, a coastline for walking with superb views over the Bristol Channel.

The South-West Peninsula Coast path tracks the coast throughout and by following the contours at about 400 feet, it avoids many of the steeper gradients encountered by motorists. The path begins (or ends) at Minehead just east of the Exmoor national park and continues for 512 miles to Poole Harbour.

However, other paths can be combined to produce more modest circuits. Much of the land between Minehead in the east and Combe Martin in the west is owned by the National Trust; only around Selworthy or in the Valley of the Rocks are you likely to encounter summer crowds away from the main roads. The only

substantial breach in the hills occurs at Porlock Bay where a shingle beach protects fertile agricultural land. It is the juxtaposition of uplands and coast that give this area its unique character. Nowhere else in England are the cliffs so high and so densely wooded — and with popular resorts such as Minehead and Ilfracombe as the gateways to the Exmoor coast, it offers easy accessibility with an unspoilt natural beauty rare in southwest England.

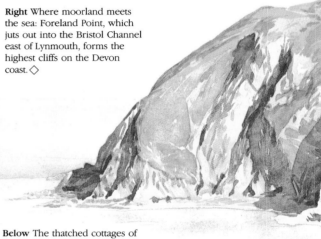

Right Where moorland meets the sea: Foreland Point, which juts out into the Bristol Channel east of Lynmouth, forms the highest cliffs on the Devon coast. ◇

Below The thatched cottages of Selworthy, one of the prettiest villages in England, overlook the magnificent Somerset countryside. ◇

Culbone Church

Above Culbone church is only 34 feet long and 12 feet wide — the smallest active church in England. The vicar comes by land rover, otherwise it's a two mile walk from Porlock Weir. ◇

Exploring the coast · 1
Minehead is a town with two faces: a conventional seaside resort onto which a vast holiday camp was grafted and the older Higher Town where colour-washed cottages huddle between cobbled streets. The Exmoor national park boundary begins just west of the town where footpaths take over from dead-end roads. Although the paths avoid some unstable sea-facing slopes, the views can be remarkable — as far as Wales in one direction or across to Dunkery Beacon on Exmoor. Where the roads end a variety of walks begin: around Church Combe to Bossington Hill with its view across Porlock Bay or downhill through the woods to Allerford and Selworthy.
The highest point is Selworthy Beacon at 1,013 feet and this, like much of the area, is owned by the National Trust as part of its Holnicote estate. Skylarks, meadow pipits and whinchats are the common birds. The vegetation is mostly gorse, ling heather and bracken but tormentil and milkwort are also on display during the summer. ◇

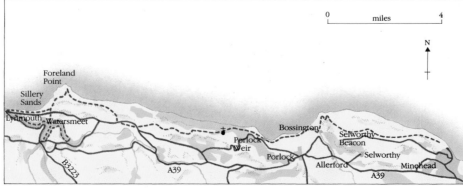

Exploring the coast · 2

Porlock Weir marks a dramatic change in the scenery for the traveller heading west. Behind him is the Vale of Porlock, two miles of lush pasture land; ahead are the 'hog's back' cliffs of Exmoor. Almost immediately the coastal path plunges into thick woodland, mostly oak, but the walking is surprisingly easy; while cars are grinding up the notorious 1 in 4 slopes of Porlock Hill a little inland, the walker meanders round the 400-foot contour line.

Two miles beyond Porlock is what is claimed to be England's smallest church, at Culbone. It measures just 34 by 12 feet with seats for 30 people. Services are still held regularly, with the vicar arriving by land rover.

Beyond Culbone, there is a high-level path through farmland or a woodland route along what is probably the most unspoilt stretch of the Exmoor coastal path. Apart from the zigzag path down to the shore at the Glenthorne Valley, there is no escape until the two routes meet up again shortly before Foreland Point on Countisbury Hill. ◇

Right Sea milkwort, a creeping plant, is common by sea and saltmarsh. Its tiny pink flowers, growing on leafy spikes, have no petals but petal-like sepals. ◇

Sea Milkwort

Right Whinchats are among Britain's earliest summer visitors. On Exmoor they tend to congregate where the heath and gorse of the moors merge with the farmland. ◇

Whinchat

Exploring the coast · 3

Foreland Point juts out into the Bristol Channel to produce the highest cliffs in Devon. A lighthouse is perched on the headland, but so steeply does the land rise to Countisbury Hill beyond that this is reached by a *descent* of terrifying gradients down arid, scree-sided Caddow Combe. The lighthouse is by no means the first attempt to exploit these heights. A mile away, on Wind Hill, just west of the hamlet of Countisbury, the ramparts of an Iron Age hill fort still remain. As a viewpoint, Wind Hill has much to commend it: to the north the open grassland of Foreland Point and the sea, to the south the wooded valley of the East Lyn river. Much of the area is owned by the National Trust with public access possible not only to the lighthouse (for walkers) but also down to the shore at Sillery Sands. This is one of the few beaches along the Exmoor coast, although the climb is inevitably steep. However the cliffs themselves can be dangerous. Walkers are therefore advised to stick to the paths described in a Trust leaflet. ◇

17

Exmoor

Immediately west of Lynmouth (and its sister town of Lynton on top of the hill) lies the Valley of Rocks: a strange amphitheatre or dry valley of rocky outcrops which can hardly claim to be remote in midsummer. This is partly because a minor road heads into the eastern end of a valley that is utterly unlike anything else along the 28 miles of the Exmoor coast. It is also relatively flat for this coast, running for about a mile west of Lynton, almost parallel to the shore. The valley was probably formed during the Ice Age either as a result of ice blocking the pre-glacial course of the Lyn rivers or by meltwater pouring off the frozen Bristol Channel. Whatever the cause, the valley was left stranded 800 feet above the sea over which jagged, frost-eroded rocks form almost sheer cliffs.

Beyond the Valley of Rocks (and 19th-century Lee Abbey) lies Woody Bay, where the National Trust's holdings begin again. A path leads to a sandy shore where the stumpy remains of a pier are all that is left of a plan to turn Woody Bay into a resort served by paddle steamers. One mile further west is Heddon Valley where the sea can be reached without the steep climbs encountered at Woody Bay. However at both Heddon's Mouth and Woody Bay the lower cliffs have been undercut by the sea and can be dangerous. The two areas are linked by two paths along the cliffs, one higher than the other, to form an enjoyable circuit of three miles combining some of Exmoor's most memorable coast, woodland and moorland. There is also the site of a Roman fortlet near the higher path, while valley paths offer sheltered walking when bad weather makes the clifftops perhaps too bracing. The paths form part of the 512-mile coastal route from Minehead in Somerset to Poole Harbour in Dorset.

From Heddon the coastal path heads westward along the exposed moorland of Trentishoe Down, past a curious isolated oak wood called Neck Wood clinging tenaciously to a 1 in 2 slope. Trentishoe and Holdstone Downs are both over 1,000 feet high and bear Bronze Age barrows on their summits. The last lap of the westward journey is reached as you cross Sherry Combe and climb the Great Hangman. This, too, is owned by the Trust as is the Little Hangman nearer Combe Martin where Exmoor's coast gloriously ends.

Discovering the wildlife

Only rarely does the bare rock show itself along the Exmoor coast. Mostly the slopes below the moorland plateau are covered by trees, sometimes — as at Woody Bay — virtually beginning at sea level. The steepness of the slopes, which has precluded both agriculture and settlement, has also deterred foresters so that the woodland we see today is mostly naturally-regenerating sessile oak. Although the woodland is traditional it is also vulnerable. The thin and rocky soils rarely allow deep roots to grow so that winter storms can flatten acres of woodland.

Nevertheless, enough oak remains for this to exercise a profound influence on the wild-life as well as the scenery. Thus the red deer as well as badgers and foxes find shelter in wooded areas surprisingly close to the shore. And birdlife is also more varied than is customary along the seashore. However, the lack of rocky ledges and stacks does make the Exmoor coast somewhat inhospitable to seabirds. In fact, the areas west of the Foreland offer the most suitable sites for breeding, so it's around places such as Heddon's Mouth that you see gulls, auks, guillemots, fulmars and kittiwakes. ◇

Japanese Knotweed

Above Japanese knotweed is an impressively tall plant which grows in clumps; its reddish stems bear heart-shaped leaves and small creamy flowers which bloom in late summer. ◇

Irish Spurge

Above Irish spurge, common in southwest Ireland, makes a guest appearance here and in Cornwall. Its flowerhead is, appropriately, bright green. Beware of the stem, it contains poisonous juice. ◇

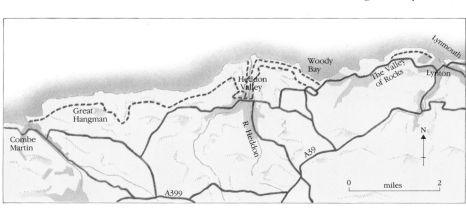

Below The Valley of the Rocks, west of Lynton and Lynmouth, is aptly named. Jagged frost-eroded rocks form crags overlooking not only the valley itself, but also the tossing sea 800 feet below. ◇

Above The gentler, wooded slopes of Heddon Valley offer a stark contrast to the Valley of the Rocks further east—and also a safe route to the shore. ◇

Left Moorland and sea are never far apart along Exmoor's coast but they are never more gloriously separated than at Watersmeet where the East Lyn river carves a wooded gorge to the sea. ◇

Worth a detour

Arlington Court 19th-century house with lake and woodland. Nature walk, stables with collection of horse-drawn vehicles. 7 miles NE of Barnstaple. NT.
Coleridge Cottage The house in Lime Street, Nether Stowey, where Coleridge wrote part of *The Ancient Mariner*. 8 miles W of Bridgwater on A39. NT.
Dunster Attractive village dominated by its castle, a 13th-century building remodelled in the 19th (NT). Outstanding 17th-century octagonal market, old watermills, packhorse bridges and inns. 2 miles SE of Minehead.
Lundy Island 11 miles offshore, totally unspoilt (no cars), interesting birdlife. Occasional daytrips from Ilfracombe and Bideford.

Exploring the countryside

There are no great rivers and no great estuaries along the north Devon coast east of Ilfracombe. The 'watershed' on Exmoor is too close to the shore for the rivers to acquire either length or width. However they race down the steep slopes of the Exmoor coast with a ferocity not found anywhere else in southwest England. Nowhere is this more evident or more accessible than in the valley of the East Lyn near Lynmouth.

This is one of two rivers which meet to form the only valley of any significance along the main stretch of Exmoor's coast. For the last two miles of its course the East Lyn tumbles down a lush, wooded gorge almost entirely owned by the National Trust. At the heart of its estate, at the confluence of the East Lyn and Hoaroak Water, the Trust has converted a Victorian fishing lodge into a visitor centre and summer café appropriately known as Watersmeet. From here paths lead in all directions, some past waterfalls and over rustic bridges at stream level, others climbing high through the oak trees to the moors and farmland beyond.

There are rare flowers such as Irish spurge and unusual trees such as the Devon whitebeam. Indeed, the flora generally — from the lichens of the scree slopes to the ferns and mosses of the wetter areas — is of great interest to naturalists. Birdlife is similarly rich, with the dipper and the grey wagtail often in evidence, bobbing around on the fast-flowing waters. ◇

19

Brownsea

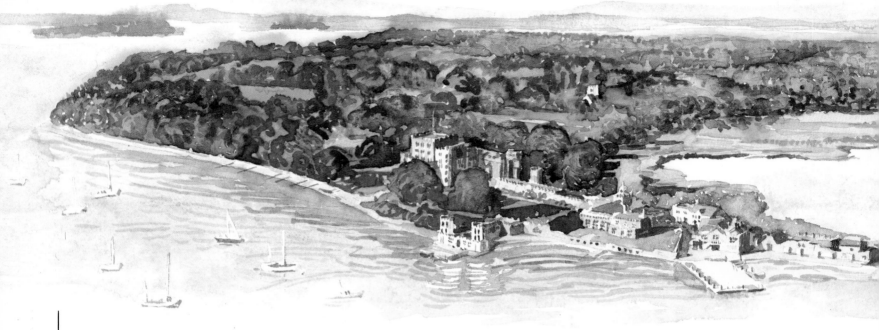

Map OS map 15 in
Outdoor Leisure series

Brownsea lies barely a quarter of a mile offshore, astride the narrow neck of Poole Harbour: close enough for boats to make frequent trips in summer yet far enough to ensure that the island remains an oasis of relative tranquillity compared to the busy beaches of neighbouring Bournemouth and Studland. Even those who do make the short crossing tend to congregate in the east, leaving western beaches less visited.

Although Brownsea is small — 1½ miles long and ¾ mile wide — it contains a wide range of habitats. There are pine woods as well as deciduous trees, saltmarshes and cliffs, freshwater lakes and a lagoon in addition to the sandy beaches. Yet the unspoilt nature of Brownsea, which is its greatest attraction, is both more recent and less natural than it might seem. It only became an island some 10,000 years ago when sea levels rose after the Ice Age to flood the low-lying heath, thus forming Poole Harbour. And until 200 years ago Brownsea had remained typical of heath and marshland, with a little clay quarrying.

In the 18th century, however, much of the heath was reclaimed and cultivated. Peat was dug to form two lakes, a million conifers planted and saltmarsh reclaimed. By 1900, much of the island was arable or pasture; wild daffodils today reflect the market gardening of that time. Branksea Castle had by then been built, as a Gothic casing for Henry VIII's fortress, along with the church and harbour cottages.

Private ownership was not always benevolent and in the 20th century prosperity waned, reversing to some extent the earlier processes of reclamation. The lagoon, for instance, was once reclaimed pasture. Marsh has returned although, like the heathland, it has to be maintained in order to curb the natural invasion of scrub and woodland. Since 1962 the responsibility for maintaining this fragile balance between nature and man has rested with the National Trust, although part of the island is leased to the Dorset Naturalists' Trust as a nature reserve.

Access to the island is limited to six months a year,

Discovering the wildlife
Woodland and water provide the foundation for the rich array of wildlife on Brownsea Island. The mixture of trees, from Scots pine to beech and oak, attracts most of the common woodland birds such as chaffinches, wrens, robins and various tits in addition to the birds shown here. Although the red squirrel is perhaps the most rewarding sight among the animals, Sika deer have swum across from the mainland to set up a colony on the island.
The natural attraction of the lagoon has been enhanced by

the construction of man-made islands which resemble shingle banks; these have successfully attracted common terns which breed there every summer. Herring and black-headed gulls join the oystercatchers nesting along the shore while grebes and tufted ducks prefer the freshwater lakes to be found inland. In the marsh bordering the lagoon, reed and sedge warblers can often be heard singing on warm summer days. More exotic, however, are the peacocks and golden pheasants wandering about on the island. ◇

Right Shoveler and wigeon are among winter visitors to the lagoon, both breeding further north. Also seen in winter are pintail, shelduck and avocet. ◇

Oystercatcher

Dunlin

Bar-tailed Godwit

Left Oystercatchers nest along the lagoon shore in the summer while terns breed on specially-built banks. Late summer sees dunlins and bar-tailed godwits. ◇

Wigeon

Shoveler

Left Brownsea Island is the largest of five islands within yacht-bedecked Poole Harbour — and the only one which the public is allowed to visit. ◇

Lord Robert Baden-Powell

from April to September. Boats operate from Poole Quay and Sandbanks to Brownsea's eastern quay where there is a Trust information centre. Tracks lead to the woods and beaches in the west. These paths plus stretches of beach can be used to make a four-mile circuit of an island small in size but wide in appeal.

Above Lord Robert Baden-Powell, the hero of Mafeking, took a party of 20 boys to Brownsea in August, 1907. They were an unlikely bunch, from backgrounds as diverse as Eton and London's East End, and their activities must have seemed just as unusual: living in the open, imitating birdcalls and stalking animals. But their ten-day camp became the model for the scouting (and guide) movement. A monument now marks the site of this first scout camp. ◇

Red Squirrel

Above The Church of St Mary the Virgin was built in 1854, a time of great activity on the island, when attempts were made to exploit clay deposits. A large pottery was built along with a new pier, a model village and, nearby, this parish church. ◇

Heron

Above The red squirrel is common on Brownsea but now rare in England. **Below** The blue-eared peacock is one of the rarest species in the world. ◇

Nightjar

Peacock

Right The grey heron wades in water yet breeds in the pine trees of Brownsea. Also nesting there is the nightjar **above**, an elusive bird most likely to be seen around dusk. ◇

Worth a detour
Corfe Castle Ruins of former royalist stronghold overlooking attractive village 4½ miles SE of Wareham. NT.
Hardy's Cottage Birth-place of Thomas Hardy whose novels disguised Dorset as 'Wessex'. 3 miles NE of Dorchester S off A35. NT.
Clouds Hill Home of T.E. Lawrence (of Arabia). 9 miles E of Dorchester, 1 mile N of Bovington Camp. NT.

Seven Sisters

The Seven Sisters are where the South Downs hit the coast between Newhaven and Eastbourne to form sheer white cliffs up to 500 feet high. The 'Sisters' are the hills between the riverless valleys of the chalk downs although, to be strictly accurate, there are eight such peaks rather than seven. The National Trust owns four of these miscounted Sisters in what has come to be regarded as quintessential downland: short springy turf, flecked by wild flowers and grazed by sheep.

Yet it has not always been so and the agricultural revolution of the 20th century has made such downland a diminishing asset. Large swathes of the Downs which, a generation ago, would have been nothing but grass have now been ploughed. As many as 40 species of flowers can grow within a square yard of sheep-grazed grassland. Ploughs, pesticides and fertilizers can

Map OS map TV49/69 in
1:25000 series

Below The little tern, Europe's smallest, is easy to distinguish: apart from its size — it's about half the size of most other terns, with a dainty wingspan of 24 centimetres—it has a stubby, squared-off tail and a yellow bill and legs. It nests in colonies. ◇

Below The chalk cliffs of the Seven Sisters, seen here from Seaford, rise sheer from the sea for up to 500 feet to form one of England's most renowned coastlines. ◇

Little Tern

Below Chalk grassland is highly regarded for its flowers. Many otherwise rare species survive in colonies here, including pyramidal and fragrant orchids. ◇

Fragrant Orchid

Pyramidal Orchid

Chalkhill Blue Butterfly

Marbled White Butterfly

Discovering the wildlife
Chalk down vegetation is soft, springy and short. It has been produced by a combination of sheep-grazing and a soil low in nutrients. This inhibits tall species which would otherwise smother the more delicate herbs and flowers. The grass itself is composed of several species, mostly fine-leaved fescues, which are interspersed with herbs such as thyme and salad burnet. Slight variations in winter frost and spring rainfall are sufficient to alter the variety and timing of the downland flora. However the first flowers to appear are usually the yellows of cowslip, horseshoe vetch, field fleawort and kidney vetch. Blues, pinks and white follow with plants such as squinancywort, viper's bugloss and rampion. Late summer is the time for the purples of stemless thistles, autumn gentian or felwort and common centaury. Then there are the orchids. These thrive on dry chalk or limestone and among many species found here are the pyramidal and common spotted varieties. Early purple orchid is the first to appear, with the white rosettes of lady's tresses usually the last in autumn.
The rich flora of the downland attracts similarly varied insect life — notably butterflies such as the

destroy them all. The Seven Sisters have therefore become an area of great ecological importance as well as one of outstanding beauty.

Sheep-grazing is ideal as the nibbling keeps grass short thereby enabling small flowers to get the sunshine and light necessary for growth. Cattle tend to trample on such flowers and tear up grass in clumps. But cattle-grazing does have a role to play in the management of the downs. Left to itself the grass would revert in time to woodland, via intermediate stages of longer grass and scrubland such as bramble and hawthorn. Cattle can be used to control scrub, just as sheep provide natural 'mowing' of the turf.

The open pasture of the Downs is one of their great attractions. Much of the area is open to public access without restriction to specific paths, but the South Downs Way does follow the clifftops and this enables visitors to get away from the crowds which congregate near Birling Gap and Beachy Head, where the road touches the shoreline. Most of the National Trust land lies west of Birling Gap and it has its own small car park at Crowlink, west of Eastdean. Further west still is Seven Sisters country park where the cliffs taper into the Cuckmere Valley — one of the last undeveloped river estuaries in southeast England. But it is the cliffs themselves which make this one of the most memorable coastlines in the south. Originally they would have extended further south but the sea has undercut their base. The chalk falls in chunks, producing sheer cliff faces and leaving dry valleys hanging high over the sea. And the erosion continues: on average the cliffs recede by 18 inches every year.

Skylark

Above The skylark, Shelley's blithe spirit, delivers its haunting, ethereal song — actually a territorial device — from high up, often beyond human sight. Few sounds can be more evocative of spring. ◇

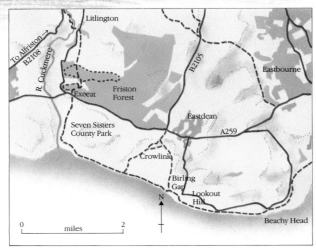

marbled white and chalkhill blue species, **left** — but the grass is too short for many birds to breed. Skylark, meadow pipit and corn bunting do nest here, though, and in winter they are joined by lapwing and redwing. Birdlife is richer where the grass is longer or merges into scrub. Here you will find linnet, stonechat, yellowhammer and dunnock. On the cliffs themselves, fulmars and herring gulls nest precariously. Totally contrasting habitats are offered by the Cuckmere Valley where a lake was made, shallow enough for waders but with artificial 'islands' to lure breeding birds such as terns and ringed plovers. ◇

Below Only a mile from the sea, Friston Forest covers 1,967 acres of chalk downland which have been extensively planted by the Forestry Commission. Walks of 1½ or 2¾ miles begin from a car park off the minor road north of Exceat. ◇

Seven Sisters

Seven Sisters country park
Seven Sisters has one of the biggest and best of Britain's country parks. It covers 692 acres and offers attractions as diverse as the breathtaking cliffs and the peaceful, unspoilt Cuckmere Estuary. There is also shingle beach, saltmarsh, river meadow, downland and scrub to provide a great range of scenery and wildlife. Activities can be equally varied. In addition to the trail for walkers, there is free access over most of the park and many come simply to picnic and admire the views. Others come to watch birds (especially in winter) or, with permission, to fish or canoe along the meanders of the Cuckmere. An excellent information centre is housed in a converted barn just opposite the main car park at Exceat.◇

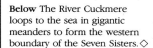

Below The River Cuckmere loops to the sea in gigantic meanders to form the western boundary of the Seven Sisters.◇

Nowhere as famous as Seven Sisters can be truly off the beaten track. Yet the area is large enough to enable anyone willing to leave their car to find tranquillity as well as beauty.

Downland walks The long-distance South Downs Way is the highway of the Downs. It follows the cliff edge from Eastbourne to Cuckmere Haven where it turns inland via Seven Sisters park to Alfriston. The clifftop section is an exhilarating seven miles although the climbs up and down each of the Sisters can be tiring.

Large tracts of downland are open for public access, notably the National Trust land south of its Crowlink car park and within the Seven Sisters country park. Quite short circuits can thus be devised based on these areas. More ambitiously, an 18-mile circuit can be made by combining two parts of the South Downs Way — starting from Eastbourne via the coastal path to Alfriston and then returning on the inland bridlepath past Jevington to Eastbourne.

Nature walks A three-mile trail has been laid out in Seven Sisters country park which, with its explanatory leaflet, offers an excellent introduction to the varied habitats of the park. It begins on open downland, with fine views over the meandering river, before reaching the cliffs. The trail returns via the shingle beach, lakes and saltmarshes of the valley. The circuit can be easily shortened and picnicking is possible virtually anywhere in the park. Two woodland walks can be found in adjoining Friston Forest.

Coastal walks The sea is best viewed from the cliffs. Walking along the seashore itself is both difficult and dangerous because of falling rocks and incoming tides. There is access to the shore at Birling Gap and Cuckmere Haven.

Man and the Downs
The natural history of Seven Sisters is by no means totally natural. Originally the downs were covered by trees; these were removed about 4,000 years ago, first as fuel and then to clear the ground.

Below and below right The meanders of the Cuckmere are spectacular but not unusual. What initiates a meander is not known, but their development is shown in the diagrams. The main current erodes the banks at the points indicated by the arrows, 1. At the same time the slower-moving parts of the river deposit silt on opposite banks, 2. These processes make the meander more pronounced and narrow the neck of land between the arms of the meander, 3. This is ultimately breached, temporarily straightening the river course, 4, and the former meander is cut off from the river to form an ox-bow lake, 5.

Ramparts of an Iron Age fort can be seen around Lookout Hill, east of Birling Gap. Better technology has elsewhere tilted the agricultural balance to arable farmland, but the Seven Sisters will be protected to preserve the open downland. ◇

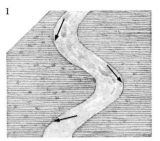

Below Sheep-grazing keeps grass short which enables flowers to flourish on the downland. Grass grazed by cattle is longer and bruised by their great weight. Sheep farming, and subsequently well-cropped downland became predominant in this area only in the last century. ◇

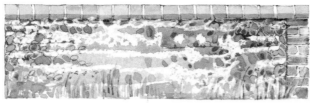

Corsican Pine

Left Flints from the chalk are used in local buildings and walls; in Stone Age times they provided tools and weapons. ◇

Below The Long Man of Wilmington was carved into the chalk; it is reported to be Saxon but may be younger. ◇

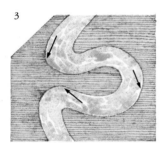

Above The Corsican pine is one of the most common trees in the Friston Forest, just as it is in other Forestry Commission plantations. In Friston Forest, the role of the pine is to protect young beech from the corrosive effects of salt-laden winds. Gradually the pine will be removed as the broadleaved woodland takes root. ◇

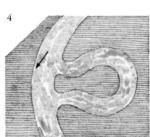

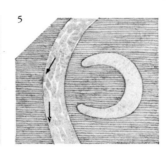

3 4 5

Worth a detour

Alfriston Thatched and half-timbered 14th-century clergy house in an attractive village four miles N of Seaford. NT. *Literary shrines* Three homes of famous writers are now owned by the NT in East Sussex. *Bateman's* south of Burwash belonged to Rudyard Kipling; *Monk's House*, at Rodmell SE of Lewes, where Leonard and Virginia Woolf held court, and *Lamb House* in Rye was the home of Henry James. The two latter have limited opening hours.

Dale Peninsula

Map OS map 157 in 1:50000 series

Below The broad sweep of Marloes Sands, here looking south towards the rest of the Dale peninsula, is Pembrokeshire at its best: sandy beaches, rocky crags and ocean waves ideal for surfing. ◇

Nobody passes through peninsulas. They are, of necessity, a destination in themselves and never a staging post. They can thus acquire characteristics more commonly associated with islands: isolation, tranquillity and an absence of crowds. The Dale Peninsula is such a place. Not that anywhere along the Pembrokeshire coast is totally undiscovered: the entire 167-mile coastline has been designated as a national park and is tracked by a footpath. Yet Dale offers a glorious introduction to some of Britain's most renowned coasts without the risk of fighting for space on the beaches. This survey will interpret the boundaries of the Dale Peninsula somewhat loosely to embrace National Trust holdings around Marloes Sands and on the islands. The complex geology of the areas has produced diverse scenery with red sandstone cliffs south of Dale at St Ann's Head and volcanic outcrops around Marloes which also produced some islands. Perhaps the best vantage point is the clifftop path where the scent and colour of wild flowers add their own beauty in late spring or early summer.

The peninsula provides two contrasting faces: the more rugged western shore takes the full brunt of westerly winds and seas while the cliffs of St Ann's Head protect the bays of the eastern shore. This contrast is nowhere more pronounced than around the village of Dale itself. It stands on a narrow neck of land no more than a mile across. Pretty harbourside cottages overlook a shingle beach and safe anchorage for yachtsmen afforded by the protected waters of the Dale Roads. One mile away to the west, Atlantic waves crash onto the sands of West Dale Bay to the delight of surfers. Dale's exposed position on the southwest tip of Wales has made it one of the windiest places in Britain; but an annual average of 1,800 hours of sunshine also makes it the sunniest place in Wales and among the sunniest in Britain.

Nowadays Dale seems an out-of-the-way place; that, indeed, is its charm. Yet the area has a long history of settlement. Two Iron Age forts stand to the west and east of Dale while the name of the village betrays its own origins: *dale* is Norse for valley and relates to the village's location in a geological fault at the neck of the peninsula. The names of the islands also reflect the forceful presence of Vikings who raided this shoreline in the ninth century. Twentieth-century visitors are more likely to be peaceable: ramblers and birdwatchers, surfers and sailors.

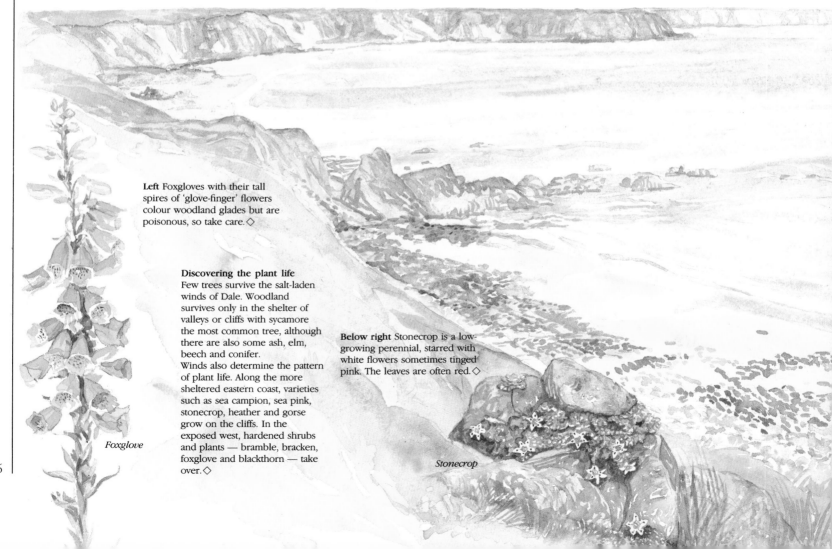

Left Foxgloves with their tall spires of 'glove-finger' flowers colour woodland glades but are poisonous, so take care. ◇

Discovering the plant life
Few trees survive the salt-laden winds of Dale. Woodland survives only in the shelter of valleys or cliffs with sycamore the most common tree, although there are also some ash, elm, beech and conifer.
Winds also determine the pattern of plant life. Along the more sheltered eastern coast, varieties such as sea campion, sea pink, stonecrop, heather and gorse grow on the cliffs. In the exposed west, hardened shrubs and plants — bramble, bracken, foxglove and blackthorn — take over. ◇

Foxglove

Below right Stonecrop is a low-growing perennial, starred with white flowers sometimes tinged pink. The leaves are often red. ◇

Stonecrop

Right This row of cottages from the 17th and 18th centuries overlooks Dale's shingle beach and once lined what used to be the quay.

Nowadays the sheltered anchorage of Dale's tiny harbour is used mostly by yachtsmen and many of the cottages are holiday homes. ◇

17th- and 18th-century cottages

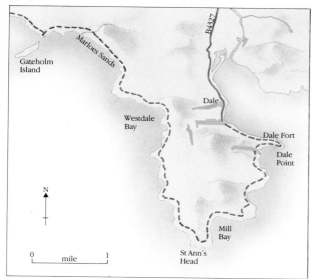

Right The tiny cove of Mill Bay is an unlikely footnote in the story of English royalty. Yet here, on Sunday 7 August 1485, Henry Tudor landed from France to begin his march to power and the throne of England. Within two weeks it had taken him to Bosworth Field where he defeated Richard III to become King Henry VII of England and found the Tudor dynasty (which was not bad for a man with barely 200 followers — and a Welshman at that). Harri Tudur, as he was known in Wales, had thus claimed the English crown just 80 years after the defeat of Owain Glyndwr, the last of the great Welsh rebel princes. Among Harri's first encounters on the road from Mill Bay to London was one with a Welsh nobleman Sir Rhys ap Thomas. The knight had promised King Richard that 'only over his body would such an invasion take place.' Sir Rhys, if legend is to be believed, was true to the words if not the spirit of his oath. He is said to have lain underneath the bridge over Mullock Brook two miles north of Dale as Harri passed. A bridge still crosses the brook, but the road is called more prosaically, B4327. ◇

Henry VII

Exploring the coast
For long-distance walkers a path runs the entire length of Pembrokeshire's coastline. Daytrippers can sample the splendours of the coast via a more modest circuit of seven miles based on Dale. The path hugs the cliffs around the peninsula to and from St Ann's Head with its lighthouse and coastguard station. An excellent national park area guide describes the history, geography and ecology of the peninsula and points out highlights of the walk. These include Dale Fort, Henry Tudor's landing place at Mill Bay and two Iron Age forts. Away from the coast, the path back to the village passes Dale Castle and church, both of which have Norman origins. But for most, the memories will be of natural rather than man-made beauty: the old red sandstone rocks at Castlebeach, the grandstand views over the mouth of Milford Haven, the cliffs of the NT's Kete coastline west of Dale and — always — the surging power of the mighty Atlantic thundering far below. ◇

Left Dale Castle has occupied this site since Norman times, although nothing original is thought to remain except some foundation stones. The castle stands in the middle of the narrow neck of land where Dale Peninsula juts southward towards the sea. Nearby is a church, also on a Norman site and also much rebuilt in the 19th century. The 'castle' is privately owned and has been in the same family for more than 150 years. ◇

Below Thrift or sea pink, with its abundance of small, pink fragrant flowers, is a widespread sea cliff inhabitant. ◇

Thrift

Dale Peninsula

Manx Shearwater

Above The manx shearwater, a relative of the albatross, spends most of its life at sea coming to land briefly for breeding, and then only at night. ◇

Below The razorbill's thick horny bill makes it easy to identify. It nests in crevices on sea cliffs, but stays away from land outside the breeding season. ◇

Razorbill

The coastline of the Dale peninsula provides sandy beaches for bathers, Atlantic waves for surfers, safe anchorages for sailors and cliffs for walkers. But above all else it is renowned for its birdlife, especially on the islands that lie a little distance offshore. The Skomer Islands owe their names to the Norsemen who raided this coastline in the ninth century and their origin to the complex geology of the area. Rocks vary in their resistance to the erosive power of the sea and this has led to the formation of numerous stacks and islands off the coast between Milford Haven and St Bride's Bay. None of the islands is particularly large and one can be explored by land at low tide. Access to other islands varies, partly according to the season, but the islands and their bird colonies remain an integral attraction of the peninsula even when viewed from the mainland.

Skomer is the largest of the islands and also the most accessible. Daily boat trips operate from Martin's Haven on the Marloes Peninsula from Easter to September, weather permitting. The crossing takes about 20 minutes. Occasionally boats can be hired from Dale. The island was made famous in the 1930s by the bird studies of the naturalist R.M. Lockley and it is now a national nature reserve owned by the Nature Conser-

vancy and leased to the West Wales Naturalist Trust. The island, a grey mass of volcanic rock, extends to some 722 acres and, in fact, is almost two islands. Geological faulting has created two inlets —North and South Haven — which virtually cut off the eastern end of the island. There are no visitor facilities on the island, other than a Naturalist Trust nature trail.

Skokholm, a little to the south, is composed of red sandstone which forms spectacular cliffs. But here, too, it is the birds which are the greatest attraction. The first bird observatory in Britain was established here and it remains a centre for research into species such as manx shearwaters and storm petrels. Boat trips operate to Skokholm during the summer, but only for people taking study courses on the islands; no daytrippers are allowed. Nor is there access to Grassholm, the smallest and most distant of the islands.

Gateholm, by contrast, is attached to the mainland at low tide. The island is owned by the National Trust and can be approached from the magnificent beach of Marloes Sands, west of Dale. Traces of what must have been a sizeable prehistoric settlement can be found at Gateholm. Now, like the other islands in the Skomer group, it is strictly for the birds.

Above The cerulean waters of Martin's Haven are crossed most days, weather permitting, by the ferry to Skomer Island. A small beach acts as the port of embarkation for visitors wishing to explore the island. Martin's Haven, near Marloes, is 15 miles southwest of Haverfordwest via the B4327. ◇

Above The sheer cliffs along Haven Point overlooking St Bride's Bay almost dwarf the ferry plying its way to Skomer Island. Skomer is open to the public every day except Monday in the summer. The ferry or 'island boat' crosses from Martin's Haven. A landing fee is payable upon arrival. ◇

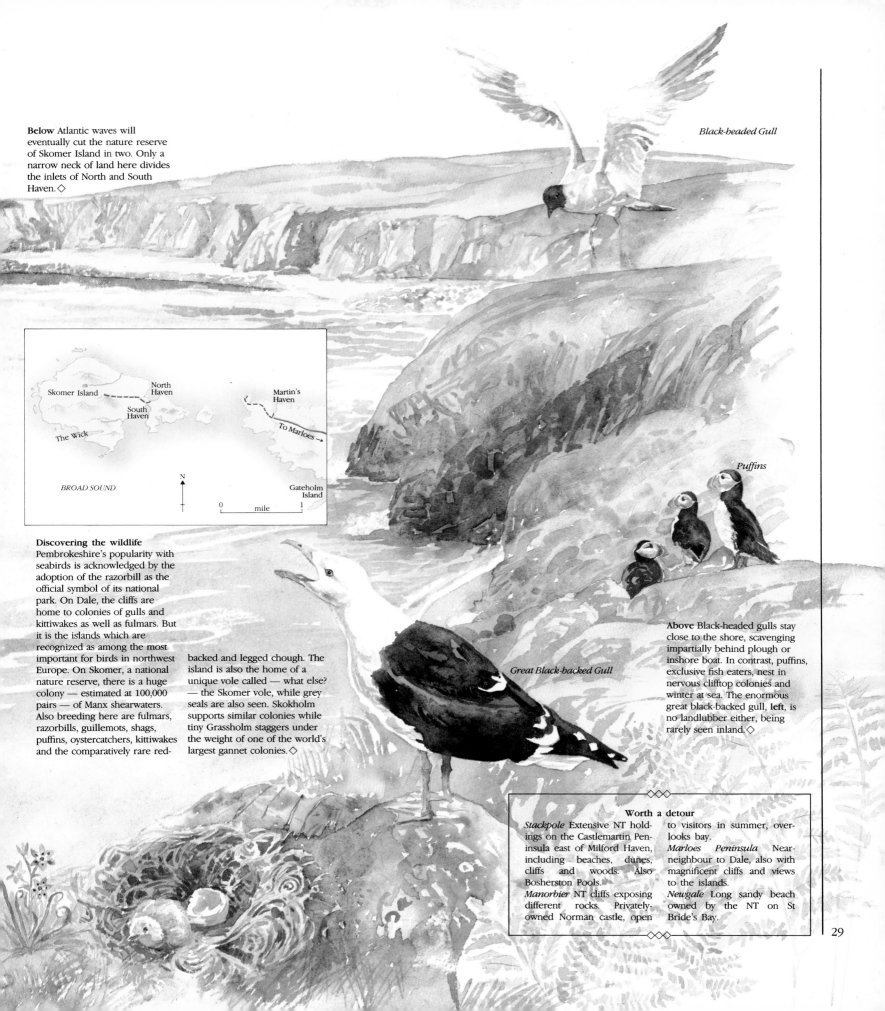

Below Atlantic waves will eventually cut the nature reserve of Skomer Island in two. Only a narrow neck of land here divides the inlets of North and South Haven. ◇

Black-headed Gull

North Haven

Skomer Island

South Haven

Martin's Haven

The Wick

To Marloes →

BROAD SOUND

N

0   mile   1

Gateholm Island

Puffins

Discovering the wildlife
Pembrokeshire's popularity with seabirds is acknowledged by the adoption of the razorbill as the official symbol of its national park. On Dale, the cliffs are home to colonies of gulls and kittiwakes as well as fulmars. But it is the islands which are recognized as among the most important for birds in northwest Europe. On Skomer, a national nature reserve, there is a huge colony — estimated at 100,000 pairs — of Manx shearwaters. Also breeding here are fulmars, razorbills, guillemots, shags, puffins, oystercatchers, kittiwakes and the comparatively rare red- backed and legged chough. The island is also the home of a unique vole called — what else? — the Skomer vole, while grey seals are also seen. Skokholm supports similar colonies while tiny Grassholm staggers under the weight of one of the world's largest gannet colonies. ◇

Great Black-backed Gull

Above Black-headed gulls stay close to the shore, scavenging impartially behind plough or inshore boat. In contrast, puffins, exclusive fish eaters, nest in nervous clifftop colonies and winter at sea. The enormous great black-backed gull, **left**, is no landlubber either, being rarely seen inland. ◇

Worth a detour
Stackpole Extensive NT hold- ings on the Castlemartin Pen- insula east of Milford Haven, including beaches, dunes, cliffs and woods. Also Bosherston Pools.
Manorbier NT cliffs exposing different rocks. Privately- owned Norman castle, open to visitors in summer, over- looks bay.
Marloes Peninsula Near- neighbour to Dale, also with magnificent cliffs and views to the islands.
Newgale Long sandy beach owned by the NT on St Bride's Bay.

Tywi Estuary

Map OS map 159 in
1:50000 series

*Gatekeeper
Butterfly*

*Meadow Brown
Butterfly*

*Evening
Primrose*

Above The orange-winged gatekeeper butterfly patrols the hedgerows, while the commoner meadow brown sticks to open grassland, flying even in dull weather. Evening primrose thrives on the roadside and the dunes. ◇

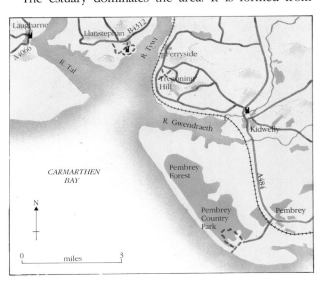

Anyone who has read Dylan Thomas will have a rough idea of what to expect from the Tywi Estuary. The fields, farmhouses and waterways around the rivers of the estuary are closely identified with his life and work. Laugharne, on the 'heron-priested shore' of the Taf, became his adopted home and not even posthumous fame has yet disturbed the calm of the village which beguiled the turbulent poet. This bypassed corner of old Carmarthenshire retains an undisturbed face.

The estuary dominates the area. It is formed from three rivers — the Tywi, Taf and Gwendraeth — which swirl together into Carmarthen Bay. It is a gentle, pastoral landscape: the peaks of the Brecon Beacons to the east have subsided into undulating hills such as the National Trust's Tregoning Hill overlooking the mouth of the Tywi; the dramatic seascapes of Pembrokeshire to the west have yet to emerge so that dunes, salt-marshes and sands rather than cliffs border the three-pronged estuary.

Laugharne Sands marks the eastern end of one of the longest beaches in Wales — the seven-mile stretch of sand beginning at Pendine once used for land-speed record attempts. Another seven-mile beach lies across the estuary. Cefn Sidan Sands borders what is now a country park where pine trees have been planted to prevent wind erosion of the dunes. The combination of forest, beach and dunes is as attractive as it is unusual, and among many activities to be enjoyed in the country park are four waymarked trails exploring the contrasting species of wildlife. The rarest plants, though, are found among the marshes, dunes and mudflats of Tywyn Burrows, north of the park along the southern shore of the Gwendraeth Estuary.

However, the countryside is mostly farmland, its villages hidden along a maze of backroads. Only the ruined castles at Kidwelly — which is among the best-preserved in Wales — and Llanstephan and Laugharne inject drama and romance into towns which are now as sleepy as the landscapes they were built to protect.

Left The castles of South Wales tend to be neglected in favour of the 13th-century castles in the north. Yet they are no less fascinating as examples of medieval military building and, as Llanstephan Castle shown here demonstrates, they can command equally dramatic locations. Three castles — at Llanstephan, Laugharne and Kidwelly — protect the estuaries of the Tywi, Taf and Gwendraeth. Kidwelly is the best-preserved of the three, with its curtain walls and towers virtually intact and a massive gatehouse which enhances its natural defensive position on a scarp above the Gwendraeth. The present Kidwelly Castle dates from the late 13th century but Llanstephan occupies a position which has been defended since prehistoric times. The present fortifications date from 1192. Laugharne Castle, dating from about 1300, was also built on an earlier site. ◊

Above Desert and forest is the unlikely combination found at Pembrey where Corsican pine has been planted to prevent erosion of dunes bordering the estuary. ◊

Right A plain white cross marks the resting place of Dylan Thomas. He was born in Swansea but spent his most contented and productive years in this village where he lived in a Georgian boathouse set amid wooded cliffs overlooking the Taf Estuary. He settled here in 1949, four years before his death, and drew much inspiration from the people and places. Laugharne was his 'timeless, mild, beguiling island of a town', where he would help his father with a crossword puzzle, drink beer at Brown's Hotel and lock himself away to write in a small shed along the lane from the boathouse. His most celebrated work, *Under Milk Wood*, was set in a fictitious village of Llareggub (spell it backwards) and partly based on the times he spent around Laugharne. Today the boathouse is a museum dedicated to the life and work of Dylan Thomas. It is open from Easter to late October. ◊

Dylan Thomas

Worth a detour
Colby Lodge Gardens in a wooded valley on the coast at Amroth W of Pendine. NT.
Gower Extensive NT areas on peninsula renowned for spectacular beaches.
Kidwelly As well as the castle, an industrial museum one mile NW of the town.
Pembrey Country park with woodland and nature trails, ponytrekking and picnic areas in forest and grassland bordering 7 miles of magnificent sandy beach. Good leaflets on nature trails. S off A484 W of Pembrey.

31

North Norfolk

Map OS map 132 in the 1:50000 series covers the coast west of Blakeney; map 133 covers the coast eastward

Lord Nelson

Above Lord Nelson is one of four admirals born and raised along this harbourless coast. He is so famous locally that many pubs are named *The Hero* without feeling any further need to identify his portrait. The rectory at Burnham Thorpe, where he was born in 1758, has gone but the church in which he was christened still remains, a little outside the village. It contains a crucifix made of wood from HMS *Victory*.◇

North Norfolk is unlike any other coastline in the United Kingdom. It is not merely very flat, as Noël Coward pointed out, it is also very new. From Hunstanton in the west, where the coast turns south towards the Wash, to Cromer in the east there are 34 miles of shingle, dunes, mudflats and saltmarshes — and not a deep-water harbour in sight. True, there are quays at several villages but only Wells can accommodate more than fishing boats or yachts. And the place names are clues to the changes along this coastline.

Wells-next-the-Sea and Cley-next-the-Sea are not merely quaint but inaccurate. Nowadays the sea is a mile to the north and has cut off completely many of the medieval ports. The old shoreline is traced by the modern A149 road which mostly follows the line of slightly higher ground where the villages grew between land and sea. In some places agricultural land has been reclaimed from the sea and cattle now graze where a few centuries ago was water or marsh. But some 30 miles of the coast are protected by a series of nature reserves, for the combination of shingle and marsh has made North Norfolk a mecca for birdwatchers. Several reserves are owned by the National Trust.

To some extent, therefore, man is trying to manage the forces of nature in order to maintain the area's present ecological balance. But how, and why, did the coastline alter so dramatically in what, geologically speaking, is a mere flicker of time? For the changes have occurred since the last Ice Age ended some 10,000 years ago.

The first change was the appearance of shingle banks, perhaps derived from the rapidly eroding sandstone cliffs east of Cromer but also from material swept up from the sea beds during the post-glacial rise in sea levels. The sand in the shingle, drying out between tides, was caught up by the wind and deposited further downwind. Thus the shingle banks grew. In some places, grasses grew through the sand, encouraging more sand grains to settle, so that in a surprisingly short time dunes up to 50 feet high had built up.

These shingle banks and dunes did not grow close to the shore but mostly a mile or more out to sea, leaving sheltered water behind them cut off from normal tides. Except where rivers flowed out to sea,

Left The crossbill is a bird of conifers, using its unique crossed bill to pick out seeds from pine cones. The males are red when mature, the females a greenish yellow.◇

Crossbill

32

Redshank

Above The distinctive redshank is a common and mostly gregarious bird, happy to share seashores with other waders. But redshanks will breed alone, usually on marshy ground. ◇

Left Salt marsh and shingle combine to produce a seascape in North Norfolk where the boundary between land and sea is ever blurred and ever changing. ◇

Discovering the wildlife
Hunstanton marks the westerly end of the North Norfolk coast and is also the only resort on England's east coast that actually faces *west*. But for birdwatchers the first point of interest is Holme where there is a bird observatory and a nature reserve extending over 600 acres of dunes and marsh. There are observation hides and a mile-long trail at the bird observatory

where no fewer than 279 species have been identified. The adjacent reserve also shelters several types of waders, both breeding species and winter migrants. Plant life is similarly rich with sea buckthorn abundant. The reserve also has a nature trail and joint permits are available for the two areas. The approach road is rough but you can get there along the sea wall from Thornham Staithe. ◇

Exploring the coast · 1
Titchwell Marsh and Scolt Head, further to the east of Holme, are respectively the youngest and the oldest reserves along the coast. Titchwell, established by the Royal Society for the Protection of Birds in 1973, is a 400-acre tract of marsh now protected by a sea wall. This allows water levels to be controlled so that habitats now include freshwater pools and reed beds as well as saltwater zones. The fresh water

attracts marsh harriers, bitterns and bearded tits among the reeds. Scolt Head has been a national nature reserve since 1923. It has a wide range of plant and birdlife but is best known for its large nesting colony of Sandwich terns. A trail operates during the summer but the ternery is closed during breeding. You can walk to the island at low tide, but it is dangerous; boats operate around high tide from Brancaster Staithe. ◇

Left Man has left little imprint on the coast — except for one three-mile stretch west of Wells and one family, the Cokes of Holkham Hall. Their imposing palladian mansion was designed by William Kent in the 18th century. By then the family had begun to reclaim saltmarsh and turn it into pasture. Later generations developed new methods of crop rotation and planted pines to protect the reclaimed land. Ironically, the dunes are now a nature reserve. ◇

silt settled and, again with the help of various plants, the mudflats grew into saltmarshes. These have stabilized at about nine feet above sea level which is low enough to be covered by about 100 tides a year.

The reshaping of the coastline stranded ports such as Blakeney and Cley inland, although fishing remains an important occupation. It is a holiday coast, too, but the villages are small and uncommercialized, their flint-walled churches and cottages as distinctive as the now-distant shore. Norfolk has always been something of a world apart. Once cut off by fen or forest from much of England, it now possesses the most rapidly-changing coastline in the country.

Flint Cottages

Above The flint in these cottages is characteristic of Norfolk; nowhere else in England has it been used more as a basic building material, most notably for distinctive round church towers. Flint is found in the underlying chalk and even as pebbles on the shore near Cromer. ◇

Exploring the coast · 2
Wells-next-the-Sea is the only port on the coast which can still take coasters of up to 400 tons. Yet it is a mile from its beach to the north — and the beach can be a mile wide at low tide. There is an excellent walk through the contrasting habitats of beach and pinewoods from the beach car park or from where Lady Ann's Road from the Holkham estate reaches the shore. Either way it is a round trip of three miles. From the beach you pass a shingle bank, with new dunes, where oystercatchers, terns and ringed

plovers sometimes nest. The beach is rich in marine shells, not just cockles and oysters but rarer species such as blunt gapers and variegated scallops. Along the shoreline look out, too, for two specialized plants, the pale violet sea rocket and, in late summer, prickly saltwort. Most of the pines are Corsican pine though there are also Maritime pines. Silver birch grows in more open areas; here there are also polypody ferns and many fungi, especially in autumn. Among the birds is the crossbill, attracted by the abundant pinecones. ◇

Goldcrest

Above The goldcrest, at 3½ inches long, is the smallest European bird and an active woodland resident. Only the mature male wears the gold crest. ◇

33

North Norfolk

Garganey

Above The garganey is chiefly a summer visitor to Britain but among its few breeding grounds here are the Norfolk marshes. It is by far the rarest British duck. ◇

Avocet

Above The avocet is the marshland aristocrat, with its slender upcurved bill and long, spindly legs. Avocets nest in colonies, laying eggs in May. ◇

Ruff

Above The male ruff acquires the plumage which gives the bird its name during the breeding season. Usually a migrant, but now recolonizing in East Anglia. ◇

Shingle, sand and saltmarsh are the predominant characteristics of the North Norfolk coast but east of Wells they eventually give way to low sandstone cliffs where the Cromer Ridge reaches the shore. Nevertheless this eastern half of the coast still contains some of the largest and most notable nature reserves in the country while the Cromer Ridge itself offers contrasting rewards for exploration.

There are no major towns. The holiday resorts of Sheringham and Cromer contrive to be genteel rather than brash while Blakeney and Wells revolve around their small harbours, nowadays crammed by sailing dinghies rather than fishing boats.

East of Wells stretches the Holkham national nature reserve. This then merges with the Morston and Stiffkey Marshes owned by the National Trust — in all seven miles of undisturbed saltmarsh. The plants growing here are very special ones, able to tolerate salt water. As the seasons pass, different species seem to dominate: in June, thrift or sea pink; in July and early August, sea lavender; in late August and September, sea aster which in Norfolk appears totally yellow, looking like michaelmas daisy without the violet outer florets. In late summer, the marsh samphire or glasswort can be found — and even eaten, as it is sold in local fish shops.

It is possible to walk from Wells along the Heritage Coast path by the sea wall out onto the marshes and all the way to Morston Quay, but do not venture off the path if the tide is coming in. Other paths offer short cuts back to Warham and Stiffkey.

Opposite Morston Marsh is the elongated arm of Blakeney Point, another National Trust reserve. You can reach Blakeney Point by boat from Morston or Blakeney, usually between two hours either side of high tide. It is also accessible by land from Cley beach car park, four miles to the east. Walking along the shingle is sometimes hard going but does offer opportunities to see shingle plants such as the yellow horned poppy, sea campion and sea pea. The route alongside the saltmarsh is somewhat easier, but both routes eventually lead to the dunes. Among the marram grass growing here are sea bindweed and clumps of blue hairgrass. But the birdlife of Blakeney Point is its greatest attraction. Little terns breed here, as well as the more common Sandwich and common terns. Other

Right North Norfolk now has the largest colony of little terns — the rarest and smallest of our breeding terns — in Britain. It is characterized by a white patch on its otherwise black forehead. ◇

breeding birds include oystercatcher, ringed plover, redshank and shelduck, while autumn brings many migrants.

Cromer Ridge is not particularly high at little more than 300 feet, although in Norfolk this appears more impressive than it would elsewhere. The ridge is a *moraine* of glacial material dumped as the ice melted and the glaciers retreated. East of Cromer this has produced 100-foot cliffs, often sheer, which are being eroded by the sea. There is a two-mile clifftop walk between Cromer and Overstrand but further east access has been closed because the cliff edges are so dangerous. Inland the Cromer ridge stretches as far west as Salthouse and Holt, sloping more gently to the south than it does to the north. Part of the ridge between Cromer and Sheringham is owned by the National Trust, including the Beacon (or Roman Camp) which at 329 feet is the highest point in Norfolk. It is a blend of heath and natural woodland with several paths and viewpoints north towards the North Sea.

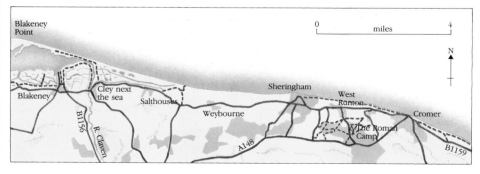

Sea Rocket

Below Peddar's Way is one of the newer long-distance footpaths but one of the oldest routeways in the country. It was almost certainly a prehistoric track which was then improved by the Romans, cutting a conspicuously straight course to Holme-next-the-Sea. Nothing remains of the Romans' metalled surface, but fine stretches of 'green road' for walking abound, notably near Fring, south of Hunstanton and, further afield, south from Great Palgrave and North Pickenham towards the flint mines of Grime's Graves. ◇

Right Sea rocket leads the vanguard which defends the shoreline, growing valiantly between dunes and encroaching sea.◇

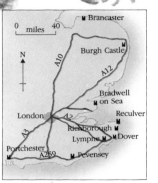

Sea Bindweed

Above Sea bindweed commonly sprawls over the shingle or on recently established sand dunes. Its large, pink bell-shaped flowers are sometimes striped with white. ◇

Roman Norfolk

There is a hilltop called Roman Camp in North Norfolk which never saw any legionaries. However there was a Roman fort of which nothings remains. The so-called Roman Camp is the highest point of the Cromer Ridge but how it acquired its name baffles even the National Trust, its owners; no traces of either a civilian or military settlement have been found for miles. By far the most important Roman establishment in Norfolk was the sea fort of *Branodunum*, as Brancaster was originally known. This formed the most northerly of a chain of nine defences known as the Forts of the Saxon Shore. These stretched from Brancaster in the north to Portchester off the Solent. They were built quite late in the lifetime of the Roman empire, probably in the fourth century, when it began to be threatened by invaders from across the sea. Only the site remains at Brancaster. See map, **left**. ◇

Worth a detour
Blickling Hall 17th-century house with Jacobean ceiling, gardens and lake. 10 miles S of Cromer on A140. NT.
Castle Acre Small town with remains of Norman castle, 11th-century priory. 4 miles N of Swaffham off A1065.
Felbrigg Hall Fine partly 17th-century house with walled garden and nature trail in wooded grounds. 2 miles SW of Cromer. NT.
Houghton Hall Palladian mansion built in 1720s for Sir Robert Walpole. Extensive parkland. 13 miles E of King's Lynn off A148. Not NT.
Oxburgh Hall 15th-century moated hall with fine tapestries. 7 miles SW of Swaffham off Stoke Ferry road. NT.

Llŷn

Map OS map 123 in
1:50000 series

David Lloyd George

Above David Lloyd George is
one of the most controversial
political figures of the 20th
century. He was brought up in
the village of Llanystumdwy, a
little to the east of Llŷn's south
coast and for 54 years was
Liberal MP for Caernarfon. Lloyd
George became Chancellor of
the Exchequer in 1908 and was
Prime Minister from 1916 to
1922. He died in 1945 and is
buried beside the river at
Llanystumdwy, where a summer
museum records his life.
Although not a son of Llŷn
proper, Lloyd George remains
identified with this northwest
corner of Wales. ◇

Those who understand Welsh will know that it is
superfluous to refer to Llŷn as a peninsula. The name,
sometimes represented on older maps as Lleyn, em-
bodies its geographic status and reflects the fact that
this long, crooked finger of land which points force-
fully into the Irish Sea is Wales's most pronounced
promontory.

The northern approach to the peninsula is dominated by the peaks of Yr Eifl which rise 1,850 feet from
the sea on the remote coast near Llanaelhaearn. The
landward peak is crowned by the abundant remains of
what must have been one of Britain's most impreg-
nable hill forts. It is an uncompromising landscape
where nature is swift to cover the scars of old quarries,
leaving decaying jetties as often the only reminders of
man's more recent presence.

Further west, the coastline becomes ever more
rugged and remote. Towering cliffs shelter tiny coves
which are rarely approached by even minor roads. The
pounding sea has eroded weaker layers of the rock to
form caves within the cliffs and rock stacks ashore.
Twenty-four miles of the coast are protected as an Area
of Outstanding Natural Beauty with extensive tracts
owned by the National Trust, mainly in the far southwest. Here the headland of Braich-y-Pwll is a good
example of Llŷn at its most elemental: spectacular,
often sheer cliffs overlooking the treacherous waters of
Bardsey Sound. Like many places in Llŷn the cliffs can
be reached only on foot. This lack of communications
has helped to maintain not only its tranquillity but has
also bolstered a cultural resilience that makes Llŷn a
bastion of the Welsh language.

There are bustling yet modest holiday resorts at
Abersoch and Aberdaron where roads do reach the
coast but mostly settlement is sparse. Llŷn as a whole is
remarkably untouched by the trappings of tourism,
perhaps because headlands such as Braich-y-Pwll and
beaches such as the 'whistling sands' of Porth Oer
require the final leg to be undertaken on foot. There is
no coastal footpath here as in Pembrokeshire or Cornwall, but there are plenty of paths to enable walkers to
plot individual routes round the peninsula. And the
unspoilt nature of the countryside brings with it com-
parably rich wildlife, most notably the large number of
seabirds which nest along the precipitous cliffs.

Above and left It would be hard to find a port more unlike Holyhead than the tiny harbour of Porth Dinllaen. Yet in the 19th century they were rivals in the race to be the prime port for Irish ferries. A company was formed in 1806 to develop Porth Dinllaen's fine sheltered harbour and a new road built to Pwllheli — but parliament backed Holyhead. In the railway age the scheme was revived, with plans for a link to the Great Western line at Worcester. But the line between Chester and Holyhead was built first, relegating Port Dinllaen to a backwater. ◇

Above Tre'r Ceiri was a fortified town which continued to be occupied through Roman times. Because it was built from stone rather than timber (and because it is so inaccessible) the remains are substantial. The five-acre site was protected by walls as well as ramparts. Some parts of this wall are still six feet high. Within the walls are the remains of numerous stone huts while outside were the cattle pounds. The steep climb to the site (from the B4417 west of Llanaelhaearn) reveals its strengths and weaknesses: easy to defend in war, difficult to eke out a living during peace.

Llŷn's history, like its scenery, is peppered with things remote and spectacular. Evidence of prehistoric settlement is found at several places. The summit of Mynydd Rhiw above Plas-yn-Rhiw contains remains of a stone axe factory with workings dated at 2,000 BC. A nearby site at Mynydd-y-Graig was later used as an Iron Age hill fort. But quite the most remarkable site — and one of the finest to be found in Britain — is Tre'r Ceiri 1,800 feet above sea level amid the rocky heights of Yr Eifl near Llanaelhaearn. ◇

*Linnet
(male)*

*Linnet
(female)*

Above Linnets belong to the finch family and are gregarious birds, often nesting in sociable groups and flocking with other finches. The cock linnet sports splendid crimson crown and breast feathers in summer. ◇

Llŷn

Inland Llŷn is an attractive landscape of small fields where lanes wind between earth and stone hedges to form a pattern little changed in places for a thousand years. But it is the coast for which the peninsula is justly renowned. And whether the attraction is an un-crowded beach or a rich array of seabirds, Llŷn has much to offer.

One characteristic feature of Llŷn beaches is their remoteness, for only rarely do roads touch the shoreline. However, this can make them less crowded and many are also protected by headlands from the prevailing westerly winds. The most spectacular bay is Porth Neigwl, four miles of sand backed by cliffs of boulder clay between Aberdaron and Abersoch. It can be reached only from either end and once seen on a stormy day fully justifies its other name of Hell's Mouth.

Other beaches are smaller but no less impressive. Among them are Porth Ysgaden, Traeth Penllech and Porth Oer on the northern coast and Ysgo and Porth Ceiriad on the southern shore. Of these, Porth Oer is perhaps the most celebrated because of its allegedly 'whistling sand'. Reliable witnesses have confirmed that the sand granules do indeed squeak, if not whistle, when walked upon at certain states of the tide, but the cove is attractive even when mute.

Many species of seabirds and some land-nesting birds breed along Llŷn's cliffs. Mynydd Penarfynydd, a NT headland west of Porth Neigwl, is particularly important. Seabirds such as fulmar, cormorant, shag, kit-tiwake, razorbill and guillemot nest in the cliffs here while the chough, a rare member of the crow family, has adapted to feed on the short grassland and gorse above the headland. Kestrel, raven, meadow pipit, rock pipit and linnet are other land-based birds seen above the cliffs. Look out for pink thrift on the cliff faces in early summer and the blue spring or vernal squill on the cliff tops during August. Porth Ysgo, with its water-falls and grassy cliffs, is especially rich in flora.

Island of the saints

Monks from Bangor-is-Coed near Chester chose the remote and inhospitable Bardsey island as a refuge from the hostility of Dark Age Britain. They set up a community there in AD 615, although little remains of their abbey except a much later tower. Bardsey became known as the 'isle of 20,000 saints' and such was its fame and sanctity that three visits to Bardsey came to equal one pilgrimage to Rome. This was sometimes easier said than done.

The island's Welsh name of Ynys Enlli means 'island of the currents or eddies' and aptly describes the treacherous waters of Bardsey Sound. Even today the island can be cut off for days. The island is now owned by a trust which has been formed to protect and conserve it. Day trips operate during the summer (weather permitting) from Aberdaron, but landing fees are charged and visiting time is restricted. At the beginning of the century, there was a population of around 100 who scratched a living from farming and fishing. Now, after years of decline, the Bardsey Island Trust has found new tenants for a farm, and restored cottages to be let as holiday homes.

The main features of the island can be seen from the Trust property of Braich-y-Pwll west of Aberdaron. A single-track road to a coastguard lookout on Mynydd Mawr and a path leads to the summit of Mynydd y Gwydded. Between these two a path leads down to St Mary's Well, culminating in some stone steps to the foot of the cliff, where a holy well spills fresh water into the sea at low tide. Hidden in the bracken on the headland above the well are the ruined walls of St Mary's church, once visited by pilgrims on their way to Bardsey. ◇

Above This dramatic sweep of coastline is Port Oer. Listen carefully as you walk along the beach — your steps will cause small grains of sand to rub together which can create a whistling sound. ◇

Below The painted lady butterfly is a spring immigrant from the Mediterranean, often laying eggs on thistles such as the spear and spindle species. The thistles bloom between July and September which is also the best time to look out for the butterfly. ◇

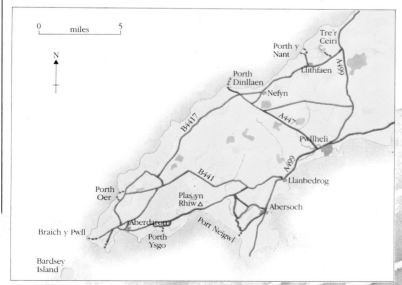

Spear Thistle

Painted Lady Butterfly

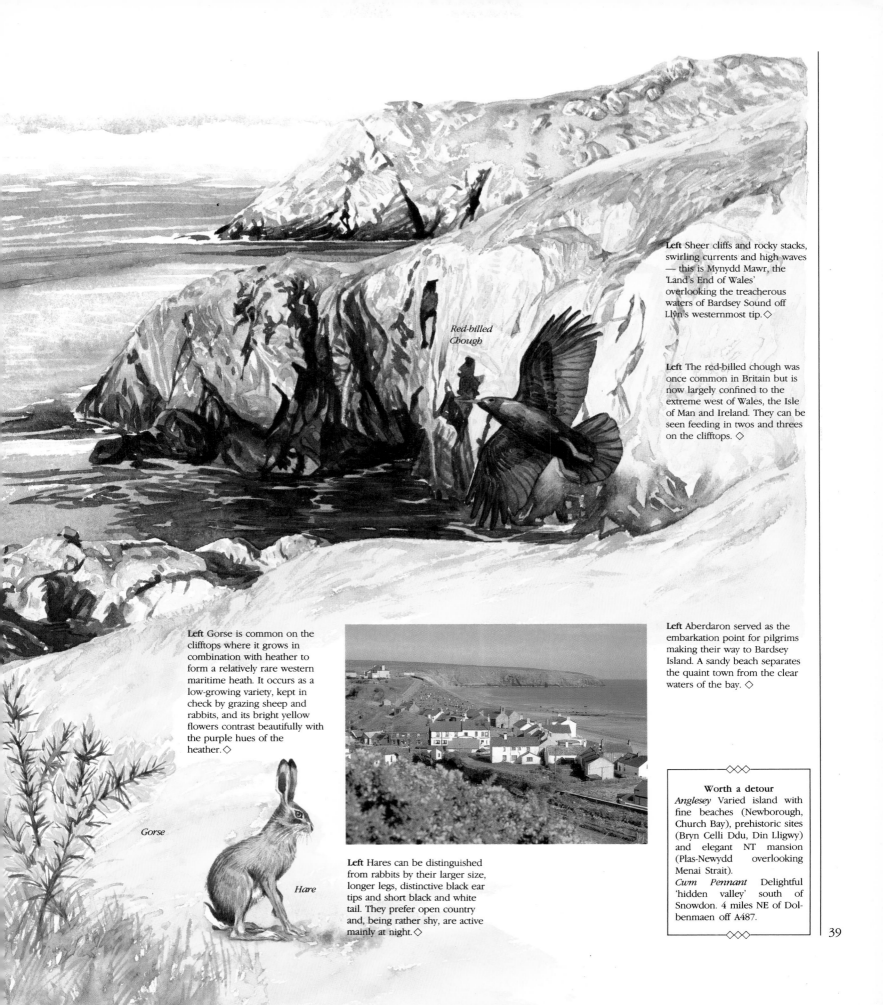

Red-billed Chough

Left Sheer cliffs and rocky stacks, swirling currents and high waves — this is Mynydd Mawr, the 'Land's End of Wales' overlooking the treacherous waters of Bardsey Sound off Llŷn's westernmost tip. ◇

Left The red-billed chough was once common in Britain but is now largely confined to the extreme west of Wales, the Isle of Man and Ireland. They can be seen feeding in twos and threes on the clifftops. ◇

Left Gorse is common on the clifftops where it grows in combination with heather to form a relatively rare western maritime heath. It occurs as a low-growing variety, kept in check by grazing sheep and rabbits, and its bright yellow flowers contrast beautifully with the purple hues of the heather. ◇

Left Aberdaron served as the embarkation point for pilgrims making their way to Bardsey Island. A sandy beach separates the quaint town from the clear waters of the bay. ◇

Gorse

Hare

Left Hares can be distinguished from rabbits by their larger size, longer legs, distinctive black ear tips and short black and white tail. They prefer open country and, being rather shy, are active mainly at night. ◇

◇◇◇

Worth a detour
Anglesey Varied island with fine beaches (Newborough, Church Bay), prehistoric sites (Bryn Celli Ddu, Din Lligwy) and elegant NT mansion (Plas-Newydd overlooking Menai Strait).
Cwm Pennant Delightful 'hidden valley' south of Snowdon. 4 miles NE of Dolbenmaen off A487.

◇◇◇

39

Northumberland

Northumberland is border country, where castles and fortified houses (or pele towers) are testimony to centuries of conflict. Once Northumbria was a kingdom in its own right and even the Romans built their great defensive wall along its southern border. Yet the landscape is not particularly hostile; inland the hills are high, but grassy or forested, while the coast is rarely rugged, with rolling sand dunes as conspicuous as the cliffs or crags. The few settlements along this coast grew around either castles or fishing harbours. Mostly, however, it is a shore that is unspoilt and undeveloped by man.

More than 50 miles of the coast, from Amble to Berwick-upon-Tweed, are now protected as an Area of Outstanding Natural Beauty. Some of the finest stretches are owned by the National Trust as are the offshore Farne Islands, now a nature reserve of international importance. Only between Bamburgh and Beadnell does a road follow the shore, so although minor roads are never far away the coast has retained an unspoilt appeal.

Much of its beauty stems from the contrasts between the wide bays backed by sand dunes and the rocky headlands. These headlands are outcrops of a dark volcanic rock known as the Whin Sill. This has intruded into the sandstone and limestones to form ridges of harder rugged outcrops well-suited to accommodate fortifications whether they be castles (as on the coast) or walls (as at Housesteads along Hadrian's Wall). The Farnes themselves are outcrops of the Whin Sill which have withstood the erosive power of the sea better than the softer rocks which must once have surrounded them. Similarly, on the mainland, the bays have been formed as the sea eroded the softer sandstone lying between the igneous headlands.

Puffin

The result is a coastline full of contrast with miles of sand interspersed by columnar cliffs and dark-cobbled beaches. Inland, the flat farmland between the coast and the A1 — never more than six miles from the sea — adds a pastoral flavour. Hedged arable fields, with some cattle grazing and shelter belts of trees provide a pleasantly traditional chequered landscape. Natural beauty allied to accessibility is always a potent combination but here the appeal is further enhanced by the richness of history and wildlife.

Castles at Dunstanburgh or Bamburgh and the seal and seabird colonies of the Farnes lure many visitors; Lindisfarne (or Holy Island) even manages to offer both a castle and a nature reserve. Harbours such as Craster and Seahouses now have a flourishing summer tourist trade but retain both their fishing fleets and their charm. And the coast is extensive enough to remain little scarred by excessive commercialization: miles of paths lead to beaches beyond the reach of the motor car or mammon.

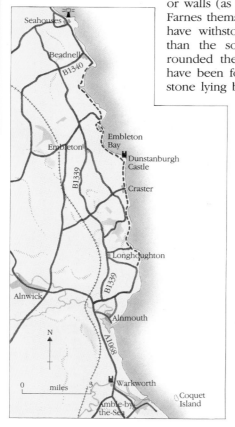

Above The fishing village of Craster, noted for its smoked kippers, today nets as many tourists as herrings or crabs. ◇

Right Grey seals come to land for their autumn breeding season in their main British breeding grounds—the Farnes. ◇

Grey Seal

Exploring the coast
One of the finest stretches of the Northumberland coast is the four miles between Craster and Low Newton. It is either owned or protected by the National Trust which has produced an excellent leaflet to describe in detail the scenery and wildlife to be seen along the coastal footpath. Craster is best known for its kippers, and it has an attractive harbour where crab, lobsters and salmon are often sold. But the coastline is dominated by the

Left Dunstanburgh Castle, splendid in its isolation, retains but a shadow of its former glory yet still dominates the sand and cobbles of Embleton Bay.◇

Historic Northumberland

Northumberland was for centuries a battleground between English kings and the Scots. It also faced directly across the North Sea towards the maurauding fleets of the Vikings. The result is probably the richest legacy of castles of any county. Several of the castles have been heavily rebuilt, as at Bamburgh and Warkworth. But they are nonetheless impressive, not least because they were mostly built to exploit the natural defensive positions afforded by the ridges of igneous rock known as the Whin Sill. Only Warksworth, two miles inland, lacked an outcrop of Whin Sill but here a huge meander of the River Coquet offered alternative defences. Warkworth castle was begun in the 12th century but the medieval fortress occupied a much earlier Saxon site. So, too, does the castle at Bamburgh which towers over the village and surrounding sand dunes. The castle was much rebuilt in the 19th century but it retains not only its 12th century keep but also a well thought to date from the 18th century. Then Bamburgh was the capital of the kingdom of Northumbria and its castle the most important along the coast. Viking raids and the new Norman castles at Warkworth and inland Alnwick diminished its importance.

Dunstanburgh Castle, between Bamburgh and Warkworth, is now no more than a ruin accessible only on foot. It, too, is perched on an outcrop of Whin Sill and was built in the 14th century. The earthworks indicate the former size of the castle which was destroyed after the Wars of the Roses.◇

Bamburgh Castle

gaunt remains of Dunstanburgh Castle 1½ miles to the north. The castle can only be reached on foot and it is an easy walk above a rocky foreshore, rich in birdlife, even for those who do not wish to tackle the full four miles to Low Newton.

The castle was built upon an outcrop of the Whin Sill and the cliffs now support breeding colonies of kittiwakes and fulmars.

North of the castle paths either skirt the western edge of a golf course or traverse the dunes between the fairways and the sand of Embleton Bay. Marram grass and the blue-tinged lyme grass are now colonizing the dunes. Beyond the broad sweep of the bay is the nature reserve of Newton Pool, a freshwater lake with two observation hides for watching the many birds which it attracts. From February to August these are dominated by 800 pairs of black-headed gulls, but many others breed or winter here.◇

Northumberland

Eider Ducks (female)

(male)

Above Eider ducks are among the birds which live throughout the year on the Farne Islands, breeding on the flatter shores rather than the stacks and cliffs favoured by other seabirds. ◇

There are 28 islands in the group known as the Farnes off the Northumberland coast east of Bamburgh. Some are little more than large rock stacks and half are fully submerged at high tide. They are all outcrops of the igneous Whin Sill found on the mainland, here producing steep cliffs on the south and west with gentler gradients on the north and east to form beaches. Boat trips operate to the islands from Seahouses but only three islands can be visited: Inner Farne, Staple Island and Longstone.

Seventeen species of birds breed on the islands making it an internationally renowned nature reserve. The ledges and columns of the Whin Sill cliffs provide ideal nesting grounds free from human disturbance. The summer visitors are common and Sandwich terns, kittiwake, razorbill, fulmar, puffin and ringed plover; additional year-round birds are oystercatcher, herring and lesser black-backed gulls. Visitors to Inner Farne, the largest of the islands, will find details posted of birds to be seen at any particular time. Obviously these will be most numerous during the May to July breeding season, although access to parts of Inner Farne and Staple Island may then be partly restricted. However some birds are resident throughout the year while winter brings not only several waders but also colonies of grey seals to the shores of Staple Island and Brownsman Island.

In order to encourage visitors to make the hour-long crossing throughout the year the National Trust, which owns the islands, has developed nature trails on Inner Farne and Staple Island. Detailed leaflets describe the flora as well as the birds, human history as well as wildlife. Longstone still has its famous (and manned) lighthouse but otherwise Inner Farne has the richest history. St Cuthbert, a seventh-century bishop of Lindisfarne to the north, went into retreat here — his cell was possibly on the site of the present 16th-century tower and a medieval monastic order built a chapel in his memory. As St Cuthbert is believed to have been the first person to protect birds rather than to kill them for food, where could be better?

How to reach the islands
Access to the Farnes or Lindisfarne is never easy or straightforward. Boats operate to the Farne Islands from Seahouses but these are dependent upon the weather. Normally the trip takes an hour. Dogs are never allowed and non-NT members pay landing fees. Lindisfarne or Holy Island is reached by a causeway from Beal but this is only possible for two or three hours at around low tide — check with tourist boards to save a wasted journey. ◇

Guillemot

Above The guillemot has a browner plumage and straighter beak than its near-relation, the razorbill. Guillemots come to the Farnes to breed on rock ledges or the cliffs before spending the rest of the year at sea. ◇

Shags

Above Shags drying their wings after a fishing expedition. They fly faster than their larger relatives, the cormorants. Mature birds are distinguished by greenish tinged plumage. ◇

Cormorant

Above The cormorant nests in colonies on cliff ledges in the Farnes. It is the largest British seabird, swimming powerfully underwater and capable of eating its own weight of fish in a day. ◇

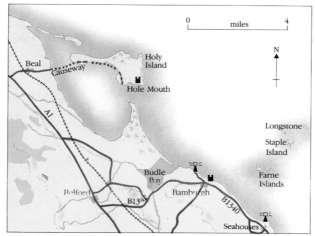

42

Below Rock stacks, such as these known as the Pinnacks off Staple Island, are common among the Farnes and offer undisturbed nesting sites for seabirds.◇

Below Lindisfarne would ooze romance even without the approach across a causeway at low tide from the mainland. It has a medieval village, a ruined priory and a castle upon a crag. These are concentrated at the southern tip of the island with a nature reserve to the north and west ends of it.

The ruined priory was built in the 11th century but stands on the site of a monastery founded by St Aidan in the year AD 634. Lindisfarne became a place of pilgrimage — which gave it the alternative and still-used name of Holy Island — until the monastery was destroyed by Viking raids. Fortunately, the Lindisfarne Gospels survived and are now kept in the British Museum as evidence of Saxon scholarship.

Benedictine monks resettled the island in 1502 until their priory was destroyed after the dissolution of the monasteries by Henry VIII. Stone from the priory was used to build a fort to guard the harbour. This fort was restored earlier this century by Sir Edwin Lutyens to form the castle we see today.◇

Below Arctic terns live in large breeding colonies established on rocky beaches and small islands. They undertake vast migrations — often as far as the Antarctic — after breeding in the Farnes.◇

Arctic Tern

Worth a detour

Castles Dunstanburgh and Lindisfarne castles are owned by the NT and open during the summer months.

Chillingham A castle now most renowned for its rare breed of white horned cattle, the famous Chillingham herd. 4 miles SE of Wooler.

Cragside A remarkable Victorian mansion which was designed mostly by Norman Shaw. It is surrounded by 900 acres of grounds which now form a country park of lakes, woodland walks and waterfalls. 13 miles SW of Alnwick. NT.

Wallington Hall A 17th-century house with 18th-century additions amid 100 acres of parkland. 12 miles W of Morpeth. NT.

Colvend

Dumfries and Galloway are full of contrasts: rich dairy pasture and coniferous forests, rock-strewn moorland and sand-clogged estuaries. What they have in common is an undiscovered tranquillity that is well represented by the Colvend coast, a peaceful stretch of the Solway shore which lies between the estuaries of the River Urr and the River Nith.

Both estuaries reach deep inland and were once thriving shipping lanes. The combination of railways on land and mudflats in the estuaries caused shipping to dwindle but the largest towns remain some distance inland at Dumfries, Dalbeattie and Castle Douglas. On the coast, commercialization is modest and mostly confined to Sandyhills where the main road reaches the shore. Elsewhere communities such as Kippford, Carsethorn and Glencaple have lost their roles as ports but found new life as small holiday or yachting resorts. And the tiny coves which once promised sanctuary to smugglers still offer peace to 20th-century visitors.

Kippford lies on the eastern shore of Rough Firth as the Urr Estuary is known. The National Trust for Scotland owns property in neighbouring Rockcliffe and between the two villages. Behind them lie a series of hummocky granite hills, rarely more than 300 feet yet high enough to give this southwest-facing shoreline a sheltered climate rich in flowers. The granite outcrops — one of which is crowned by a Dark Age fort — overlook Rough Island, a bird sanctuary half a mile offshore. Several species breed here but the coast is perhaps best known, especially east of the Nith on the Caerlaverock saltmarshes, as the prime winter haunt of thousands of barnacle geese and other wildfowl.

Map OS map 84 in 1:50000 series

Robert Burns

Above Robert Burns was born in Ayrshire but the Galloway connection is strong. He farmed for a while at Ellisland, north of Dumfries, and later visited the quays of Kingholm and Glencaple during his unlikely stint as an exciseman. There is a museum in Dumfries where the poet lived from 1759 until his death in 1796. A Heritage Trail links these and other locations. ◇

Below Each winter barnacle geese fly into the marshes of the Solway Firth, notably the Caerlaverock reserve, from their breeding grounds in the Arctic. They feed almost entirely on grass near the shore, mainly at night. ◇

Barnacle Goose

Right Rockcliffe's sandy beach on the eastern shore of Rough Firth is sheltered by a line of low granite hills which allow Riviera-like plants to grow here. ◇

Left Rough Island is a bird sanctuary reached across the mudflats at low tide. A causeway leads from northwest of Rockcliffe but this route is often equally muddy so wear rubber boots — or bare feet. ◇

Rock Pipit

Above Rock pipits are greyer than meadow or tree pipits and are found only on the coast, usually on remote and rocky shores. ◇

Natterjack Toad

Above The natterjack toad is the rarest of Britain's amphibia. It survives in southwest Scotland which is one of its few remaining habitats. ◇

Discovering the wildlife

This stretch of the Solway Firth is one of the principal British haunts of barnacle geese. Over 8,000 winter on the Caerlaverock reserve to the east of the Colvend coast. The nesting species on the 20-acre Rough Island include rock pipit, ringed plover, common gull, tern and oystercatcher. A muddy causeway links the island to the mainland from near Rockcliffe at low tide but visitors are asked not to come to the island in May and June during the breeding season. This is largely to protect birds such as the ringed plover which build their nests on the shingle and so are vulnerable to trampling feet. Among the birds to be seen on the mainland are whitethroats on the more open scrubland along Jubilee Path and crossbills among the Forestry Commission's conifer plantations. The sheltered shores of Rough Firth allied to a mild climate have encouraged many wild flowers, noted more for their profusion than their rarity. Orchids, bluebells and dryers' greenweed are most abundant. ◇

Exploring the coast

Only near Sandyhills Bay does a road run alongside the coast leaving the remaining shoreline of the Colvend coast free for walkers. A recently cleared footpath now links Rockcliffe to Sandyhills via Castlehill Point and Portling, a distance of six miles with enchanting views across the Solway towards the peaks of the Lake District.

A more modest walk links the two villages of Kippford and Rockcliffe. These villages are both cul-de-sacs overlooking Rough Firth, just one mile apart via the Jubilee Path which was cut along the hillside to celebrate Queen Victoria's Jubilee. This path can be combined with a walk to the Mote of Mark to make a three-mile circuit between the villages. The view from the Mote of Mark is particularly fine, although at low tide Rough Island is surrounded by a less-than-inviting sea of mud.

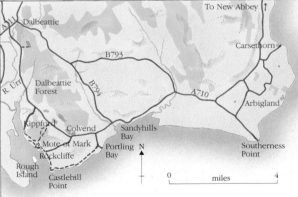

Further inland there are several walks through the woods of the Forestry Commission's Solway Forest. Forest tracks lead from the Rockcliffe end of Jubilee Path towards Auchensheen and a series of small lochs. Fishing permits are available for these lochs — details from local tourist offices which can also supply information about ponytrekking.

Local maps indicate paths through this southern fringe of the forest so that people can devise their own routes. However, three waymarked trails of between one and three miles in length start from a picnic area off the A710 one mile south of Dalbeattie town centre and lead towards a loch in the heart of the forest. ◇

Above The Mote of Mark is an example of a peculiarly Scottish form of antiquity: a vitrified fort. Exactly how these were formed remains a matter of dispute between archaeologists. However it appears that many Celtic hill forts had walls made from a mixture of timber, stone and glass; when attacked and set on fire, these materials fused together into a slaggy mass of stone to form a vitrified fort. The Mote of Mark's remains are in a hollow on the summit ridge between two granite peaks on the eastern shore of Rough Firth. It is thought to have been a Celtic stronghold between the fifth and seventh centuries AD. ◇

Worth a detour
Abbeys Remains of Cistercian monasteries at Dundrennan and New Abbey. Not NTS.
Caerlaverock A wildfowl refuge with observation points at East Park Farm — 7 miles SE of Dumfries.
Wildfowl Refuge A roosting and feeding place for wild geese and ducks on the River Dee. Nearby is Threave Garden, of interest throughout the year for its shrub roses, heaths and daffodils.
Threave 1 mile W of Castle Douglas. NTS.

St Abbs

The rugged headland of St Abbs is only a few miles north of the English-Scottish border, but it is no mere extension of the Northumberland coast. The hilly coastal grasslands of St Abbs Head drop in spectacular jagged cliffs into the North Sea. On the cliffs and on numerous stacks of rock offshore are vast numbers of nesting seabirds. Every year some 170 different species of birds are seen on or around the head which is now a national nature reserve, owned by the National Trust for Scotland and managed in cooperation with the Scottish Wildlife Trust.

Spring and early summer, between April and July, is the breeding season when kittiwakes, guillemots, fulmars, razorbills, puffins, herring gulls and shags can all be found here. At sea there is a constant stream of gannets and other seabirds moving past, while inland Mire Loch attracts freshwater birds. In spring and autumn the bird population is swollen by large numbers of migrants which use the headland as a stopover between northern Europe and the south.

However, the natural interest of St Abbs is not confined to its birdlife. The cliffs support plants which have never seen the plough or been grazed by stock. Thus in this steep wilderness grows a wide range of specialist coastal plants: thrift, sea campion, buck's horn plantain and brightly-coloured lichens are abundant with the rarer roseroot and Scots lovage in a few out-of-the-way corners. In the rolling pasture, where sheep do graze, the plants are very different. On the more acid soils the springy turf is studded with yellow tormentil and tiny white heath bedstraw while the alkaline soils of the steeper inland slopes support rock rose,

Map OS map 67 in 1:50000 series

Stonechat

Above The stonechat, a small, solid thrush, perches confidently on top of bushes or tall plants. It sings in flight, fluttering up and down 'on the spot'.◇

Exploring the coast
Although the ruggedness of St Abbs is the essence of its appeal — to human visitors as well as birds — it is easily accessible. A footpath leads from the main car park off the B6438 half a mile from St Abbs village and the whole circuit of the reserve takes barely two hours at the most leisurely of paces. A leaflet is on sale at the main car park — a smaller car park near the lighthouse is reserved for the elderly or disabled.
This accessibility has not lessened the attraction of the headland to its vast colonies of birds. It is no coincidence that so many seabirds are crowded onto St Abbs Head. The reason lies in the geology. To seek shelter from predators and man, most seabirds nest on cliffs. However the grey sedimentary rock which forms the coastline around the head does not produce cliffs as steep as the reddish volcanic rock of St Abbs. The less steep the cliff, the less protection it affords from such predators as stoats or weasels.

There are also beaches at the foot of the grey cliffs but none under the lava — and this too adds to the attraction of St Abbs. This is because juvenile guillemots and razorbills, whose flipper wings are difficult to fly with when young, jump from their ledges before they can fly, and swim out to the feeding grounds with their parents. Obviously, if the chicks are not going to damage themselves they must have a straight drop into the sea rather than onto a beach. This is why both species avoid cliffs with beaches below.◇

Right Scots lovage, savouring slightly of celery, is at the end of its southern range here. Low-growing purple milk vetch flourishes on chalk or dunes making an attractive foodplant for the common meadow blue, a small tailless butterfly.◇

Common Meadow Blue Butterfly

Purple Milk Vetch

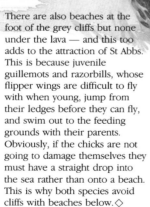

Scots Lovage

46

wild thyme and the rare spring sandwort. The wealth of plant life supports, in turn, a wealth of insects: the headland has been known for 150 years as an important site for grayling and northern brown argus butterflies, although more common species are also found. And with insects providing food for birds such as wheatears in the open grassland and migrant flycatchers around the loch, nature's cycle is complete.

Man has shaped St Abbs Head not only by introducing grazing animals but by damming a stream in 1900 to form Mire Loch. Sharp-eyed observers will also see hints of ancient ridge-and-furrow agriculture on level ground. On top of Kirk Hill low mounds mark the remains of the once important monastery of St Aebbe, a seventh-century Northumbrian princess who gave her name to the headland and the picturesque harbour.

St Abbs Lighthouse

Above So high are the St Abbs cliffs that the lighthouse does not need to be on top of a tower. ◇

Left Mire Loch was created by the construction of a dam in 1900. The valley of the Mire was formed by glacial meltwater of the last Ice Age and the freshwater loch with its trees is a pleasant diversion in a coastal nature reserve. ◇

Kittiwake

Right The kittiwake takes its name from the sound it makes and with 15,000 pairs on St Abbs Head, it does not go unheard during the nesting season. ◇

Fulmar

Above The fulmar now breeds regularly at St Abbs, just below the clifftops. ◇

Below The gannet, Britain's largest seabird, commutes past St Abbs to and from its Bass Rock breeding ground. ◇

Gannet

Above The clean, deep waters between St Abbs Head and Eyemouth have been declared a voluntary marine nature reserve to protect the rich and diverse communities of animals and plants which live underwater. The elaborate caves and tunnels underwater also make this one of Britain's most popular areas for skindiving. ◇

Worth a Detour
Preston Mill 16th-century watermill, the oldest still working in Scotland. Nearby is Phantassie Doocot, which once was home to 500 doves. Off A1 in East Linton. NTS.
Dirleton Castle Ruins of 13th-century castle with 17th-century bowling green. 3 miles W of North Berwick on A198.
Priorwood Garden Garden next to Melrose Abbey, noted for dried flowers.
Northumberland coast See feature on pages 40–43.

North Antrim

Map OS map 5 (Northern Ireland) in 1:50000

Above right White Park Bay encapsulates the beauty of the North Antrim coast — a sandy shore, rock stacks and white chalk cliffs backed by dunes. ◇

Below The cottages of Cushendun are pleasant enough, but gain some piquancy as the forerunners of Portmeirion, the Italianate village developed by their architect, Clough Williams-Ellis. ◇

Cushendun Cottages

The North Antrim coast is Northern Ireland's scenic showplace. Anywhere else in the United Kingdom it would be among the most famous, and most visited, coasts in the country. Certainly few areas can rival North Antrim for drama: deeply serrated sheer cliffs, silvery beaches, rocky stacks jutting out of sheltered bays and the extraordinary phenomenon of the Giant's Causeway.

The National Trust's interests on the coast begin at the small village of Cushendun where the slate-gabled cottages were designed by Clough Williams-Ellis, later to achieve wider renown as the architect of Portmeirion in North Wales. Between Murlough Bay and the Giant's Causeway, the Trust is mainly concerned with protecting the scenically and ecologically important coastline while providing safe public access. Much of the shoreline is, indeed difficult to reach, not least because at 600 feet the cliffs of Fair Head are the highest on the northern coast. However the views are accordingly spectacular and a clifftop path links most of the bays which are strung out along the coast like shimmering beads on a necklace — Carrick-a-Rede, Larrybane, Boheeshane, Ballintoy and White Park.

The clifftops themselves are ablaze from spring to autumn with a happy blend of coast and meadow flowers. But it is the birds which provide the most significant feature of North Antrim wildlife. The cliffs offer secure nesting sites for several species which are otherwise vulnerable to predators or disturbance. This is particularly true of Rathlin Island which is inhabited by colonies of guillemots, razorbills, puffins and kittiwakes. Apart from puffins these are found, too, along the mainland coast along with other sea birds such as shags, choughs and fulmars; peregrine falcons, buzzards and ravens are also found on the coast. Grey seals breed on the remote rocky beaches and caves of Rathlin Island but are also seen along the more rugged sections of the coast itself. Inland, the Glens of Antrim, formed by retreating glaciers, are almost as renowned as the coastline, and their rivers have become important refuges for the otter.

North Antrim thus offers much of specialist appeal to both naturalist and geologist. Most visitors, though, will be lured by the diverse attractions of the coast, whether these be the popular sandy beaches such as Portstewart, attractive harbours such as Ballycastle or the solitude of the clifftop paths and more remote bays. Broadly speaking, the more commercial areas lie west of the Causeway, a sight itself undimmed either by popularity or familiarity.

Herb Robert

Sea Sandwort

miles
0   5

N

Rathlin
Island

Benbane
Head
Dunseverick
Castle
Giant's
Causeway
B146
White Park
Bay
Ballintoy
Carrick-a-rede
Island
Kinbane
Head
Fair Head
Murlough
Bay
Dunluce
Castle
A2
Portbraddan
Port
Portballintrae
Bushmills
B17
A2
Ballycastle

Above left Herb Robert is the marathon man of the hedge banks with clear pink flowers blooming from April to November. It has a pleasant musky smell. ◇

Above right Sea sandwort or sea purslane grows out by the sea on shingle or dune edges, producing greenish white flowers and small, pea-like fruit. ◇

Right The common shore crab, a tiny crustacean about 1½ inches long, lives in rock pools or under stones, tidily scavenging dead or dying fish. ◇

Discovering the wildlife
Seabirds are the most conspicuous form of wildlife, but the bays and cliffs are home to much else of interest. Between Dunseverick and Portbraddan and on the cliffs near Dunluce the meadow crane's bill

*Common Shore
Crab*

Geranium pratense grows in such profusion that it is known as the 'blue flower of Dunluce' yet it is rare elsewhere in Ireland. Juniper and briar rose are found at Fair Head where the sides of Grey Man's Path are the home of the yellow Welsh poppy. The comparatively rare filmy fern grows around boulders and tree stumps in the moist woods of Murlough Bay which, along with Craigagh Wood at Cushendun, are the semi-natural deciduous woodlands in the area. Inland there are several conifer plantations of which Slievanorra is the largest. ◇

Exploring the coast
The North Antrim cliff path links many of the National Trust properties along the coast. At the time of writing it exists in two main sections: from Fair Head to Murlough Bay and from the Giant's Causeway to Larrybane and Carrick-a-Rede.
This latter section includes many of the most majestic tracts of the coastline: the Causeway itself (where there is a visitor centre), the ruined Norman castle at Dunseverick, the picturesque harbours of Portbraddan and Ballintoy, the silvery sands and chalk cliffs of White Park Bay and the limestone quarry at

Larrybane. It may appear possible to walk below the cliffs which separate Portbraddan from White Park Bay, however it is definitely not recommended because of the dangerous rocks and currents, it is much safer to stick to the path and road. Either way the sands, rocks and dunes are an awesome combination. At Carrick-a-Rede, a 60-foot long rope bridge sways in the wind 80 feet above the water to link the mainland to a small island with a salmon fishery during the summer. Less intrepid visitors will settle for fine views – to Rathlin Island or Islay or even mainland Scotland itself. ◇

North Antrim

The Giant's Causeway has aroused the curiosity of travellers for centuries. William Thackeray wrote: 'When the world was moulded and fashioned out of formless chaos, this must have been the bit over — a remnant of chaos'. Certainly there is no more remarkable sight in the whole of Britain or Ireland than these strangely symmetrical columns protruding into the Atlantic amidst massive amphitheatres of sheer cliffs, sea stacks and headlands. The National Trust has established four basic walks which can be modified to suit the age, fitness and inclination of the walkers.

The shortest circuit is a 1½-mile walk along the cliffs west of Causeway Head; this does not pass the columns but there are some good views and also access, for the more agile, to Portcoon, one of the coast's finest caves.

A circular two-mile walk from the visitor centre covers the most celebrated parts of the Causeway and also offers fine views from Weir's Snout and Aird Snout. It leaves the clifftops and descends the 149 steps of Shepherd's Path to the Giant's Causeway itself. The trail leads back to the visitor centre via a low-level path and then a road to the clifftops. A bus service shuttles up and down this road during the summer.

Walks three and four initially share the same clifftop path east of the visitor centre continuing past Weir's Snout and Aird Snout to the feature known as the Giant's Organ, where columns up to 40 feet high are cut deeply into the cliff face. The Organ can be seen from Aird Snout but is best viewed from the lower path. Further along the cliffs are the Chimneytops,

Common Tern

Left The common tern is a sociable seabird whose black-tipped coral red bill is the only sure way to distinguish it from the arctic and roseate terns with whom it convivially flocks. ◇

Right Legend has it that the Giant's Causeway was built by the Irish hero, Finn MacCool, in order to travel to Scotland without getting wet. Exactly how the columns were formed is not known, but geologists are sceptical about Mr MacCool. The columns clearly owe their origins to volcanic activity around 60 million years ago. Lava does not appear to have erupted violently but poured out to form layers of basalt over the white chalk. The dark basalt cooled at different rates and as it did so it contracted to produce the vertical faults and hexagonal shapes. The columns were most marked at the lower levels where cooling was slowest and they were vertical where the surface onto which the lava had poured was nearest to the horizontal — in other words, near the seashore. ◇

formed by a later lava flow. Shortly before this point, east of Aird Snout, the two walks divide: a lower path returns to the visitor centre via the Grand Causeway to complete a two-mile circuit while the clifftop path leads eastward via Berbane Head to Dunseverick. This latter route, from Causeway Head to Dunseverick and back, is nine miles long, designed for fit walkers to see the variety of scenery and geological structures of the Grand, Middle and Little Causeways.

On the causeways themselves you can explore the Giant's Loom, Wishing Chair, Honeycomb and innumerable 'seats'. Here too, the marshy vegetation fringing the columns is brightened by flashes of cuckoo flowers or lilac milkmaids while sinister hooded crows congregate on the hexagonal columns.

Above The Dunseverick Castle ruins date from the 16th century but stand on even older, possibly Iron Age, earthworks for this was traditionally one of Ireland's three great *duns* (royal forts). ◇

Some common Irish place-names and their English meanings	
Aird	Promontory
Ard	Height
Bal	Place or town
Coon	Narrow
Curragh	Marsh or plain
Dun	Castle or fort
Ennis	Island or watermeadow
Kel	Church
Lis	Enclosure
Lough	Lake
Plaiskin	High unsheltered land
Port Ganny	Sandy port
Port na Tober	Port of the well
Port Noffer	Giant's port
Portnaboe	The cow's port
Seari	Old

Above In summer, tourists willing to take their courage — and a rope — in their hands can cross a 60-foot wide chasm 80 feet above the sea to a small island at Carrick-a-Rede. ◇

Right Fair Head is as wild and rugged a headland as you would find anywhere. At over 600 feet it is the highest point on the north coast of Ireland and the closest to Scotland. The summit — reached from Ballyvoy — is a bleak heathland of rocks and heather relieved by three small loughs or lakes. One of these, Lough Fadden, has a bog of great interest to botanists for its flora, and the Grey Man's Path, a narrow cleft to the sea's edge near the headland point, is flecked by the yellow of Welsh poppy. However, the flora is much more luxuriant a short distance to the southeast as the barren plateau gives way first to open chalk downland and then to the wooded slopes of Murlough Bay.

A number of waymarked trails enable visitors to explore these contrasting areas. Two begin from Coolanlough at the end of the road leading to Fair Head; each is two miles long and they can be combined to make a circuit. One takes you thrillingly close to the cliff and the other leads inland via Lough Fadden before reaching Murlough Bay. Other walks lead from the middle car park at the bay either to the towering cliffs of Fair Head, past a maze of caves and relics of coal mines, or inland to the woodlands of Benvan. ◇

◇◇◇

Worth a detour

Ballypatrick Forest A scenic drive, picnic sites and walks by Carey River. 5 miles W of Cushendun off A2.

Barmouth Wildlife sanctuary and bird hide. 2 miles E of Castlerock at mouth of Lower Bann. NT.

Downhill Castle and Mussenden Temple High above the 7 miles of Magilligan Strand is the shell of an 18th-century mansion. 1-mile walk across landscaped grounds leads to the exquisite circular temple. 4 miles W of Coleraine off A2. NT.

Portbraddan Smallest church in Ireland, St Gobhan's is just 6 × 10 feet.

Rathlin Island Boat services operate (weather permitting) from Ballycastle. Part of island is a nature reserve.

◇◇◇

51

HILLSIDE

The uplands of the British Isles do not rank high on a global scale: the summits are at heights which in the Alps would be valley floors or nursery slopes. But they do not lack grandeur. The mountains and moorlands form Britain's last great wilderness, where even today a sense of isolation untrammelled by 'civilization' can be gained.

The highest and most remote uplands are concentrated in the north and west of Britain, where their beauty is often enhanced by their proximity to the sea. In Scotland, especially, the sea lochs or fiords form long fingers probing deep inland to inject a drama to the surrounding mountains and hills that belies any apparent lack of height. Mountains which soar sheer from the sea to more than 3,450 feet, as in northwest Scotland, have a greater impact than peaks twice as high on any upland plateau.

The Ice Ages moulded many of the most distinctive features of the British uplands. Glaciers scoured basins, known as *corries* or *cwms* which are often filled by lakes. Valleys were deepened, sometimes to leave waterfalls from side or tributary valleys, invariably to create steep slopes to challenge climbers. Lakes developed in many of the flattened valley floors and when sea levels rose, the sea flooded valleys to form fiords. Apart from the fiords, these glaciation features are characteristic of Snowdonia and the Lake District as well as Scotland.

Yet it would be wrong to imply that the north and west has a monopoly of upland beauty. The moorlands of the central Pennines and the limestone hills of the Peak District provide tracts of contrasting hill country which have nurtured a deep love of the countryside among generations of people who have grown up in the surrounding industrial conurbations of Yorkshire and Lancashire. Respect for the wildness of the uplands, is given too: walkers can, and do, die from exposure on barren hills barely 20 miles from the centre of great cities.

Further south, the mellow countryside of the limestone Cotswolds and the chalk downs of southern England may appear to be the epitome of lowland Britain. Certainly these lack the untamed quality of their more northerly and westerly counterparts: and yet, it is still possible to walk along a ridge of these hills, almost 1,000 feet above the valleys below, and escape the bustle of the world.

Hillsides have a beauty of their own and are inhabited by many of Britain's rarest flowers, birds and animals. Even the bleak fastness of a moorland will be transformed in late summer by a purple haze of heather. But it is often the views from the hills that emphasize the magnificence of Britain's contrasting countryside, whether it be from the Cotswold escarpment across the Vale of Evesham towards Wales or from the Lake District across the lush Vale of Eden towards the Pennines. These, truly, are views for all seasons.

Whether it be bare rock faces, grassy fells or heathery moors, the hillsides of the British Isles can still overwhelm man by their splendour.
Clockwise from right: The hills of the Yorkshire Dales, like many uplands, are sheep country unlike the arable fields in the lowlands; Buachaille Etive Mór, towering behind a cottage in Glen Coe, is too bleak even for sheep, although red deer may be seen in its high corries; the Cumbrian fells can provide isolation in the Lake District even at the height of summer; the North York Moors offer striking colour contrasts in early autumn; Nant Gwynant, in Snowdonia, is impressive whether viewed from the flat valley or the jagged summit ridge.

Dolaucothi

Douglas Fir

Above The Douglas fir, strongly
represented in local plantations. ◇

Below An imaginative
reconstruction of how the
Roman fort looked in AD 100. ◇

Dolaucothi meant more to Roman emperors than it does today, even in Wales. For here, amid the wooded hills of the Cothi Valley, the Romans found gold — and they built a fort to protect their mines and roads to haul the gold back to Rome. Dolaucothi was one of the three known gold mines in the Roman Empire but the only one in Britain. Although the mines were worked again intermittently from 1888 to 1938, nature has repaired many of the ravages of man, clothing mounds of debris with vegetation, so that what was once an industrial site has become once more a place of beauty and tranquillity. Yet clues to Dolaucothi's unique past can still be seen for those who know where to look and what to look for.

The mines lie just to the east of the village of Pumpsaint, among the thickly wooded hollows and jagged outcrops of rock in the hills beside the River Cothi. The river initially gave the game away: deposits of gold were found in the gravel of the river bed. The discovery prompted what is believed to have been the most technically advanced operation anywhere in Roman Britain and may explain why the Romans went to such lengths to subjugate the Welsh; they, like later empire-builders, had not come to educate and develop their colonies but to exploit the natural resources for their own profit.

The gold in the Dolaucothi hills was mined by a combination of sophisticated engineering and slave labour. The engineers built aqueducts to bring water to wash the ore and to power stone-crushing mills; one aqueduct was seven miles long and the water supply was controlled by a series of troughs, sluices and reservoirs above the mine shafts or *adits*. The slaves first dug the mine shafts and then hewed the rock by hand; some archaeologists also believe the slaves toiled on treadmills that pumped water out of the mines. At least a thousand slaves were imported to this remote site. A fort was built *c.* AD 75 to protect the mines and to house the engineers. But the gold which occurs in the veins of quartz here appears to have been too

limited to sustain this scale of operation for very long. The fort was demolished *c.* AD 140 and the Romans finally abandoned the mines some 60 years later. The gold rush was over.

Dolaucothi then subsided into a period of oblivion with only the discovery of a hoard of Roman jewellery in the 18th century to stir any curiosity. Toward the end of the 19th century, however, a second gold rush occurred. The Roman workings were extended, limited companies formed and some gold was found. But the rewards never justified either the investment or the hopes and in 1938, after several false starts, the mines were closed for good.

The mine entrances are the most obvious sign of Dolauchothi's industrial past but, for safety reasons, they are opened only for guided tours in the summer. If you look carefully, however, you can still see a shallow channel along the line of an aqueduct and the hollows of the old storage tanks. Mostly the area hides its history well. Trees and shrubs now cover mounds of mining debris and most of the old open-cast workings. Dolaucothi, once on all the maps of Rome, is a rural backwater once more.

Right 'There's gold in them there hills'—or, at least, there used to be in Roman times when the mines of Dolaucothi employed 1,000 slaves. Now only the abandoned mine entrances remain. ◇

Below Inside one of the shafts is the Roman gold mines. You can see how they were dug by hand; tool marks have been found on the roofs and walls of some mines. ◇

Roman Fort

Below Ground ivy spreads its scented flowers generously over hedges and the woodland floor in the early summer.◇

Ground Ivy

Wood Pigeon

Above The plump shape of the wood pigeon is a common sight, unlike the lesser horseshoe bat, **right**, which roosts by day in mines or caves. ◇

Lesser Horseshoe Bat

Left Woodland violet grows in glades and lane banks, producing its lilac flowers in early spring. It is not so robust-looking as its relative, the common violet, which can be seen on woodland borders. Neither are scented. ◇

Woodland Violet

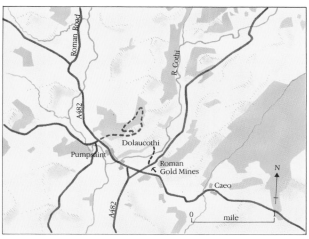

Exploring the countryside

The gold mines are by no means the only attraction of these hills, but most visitors will probably start there. Three trails have been laid out by the National Trust which now owns the area; leaflets are available from NT offices or, during the summer, a kiosk near the car park. From mid-June to mid-September guided tours also allow glimpses inside the mines themselves. Tourism is a minor element in the area's economy, however. Most of the Trust's estate is devoted to farming and forestry. A circuit of 1½ miles through the estate begins just north of Pumpsaint and gives not only fine views over the Black Mountain but also an insight into the varied land use. The path, which includes a steepish climb, leads first through broadleaved woodland of oak, beech and birch. Once oak would have covered most of the land but it was cleared for fuel and agriculture. Cattle and sheep farming can be seen on this walk but so, too, can the conifer plantations which have taken over from sheep on many more marginal upland areas. Caeo Forest is such a development with Sitka spruce, Douglas fir and larches the most planted species. A NT leaflet describes the walk in detail. ◇

Right The Pumpsaint Stone which, according to legend, represents five saints who rested their heads here during a pilgrimage. ◇

Below This Roman ornament was ploughed up near the Dolaucothi mines in the 18th century. Welsh gold is traditionally used for royal wedding rings but it is no longer mined commercially. In the 19th century, prospectors panned the Mawddach near Dolgellau, and among mines opened nearby was the Clogau which produces the royal gold. ◇

Pumpsaint Stone

Worth a detour

Gold mines An exhibition on the Roman mines can be seen at Abergwili museum near Carmarthen. Further afield the Maesgwm forest visitor centre includes an exhibition on the Mawddach mines, and the Clogau site has a display board about walks around the mine area. Maesgwm is 8 miles N of Dolgellau off A470; Clogau is at Bontddu 6 miles W of Dolgellau.

Carreg Cennen Spectacular ruined castle 4½ miles SE of Llandeilo. Not NT.

Cadair Idris

The massive escarpment of Cadair Idris rears dramatically from the Mawddach Estuary to the north. At first sight, it is easy to understand why, in the 16th century, people thought it must be the highest mountain in Britain. At 2,928 feet Cadair Idris is some 600 feet lower than Snowdon, let alone Scottish summits. But no British mountain is more imposing than this southerly sentinel to Snowdonia's national park.

Dramatic landscape evokes dramatic legend. Cadair Idris means the chair or throne of Idris, who was clearly more than your average Welsh giant: not merely a warrior but poet and philosopher, too. In fact, the kingdom of Idris is impressive enough in itself.

Map OS map 23 in Outdoor Leisure series

Left The red kite was once common in Britain. Now it is confined to small areas of Wales such as Cadair Idris where it nests in hanging oak woods on steep-sided valleys. It lives mostly on carcasses, but also kills.◇

Red Kite

Above right What Welsh mountains may lack in metres, they do not lack in grandeur. Here the gaunt plateau of Cadair Idris towers over the Cregennan lakes on its northern slopes near Dolgellau.◇

The force of glaciation
Llyn Cau nestles in a steep-sided basin called a *cwm* in Wales or *corrie* in Scotland. It was gouged by the pressure of ice which collected here in the Ice Ages. Eventually enough ice gathered to spill over the basin toward the valleys; in other words, it became a glacier. Text-book examples of the work of ice on the landscape abound in Cadair Idris: not only the cwms (some of which contain lakes and all of which retain pockets of snow long into the summer) but also the valleys. The Tal-y-llyn, for instance, was widened and flattened into the classical U-shaped profile of a glacial valley whereas river valleys are V-shaped. And the Mawddach Estuary is a drowned river valley formed when melting ice waters caused sea levels to rise 10,000 years ago. Sediment washed off the hills later softened the snow.◇

The northern escarpment rises almost like a cliff to form a sharp ridge of tough volcanic rock. The southern side has softer slates and sandstones but the slopes are not necessarily gentle. Once Cadair Idris formed part of a ring of volcanic rock which extended northwards to Snowdon. But the features we see today — the lakes high in mountain basins, the flat river valleys and wide estuaries — reflect the imprint of more recent Ice Ages. The Cadair Idris Range is bordered by the waters of Cardigan Bay and by what Wordsworth called the 'sublime' Mawddach Estuary. The main areas owned by the National Trust are on the northern slopes; Braich Ddu, Tan-y-Gader and Llyn y Gadair are unfenced properties on upper slopes. Four paths lead to the summit itself. None is easy. The upper slopes of Cadair Idris are no place for an ill-shod novice who should stick to the foothills and valleys. Even the shorter walks to lakes such as Llyn Cau or Llyn y Gadair involve steep climbs and should only be attempted by energetic walkers. Those who make it to the top will find a boulder-strewn land of precipitous screes, craggy ridges and — in summer — alpine flowers.

The gentler face of Cadair Idris is approached by the Tal-y-llyn narrow-gauge railway which puffs from the coast to Abergynolwyn south of the mountain — get off at Dolgoch for a path to some fine waterfalls in a wooded gorge. Other simple strolls are possible near Tal-y-llyn Lake and the woods and lakes of the National Trust's Cregennan estate to the north. Be warned, though: greater accessibility means greater crowds.

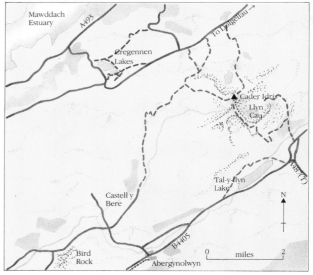

Castell-y-Bere

Starry Saxifrage

Rose-root

Marsh Fritillary Butterfly

Discovering the wildlife
The upland moors and bogs of Cadair Idris are rich in wildlife. Buzzards nest in the cliffs above Llyn y Gadair; ravens are also fairly common. Smaller birds such as the willow warbler are seen in the woods around the Cregennan lakes; beside the lakes are the nests of the coot and common sandpiper. The lake and bog habitats support a variety of insects and the mountain also has its rabbits, stoats, weasels, foxes and deer. ◇

Above and right Cadair Idris is Britain's most southerly habitat for arctic alpine plants such as rose-root and starry saxifrage as well as meadow plants such as field scabious, **below**, which support such butterflies as the marsh fritillary. ◇

Field Scabious

Polecat

Left Wales is renowned as a land of castles. Yet those attracting most attention — to the chagrin of many Welshmen — are the fortresses built by Edward I to subdue the restive Welsh. But beneath Cadair Idris stands Castell-y-Bere, a native castle built in the early 13th century by Llywelyn the Great, Prince of Gwynedd. Once it commanded a strategic route across the mountain toward Dolgellau. Now it stands, almost forgotten, off a cul-de-sac from Abergynolwyn. Even in ruins, however, it provides an atmospheric echo of the past. ◇

Above Seabirds do not normally nest five miles from the sea but the sheer-sided outcrop of Craig-yr Aderyn is an exception. The outcrop, known as Bird Rock, can be seen here beyond the Castell-y-Bere ruins and the Vale of Dysynni. Once Bird Rock was a seacliff but the silting of the Dysynni has caused the waters of Cardigan Bay to recede. Cormorants breed here as they have done for centuries. ◇

Right The polecat, a musty, semi-aquatic carnivore, was once common all over Britain, but is now confined to Wales. ◇

Worth a detour
Dolmelynllyn NT estate W of A470 5 miles N of Dolgellau, containing a spectacular waterfall, Rhaiadr Ddu, accessible by a short path from Ganllwyd.
Dinas Oleu Cliffs above Barmouth with panoramic views over sea and hills. (First-ever NT property — acquired in 1895.)
Y Lethr Remote area in Rhinog mountains 2½ miles from end of road N from Borthwnog. NT.

59

Shropshire Hills

The Shropshire Hills are among Britain's least-known designated Areas of Outstanding Natural Beauty. This is not because of any lack of either size — at 300 square miles, they are among the largest such areas — or unspoilt natural beauty. Rather it is because the name conjures up none of the stereotyped postcard images which give a place an immediate identity. It is difficult to focus the Shropshire Hills in the mind's eye, for this is quintessential border country.

When Offa built his dyke separating English from Welsh in the ninth century, he did no more than emphasize a natural division which has always influenced both the landscape and man's use of it. It is countryside where the uplands and lowlands meet; where the wilder hills of Wales spill eastward before detumescing gradually into the softer landscape of the English vales. The scenic transition is echoed by the wildlife and patterns of settlement. Of the half dozen or so distinct areas which comprise the Shropshire Hills, none better illustrate the contrasts than those in which the National Trust has a major stake: the Long Mynd and Wenlock Edge.

Though not the highest summit, the Long Mynd dominates the Shropshire Hills. Its angular bulk rises abruptly from east and west to a broad, undulating plateau of sheep-grazed moorland. Cutting deeply into the eastern flank is a series of valleys, known locally as *batches* or *hollows*, each with a tumbling stream of pure water. A small area in the south is forested and agricultural improvement of the upland grazing laps up the western and northern slopes. But 5,000 acres remain common land and, despite the popularity of parts of the hill, it is necessary to walk only a few hundred yards to find solitude. You can then share the sights and sounds of the uplands — the ravens, buzzards and curlew — much as our Bronze Age ancestors must have done as they travelled the ridgeway route of the Port Way.

Wenlock Edge, less than ten miles to the east, is quite different. It reflects its underlying rock as unmistakably as the Long Mynd but instead of a great folded block of acid shales, we see gently dipping strata of limestone. The Edge extends in an unbroken line for 15 miles from Craven Arms to the Severn Gorge, yet is barely half a mile wide. It is steep wooded escarpment facing northwest that forms the 'Edge' as such and it is here that coniferous afforestation and limestone quarrying have posed the greatest threat to the ancient broadleaved woodland; although, ironically, it is on the uneven turf clothing the older quarries that the best displays of limestone plants can now be found. Fortunately the National Trust has acquired almost five miles of the northern end of the escarpment. Not only does this acquisition present an opportunity to restore native woodland, but it also improves access to a classic feature of the English landscape of which many people have heard but very few have actually explored.

Map OS map 137 in 1:50000 series covers most of Wenlock Edge; 138 covers most of northern end.

Yew

Above Yew, a native conifer is a solemn, squat, unsociable tree rarely growing in woods. It thrives, gloomily, in limestone areas, producing seed-bearing berries: the leaves, bark and seeds are poisonous. ◇

Right The ring ouzel takes over from its relative, the blackbird, in moor and mountain areas. It is the dunce of the thrush world, singing a very dull song. ◇

Ring Ouzel

How man shaped the landscape The view up the Long Mynd's Callow Hollow appears to epitomize unspoilt beauty. Yet the appearance of these moors and valleys has been strongly influenced by the activities of man. Trees were cleared from the hills by Bronze Age men who left their notable dead in a series of round barrows or *tumuli* close to their ridgeway route along the hill. A plateau is not ideally suited to hill forts, but an Iron Age fort was built on Bodbury Hill. By late Norman times the present pattern of land use had been established with sheep grazing the hills. Grazing restricts the natural regeneration of trees, but there are a few hardy thorns and rowan, which probably became established during periods of agricultural depression. Otherwise the Long Mynd is notably devoid of trees, despite being below the altitudes at which trees can grow.

A more recent influence on the hill is its maintenance as a grouse moor, reputedly the most southerly in Britain. To encourage the red grouse that were introduced in the last century (and also to improve the sheep-grazing) the heather is now mown off periodically. This produces a distinctive patchwork look to the summit's vegetation. ◇

Right Ashes Hollow represents one of the two faces of the Long Mynd: the narrow valleys of the eastern flank contrast with the bare moorland plateau. ◇

Common Spotted Orchid

Right The common spotted orchid, a limestone enthusiast like all orchids: its leaves are spotted and the flowers may be purple, white or speckled. ◇

Below Bilberry is a moorland shrub with small, globular greenish-pink flowers which turn into the black berries used in jam and tarts. ◇

Bilberry

Discovering the wildlife
Heather dominates much of the Long Mynd, although bilberry and bracken are also common. Wiry moorland grasses such as sheep's fescue and common bent are interspersed occasionally by yellow tormentil or white clusters of bedstraw. Around the streams are bog moss and bog pimpernel. These wetter areas are also the places for the insect-eating butterwort and sundew. The streams are the home of the dipper while summer visitors to the upper valleys include the wheatear and the ring ouzel or mountain blackbird. Most dramatic of all, though, are the buzzards and ravens glowering over the summits. ◇

Exploring the countryside
The Long Mynd is made for walkers, from a short family stroll on more or less level paths to a day's hike. Minor roads give easy access to the top while there are car parks in the lower eastern valleys. Most people start with a visit to Carding Mill Valley, well signposted just north of Church Stretton. It is named after a short-lived 19th-century woollen mill and now houses a NT information centre. An easy circuit is to follow the main streamside track from the upper car park to the first major fork in the valley. Turn back on a higher path that leads to a former reservoir, New Pool Hollow. From the dam follow the stream back to the car park. Many more ambitious walks can be devised, according to time and energy, by following the theme of walking up one valley, out across the top or round the spur of the hill, and back down another valley. The still more adventurous will seek the solitude of the southern end of the Long Mynd where walks up Callow Hollow or around Little Stretton lure the agile and well-shod. ◇

Left Lightspout waterfall in Lightspout Hollow occurs at a 'nick point' which marks the upper limit of the post-glacial down-cutting which has formed the steeper and narrower middle section of the Long Mynd streams. Lower and upper reaches of the streams are gentler and more rounded. ◇

Shropshire Hills

Wenlock Edge is more wooded and more cultivated than the Long Mynd. It has also been less accessible than its western neighbour so that it is less well-established as walking territory. The major footpath is along the crest of the Edge and forms part of the unofficial long-distance route, the Shropshire Way. But as the National Trust opens up its stretch of the northern Edge, some circular routes are becoming possible.

From the Trust car park on the B4371 outside Much Wenlock, a waymarked route strikes up onto the Edge and into Harley Wood. A circuit can be taken around the wood, part of which is naturally regenerated on old limestone quarry workings. In the spring the woodland rides are edged with primroses, cowslips and violets while the shrubby undergrowth includes such lime-loving plants as spurge laurel. Early summer sees other species characteristic of limestone country — orchids. The twayblade and common spotted varieties are particularly plentiful.

For several miles south of Much Wenlock the B4371 travels along the top of Wenlock Edge and there are innumerable small parking areas with paths leading across a narrow strip of woodland and grassland to the escarpment itself. The footpath along the ridge affords excellent views into Ape Dale and across to the Stretton Hills, often from craggy promontories of bare limestone such as Major's leap and Ippikin's Rock.

Towards the foot of the escarpment the track bed of the old railway line between Much Wenlock and Craven Arms has been turned into a path through Easthope Wood and makes an ideal level walk. But local maps will indicate many other possibilities.

Wheatear

Yellow-wort

Carline Thistle

Above The wheatear's name comes from the anglo-saxon for 'white rump', the feature which makes it easy to identify in flight. Wheatears are perky birds with an upright posture and an impressive sprinting speed.◇

Above The spiny carline thistle, which looks like an armoured daisy, shares its habitat with the yellow-wort, a non-combatant whose yellow petals stay firmly closed unless the sun is shining.◇

Above Bare limestone crags, dotted with wild flowers, jut from the otherwise wooded escarpment of Wenlock Edge which looks west towards the Long Mynd.◇

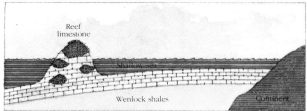

Above Geological time is hard to imagine, let alone comprehend. But in order to understand how Wenlock Edge was formed you have to go back 420 million years. Then, according to current thinking, it was being created as a barrier reef not only underneath the sea but south of the Equator. This is because the Edge is composed of limestone, which is built up of skeletons of marine creatures. Over the eons of geological time, land masses drifted north and the earth's crust has been uplifted, pushing limestone areas such as Wenlock Edge up out of the sea.
Later earth movements imparted the gentle southeasterly dip to the limestone beds which can be seen in the quarries. Erosion removed softer rocks lying above and below the limestone to create the valleys of Ape and Hope Dales. ◇

Left A springtime woodland ride in Harley Wood, southwest of Much Wenlock on Wenlock Edge. Part of the wood now covers old limestone workings and the broken ground has enabled a rich profusion of flowers and vegetation to grow amid the trees. Early summer is the best time to see the flowers in the wood which is well served by paths and rides such as this. ◇

Below The remnants of a former mill pool in Carding Mill valley. Several pools such as this one stored water for a 19th-century woollen mill. The pools thus gave the name 'New Pool Hollow' to the valley and also to a nearby reservoir. ◇

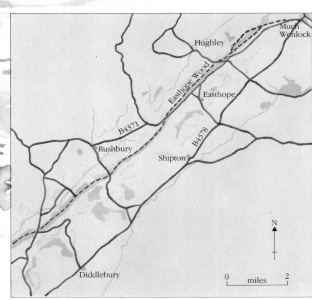

Worth a detour

Wilderhope Manor Now a youth hostel but there is limited public opening of this Elizabethan house. Walks through farmland and woods 7 miles SW of Much Wenlock. NT.

Benthall Hall 16th-century stone house plus garden. 4 miles NE of Much Wenlock near Broseley. NT.

Attingham Park 18th-century mansion set in parkland landscaped by Repton. Walks through deer park and grounds. 4 miles SE of Shrewsbury. NT.

Dudmaston Hall 17th-century house with fine furniture and paintings plus park and garden walks. 4 miles SE of Bridgnorth. NT.

Manifold Valley

Map OS map 24 in Outdoor Leisure series

Below The Manifold winding its leisurely way to confluence with its tributary the Hamps. The romantic foreground ruin is called Weag's Barn; far right is the crag of Beeston Tor. ◇

The Manifold Valley lacks the alliterative appeal of Dovedale which cuts an almost parallel valley through the southern Peak District. But in terms of beauty it is no poor relation; indeed, the lesser renown becomes an advantage in summer months when crowds clog the paths and car parks of Dovedale. In fact the two rivers are closely related. They rise within barely half a mile of each other on the eastern slopes of Axe Edge and join just below the southern gateway to Dovedale. The National Trust owns substantial portions of the most beautiful sections of the valleys. It is the Manifold which is featured here, however, and in particular the steep wooded section between Hulme End and Ilam.

The higher reaches of the Manifold are surrounded by undulating farmland but south of Hulme End — where the river breaches a tract of limestone — the landscape changes dramatically. Here the Manifold begins to carve a narrow winding valley, often 500 feet deep, with all the characteristics of limestone country: bare crags of rock, rivers that disappear through 'swallow holes', networks of caves and a rich and distinctive array of wildlife. The densely wooded slopes of the valley (and that of its tributary, the Hamps) contrast with the bare grassy uplands of the plateau. In places limestone cliffs emerge with a stark grandeur as at Beeston Tor and Thor's Cave. Beeston Tor contains several caves but Thor's is the most famous of the many caves in the Manifold Valley; in its time Thor's Cave has housed bears, hyenas, tigers — and early man. More recent evidence of man's presence in the valley can be found around Ecton where copper was mined, on and off, for eight centuries. The mines

Greater Bellflower

Cowslip

Left The greater bellflower looms over the hedge banks on its four-foot stem. In summer, its purple flowers droop regally from angled stems, the lower ones blooming first. ◇

Right The cowslip belongs to the ubiquitous primrose family, but has deeper yellow flowers. It often cross-pollinates with its paler relative to produce the false oxlip. ◇

closed around 1890 leaving a rather forlorn array of decaying shafts, adits and mine buildings. But, as with relics of limestone workings, these do not disfigure the natural beauty of the landscape.

Modern man has not settled in the valley in any great numbers; a few farms exist but the steepness of the slopes allied to the lack of surface water have ensured it retains a largely uncultivated appeal. This is enhanced by the lack of roads through the valley. For 30 years a narrow-gauge railway did penetrate the Manifold and Hamps valleys but this is now — for most of its length — reserved for walkers and cyclists. The Manifold thus combines tranquillity with accessibility for anyone willing to leave their cars. It is not only a worthy alternative to Dovedale but its caves, disappearing river and trackway cannot be matched.

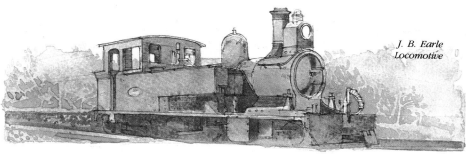

J. B. Earle Locomotive

Above It is half a century since locomotives of the Leek and Manifold Valley Light Railway puffed through the valley, but one legacy remains. The former track has been turned into an asphalt path which provides easy walking — or cycling — along a valley with few roads. Ironically, the promoters of the railway had hoped to catch some early tourist traffic when the line was opened in 1904. It ran for eight miles from Hulme End to Waterhouses where it joined the North Staffordshire Company's branch line to Leek. The idea was to ferry milk from the farms (as well as tourists) and to foster a revival of lead and copper mining around Ecton. However the Ecton copper mines, which had closed about 1890, did not reopen. Thus the picturesque narrow gauge line along the Manifold never made a profit during its 30-year life. ◇

Brown Argus Butterfly

White Letter Hairstreak Butterfly

Discovering the wildlife
Sheep-grazing on the uplands has restricted the growth of trees which are concentrated in the valleys. The soil is mostly too thin for oak, so ash is the most common species with other lime-loving shrubs such as hawthorn, elder and dogwood also evident. The relatively undisturbed nature of the valleys has enabled many comparatively rare plants to prosper; cowslip, early purple orchid, harebell,

Above The brown argus butterfly, its wings fringed with 'eyes', and the white letter hairstreak marked with a 'W', like to fly high among the trees. ◇

alpine currant and bellflower are all typical limestone plants. The woods and water attract a wide variety of birdlife with the dipper and moorhen common by the river and the tree creeper among the rarer woodland species. ◇

Above For about four miles the Manifold is a valley without a river. Just below Wetton Mill — apart from the wettest weather — the river disappears underground and resurfaces in the grounds of Ilam Hall to the south. The phenomenon reputedly baffled one early traveller. Dr. Johnson only believed it to be the same river after playing a kind of lexicographer's poohsticks, dropping corks in the stream as it poured through its 'sinks' or 'swallow holes' only to see them re-emerge at Ilam. For those four miles the river flows through a subterranean network of caverns that is characteristic of limestone areas. Limestone is a porous rock, when exposed, with vertical and horizontal joints. Water tends to flow down and along these to form caverns. It reaches the surface again when the limestone belt ends or when the valley is cut below the level which is saturated by water. ◇

Manifold Valley

Hulme End is the beginning of the Manifold Valley as the river leaves the shales of its upper course and begins to carve its deep valley through the limestone hills. It was also the end of the old railway, so that from Hulme End the former trackway now provides easy, all-weather walking along the northern section of the valley. Local maps will indicate many alternatives over the surrounding hills which provide grandstand views over the valleys and crags. The slopes, though, can be steep, and strong footwear is advised when venturing beyond the valley floor.

Valley walk This follows the trackway of the old railway. It precludes cars from all but a 1½-mile stretch between Swainsley tunnel and Redhurst crossing (where the Wetton–Butterton road crosses the valley). Cars can be parked at many places including Hulme End, Swainsley, Wetton Mill, Weag's Bridge and Beeston Tor so that walks can be varied according to energy and time available. Old packhorse routes cross the valley, sometimes now followed by minor roads. Just below one, at Wetton Mill, the river often disappears underground; just below another, at Weag's Bridge, the Manifold gains a river but loses a railway as the track follows the Hamps valley southwest. Distance: anything up to five miles along Manifold.

Cave walk Thor's Cave is the most visited attraction in the valley and can be reached simply, if strenuously, by climbing up the 100 feet from the valley floor. A more rewarding circuit might be tried from Weag's Bridge via the railway track and footbridge to the cave. Beyond the cave a path to the left leads towards Wetton village. A little to the right of where this path joins the village another heads south back to Weag's Bridge. Distance: two and a half miles.

Hill walk Slightly more ambitious, this starts from Wetton Mill and heads past Dale Farm around the left of the rock known as the Sugar Loaf. The circuit then continues around Ecton Hill, past the old copper and limestone workings, before swinging right to return via the quaintly-named Back of Ecton and Far Hill Hollow to Wetton Mill. The Hollow can be wet in winter. Distance: four miles.

Small-leaved Lime

Above The small-leaved lime tree is characteristic of the Manifold Valley. One of the few areas in Britain where it is naturally regenerating is the Trust's Hinckley Wood opposite Ilam country park. This has therefore been designated a Site of Special Scientific Interest. ◇

Below The tree creeper, a reticent bird with a startlingly systematic feeding habit, spirals up each tree in turn, gleaning insects from the bark. ◇

Tree Creeper

Below left The weasel, small but ferocious, is the scourge of voles and mice, but will also eat berries. Owls occasionally avenge the voles.

Below The grey squirrel, a rodent introduced from North America by 19th-century landowners, is an adept climber and jumper. ◇

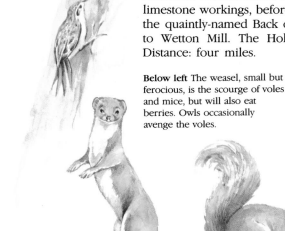
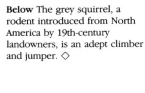

Weasel

Grey Squirrel

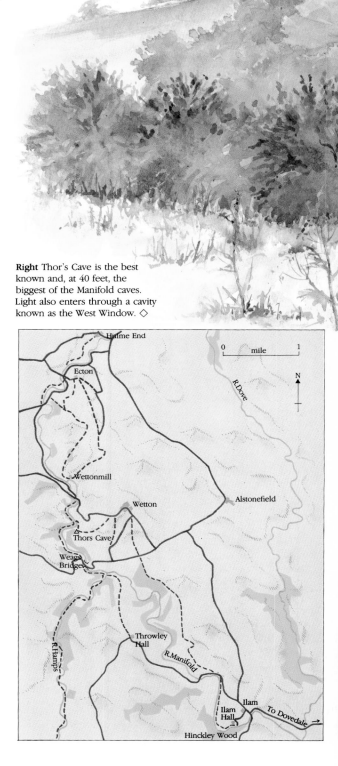

Right Thor's Cave is the best known and, at 40 feet, the biggest of the Manifold caves. Light also enters through a cavity known as the West Window. ◇

No footpath follows the southern section of the river valley between Beeston and the boundaries of Ilam country park. The railway track has swung southwest down the Hamps valley, so walkers have to head for the hills. However, two high-level paths follow each bank giving excellent views of beautiful parts of the valley. Hanging woodlands lead to small fields and isolated barns. Just below Beeston Tor, a popular rockface among climbers, there are some remnants of mining, but more impressive are the great halls of the local estates; Castern Hall and Throwley Hall date from the 17th century, Musden Grange Farm was attached to a monastery destroyed by Henry VIII. It is at Ilam Hall, though, that most visitors begin their exploration.

Short walks The grounds of Ilam Hall now form a country park with a variety of footpaths. It is here that the Manifold resurfaces through what are known as 'boil holes'. Other features are a Saxon cross, a grotto and the remains of a formal garden. The energetic can cross the river into Hinckley Wood, though the path is steep and can be slippery. Distance: up to two miles.

Long walk Ilam Hall can also be the starting point of a circuit following the two higher-level paths; the routes are shown clearly on the OS White Peak map detailed for the northern part of the valley. Essentially it involves heading north from Ilam on the east bank via Castern Hall (and a private road) to Weag's Bridge and returning on the west bank past Beeston Tor Farm, Throwley Hall and Rushley. Distance: eight miles.

Right Ilam Hall was built in its present form in the 19th century, but only part of the building survives. It now houses a youth hostel and a Trust information centre. ◇

Below The River Manifold cuts a narrow path through the hills north of Ilam. The grassy slopes of the Peak District plateau can be glimpsed above the slopes of the lower river valley. ◇

Worth a detour

Ilam Much-rebuilt church contains Norman tower and Saxon font and doorway.

Sudbury Hall Richly decorated 17th-century house with gardens, lake and a Museum of Childhood. 6 miles E of Uttoxeter off A50. NT.

Winster Market House A 17th-century building now a NT information centre. 4 miles W of Matlock on B5057.

Edale

Rowan

Above Rowan is also known as mountain ash, which correctly identifies it as a tree of the uplands. However, rowan is an adaptable species found in woods as well as on heaths and rocky slopes. It flowers in May. ◇

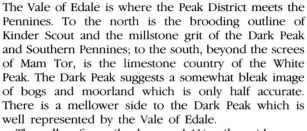

The Vale of Edale is where the Peak District meets the Pennines. To the north is the brooding outline of Kinder Scout and the millstone grit of the Dark Peak and Southern Pennines; to the south, beyond the screes of Mam Tor, is the limestone country of the White Peak. The Dark Peak suggests a somewhat bleak image of bogs and moorland which is only half accurate. There is a mellower side to the Dark Peak which is well represented by the Vale of Edale.

The valley, five miles long and 1½ miles wide, runs from west to east between two of the Peak District's most renowned summits: Kinder Scout and Mam Tor. Until the arrival of the railway in 1890, Edale remained isolated from the outside world, cut off by the Southern ridge of Mam Tor and Losehill which separated it from the parallel Hope Valley. Sheep farming has been the traditional occupation, although the number of farms has shrunk this century from more than 50 to approximately 20.

Despite this, sheep pastures dominate the lower slopes of the valley. Woodland is mostly confined to the narrow ravines (known locally as *cloughs*) from which water pours off the hills into the River Noe. The largest and most interesting area of woodland is Backside Wood on the southern slopes of Jaggers' Clough in the lower valley; here, some remnants of the ancient oak woodland remain in stark contrast to the conifers over the hill alongside Ladybower Reservoir. Backside Wood is among a number of areas now owned in the valley by the National Trust as part of its High Peak estate. Thus Edale will be spared the flooding which turned neighbouring valleys into reservoirs for surrounding cities. The woods, along with the main valley and lower cloughs, also provide gentle walking in the shadow of the hills.

However, it is more energetic rambling for which Edale has achieved a fame which belies its size. It is the southern terminus of the Pennine Way, the first of the long-distance footpaths and still the one regarded as the greatest challenge. In the 1930s people went to prison for the right of access to Kinder Scout and the Pennine moors; in the 1980s gravel with a timber underlay has had to be laid across a stretch of Kinder to prevent excessive erosion by ramblers.

The early pioneers may never have imagined that so many people would follow in their footsteps, but the Peak District, wedged between the conurbations of Lancashire and Yorkshire, has always been Britain's most visited national park. The village of Edale echoes with the clump of heavy-booted ramblers in the summer but away from the village street, and especially out of season, Edale offers uncrowded and unspoilt beauty on the doorstep of industrial England.

Exploring Upper Edale

Edale is sheep-farming country, particularly along the slopes of the upper valley where the weather is more severe and less able to support dairy or arable farming. Visitors should therefore remember to keep dogs on a lead *at all times.* Although the lower slopes are grazed, there are a number of public paths in Upper Edale. The Trust has recently opened a concessionary path which makes possible a circular route from a small car park known as 'the Tips'. Why? Because that was where railway navvies tipped the soil when burrowing Colborne tunnel in the 19th century. From the Tips it is an easy 2½-mile circuit along Whitemoor Clough, a narrow ravine which feeds into the River Noe near the hamlet of Barber Booth. The route passes Dalehead, Orchard and Highfield farms all of which are typical of the hardy sheep-grazing prevalent in the Upper Edale area. Such farms tend to have about 500 breeding ewes producing crops of both wool and meat. ◇

Above Winnats Pass, the turnpike route through the Peak District, was relegated to a minor road this century. But its replacement fell victim to landslips giving new life to the winding gorge. ◇

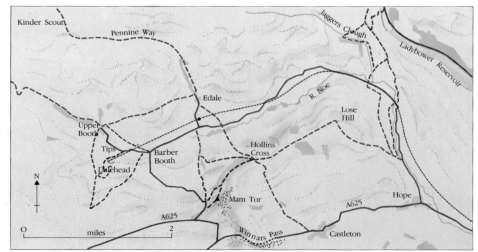

Left The Vale of Edale, where Midlands and North meet, is the heart of the Peak District national park. Its open moors, rocky crags, watery caverns and wooded ravines form an adventure playground for urban man. ◇

Little Owl

Above The little owl is not only the smallest British breeding owl but also the one most likely to be seen by day. It often perches on a post, then hops with a bounding flight and a curious bobbing of its head. ◇

Exploring Lower Edale

The valleys cut by the streams which pour off the hills of the High Peak are known as cloughs. One of the main river courses from the Kinder plateau north of the Vale of Edale is Jaggers' Clough at the eastern end of the valley. It starts on the plateau edge at about 2,000 feet amid wild heather moorland and gradually levels out into a more open valley at about 1,100 feet where the pasture begins. Almost all the land within Jaggers' Clough is owned by the National Trust, with open access to all but the enclosed fields. The moorland provides rewarding walking for the more experienced or adventurous, but the lower parts of the clough have been opened up to provide gentle strolls in the woodland.

The largest tract of woodland is Backside Wood which is also one of the oldest remaining woods in the High peak, although oaks could once have covered the area. The Trust has planted several thousand trees and banned cattle grazing in the hope that natural regeneration of the woodland will take place. The area is well served by footpaths—park at Hope or Edale End. ◇

Edale

Mass trespass on Kinder Scout in the 1930s helped to open up Britain's uplands for recreation, so it is perhaps only appropriate that Edale should have become such a centre for hillwalking. Kinder Scout itself remains a great attraction, even for many not undertaking the full 250 miles of the Pennine Way to Kirk Yetholm in the Scottish borders. However the wildness of the moors which lures visitors can also endanger them. At 2,000 feet, Kinder Scout is often blanketed by heavy mist when the valley below remains clear, and the sodden peat bogs of the open moors then become especially treacherous. It is not a coincidence, therefore, that Edale has a well-equipped mountain rescue centre.

Yet for a sensibly-clad rambler Kinder and the southern peaks offer rewarding as well as challenging walking. The footpath along the southern ridge from Mam Tor, although not easy, is less hazardous than Kinder. Mam Tor overlooks not only the Vale of Edale but also Hope Valley to the south: a strategic site recognized by the existence of an Iron Age hill fort on its summit. The 'skyline' walk, as the southern ridge route is sometimes known, thus offers spectacular views across both valleys. There is even a crossroads some 1,400 feet above sea level at Hollins Cross where a packhorse trail — from Castleton to Edale — crosses the ridgeway route. These trails enable many circular routes to be devised by walkers who want something between the rigours of Kinder Scout and the nursery slopes of the lower valley walks.

Hope Valley to the south is much busier than the Vale of Edale with a main road proving more intrusive than the railway. The head of the valley is dominated by Mam Tor, a dramatic but unstable mass of sandstones and shales which has produced so many landslips that it is sometimes known as the Shivering Mountain. Several such unexpected 'shivers' in the 1970s actually destroyed a modern road and sent traffic back to the craggy Winnats Pass.

Mam Tor stands on the border between the millstone grits of the Dark Peak and the limestone of the White Peak. However the caves below Mam Tor are more the product of mining than the underground erosion found in the limestone country to the south. The mines which once extracted lead and blue John (a type of stone) have been abandoned but many of the caves they left behind are now open to the public for exploration.

Above The curlew, Britain's largest wader, is inevitably associated with the seashore. But only in this century has it bred anywhere other than moorland and many still return to Edale to breed. ◇

Below Edale cotton mill was built in the 18th century, initially using water power but later coal. It closed in 1934 but has been restored by the Landmark Trust. ◇

Curlew

Right The 'shivering mountain' of Mam Tor is crowned by the remains of an Iron Age hill fort which exploited its dominant position at the western end of the Hope Valley and Edale. ◇

Left Ladybower reservoir is one of three in the Upper Derwent valley. When completed in 1945, it was the largest man-made lake in the country. Underneath the reservoir is the drowned village of Derwent, remnants of which may be seen in droughts. ◇

Dry stone walls are wider at the base for stability.

A good wall will have 'through stones' that shed water.

Left The Peak District is moorland country so the fields are divided not by hedges but by the dry-stone walls familiar in other upland areas such as the Lake District or Cotswolds. Building walls with neither mortar nor cement remains one of the most widespread country crafts, despite some attempt to introduce concrete fillings. A dry-stone wall is wider at its base in order to give it stability. However, many different sizes and shapes of stones are selected by a skilful dry-waller. The large stones of the outer layer are piled on each other in such a way that water will easily run off them. Long slabs known as *through stones* pass right through the wall to hold the two outer layers together, with rubble called *hearting* filling the rest of the gap between the outer stones. The wall is often topped by near-vertical slates or stones known as *coppings*; on hills these usually slope downhill and will be arranged to protrude towards the neighbour's land. A well-built wall will last for a century and some include features such as *bole* or *bogg holes* which allow young sheep to move from one field to another. Some walls also incorporate horizontal slabs forming stiles which generations of feet have worn into hollows. ◇

Discovering the wildlife

A patchwork of wildlife habitats can be found in the Vale of Edale from moorland tops to river valley. Running through them all is a network of dry-stone walls and lines of old hawthorn hedges. The hawthorn on the valley sides forms a haven for nesting birds in spring and in late autumn the clusters of crimson berries provide food for many wintering birds such as robins and fieldfares. In the valley bottom, the larger and older trees, with their gnarled trunks, are good feeding grounds for the busy little tree creepers. Bluebells and forget-me-nots carpet the woodlands in spring. Small wetland sites along the river valley provide sheltered areas where the lilac flowers of lady's smock can be seen growing among the rushes, disturbed only by the occasional moorhen, while the graceful but greedy heron feeds on trout in the river itself. ◇

Stoat

Left Stoats make their homes or dens in wooded areas, to elude their enemies — owls or hawks. Hunters themselves, they attack rats and voles as well as rabbits and hares. In winter their fur becomes white but the tip of the tail remains black. ◇

Worth a detour
Hardwick Hall Built by 'Bess of Hardwick' in the 16th century. Impressive house close to M1 and now surrounded by country park. 9½ miles SE of Chesterfield. NT.
Lyme Hall Elizabethan house with large deer park and woodland walks. 6½ miles SE of Stockport. NT.
Peveril Castle Norman castle of which the keep and walls remain on rocky outcrop above Castleton village. Not NT.

71

Duddon Valley

Norway Spruce

Above Norway spruce is best known as the Christmas tree but is also planted as a conventional timber crop. It is not native, but has been grown in Britain for around 500 years. ◇

The valley of the River Duddon is a Lakeland dale without a lake. This may be why, even at the height of summer, the valley is rarely crowded. Yet it is one of the Lake District's loveliest dales — and one that inspired many of Lakeland poet William Wordsworth's best known sonnets.

'Still glides the stream, and shall for ever glide', wrote Wordsworth in his *Valediction to the River Duddon*. And the poet would find Dunnerdale, as the valley is also known, less changed than many other places in his beloved Lake District. The occasional walker and a few cars are all you are likely to encounter amid the wooded tracts, tumbling streams and serene views of the high fells.

The Duddon rises high on Wrynose Pass, flows southwest through Seathwaite and Ulpha before reaching the sea east of Millom. The head of the valley is Forestry Commission land, an area of tiered conifers. However, the National Trust owns several smaller areas in the valley as well as most of the surrounding fells at the head of the valley reaching north to some of Lakeland's most famous peaks.

It is the river which is the most attractive feature of Duddon Valley itself; wide, tumbling and strewn with boulders and stepping stones, it is for the most part lined with trees. The valley was once self-supporting: food came from the river — including salmon and trout — and salt from the estuary; the fells provided peat and also grazing for sheep, pigs and cattle; the woods furnished nuts, fruit and timber. The bubbling waters also powered small mills so that before the industrial revolution the combination of water power and charcoal (from the woods) enabled a blast furnace to flourish ahead of its time at Duddon Bridge using iron ore shipped upstream.

Sheep farming is now the prime industry of Duddon Valley, not tourism. The lack of any major centre for visitors — the valley has no large hotel and only one small youth hostel — means that it stays quiet when most other dales without lakes, such as Langdale, are bursting with visitors. Yet it is not entirely true to say there are no lakes: there are two which can be reached only by foot and which lead off Duddon Valley. Seathwaite Tarn is two miles northeast of Seathwaite village while Devoke Water is off a minor road northwest of Ulpha. Both are worth a visit.

Although most of the keen and experienced fell-

Left Cockley Beck at the head of the Duddon Valley. Here, where 3 counties once met, the tree-lined river valley opens onto the high mountains of central Lakeland. ◇

Buzzard

Left The buzzard is one of Britain's most common birds of prey, with a deceptively effortless flight-before-pounce on anything from a beetle to a rabbit. Widespread on high ground in the north and west. ◇

Above Wrynose Pass heads east from Cockley Beck towards Windermere. It is an ancient route from the coast to the heart of Lakeland — the Romans built a fort at the adjoining Hardknott Pass — which reaches 1281 feet. ◇

walkers make for the head of the valley, there is much to explore in the dale to the south. There is no main road but narrow twisting lanes provide many viewpoints and picnic areas, such as the narrow gorge near Birks Bridge where the river has formed deep, clear pools perfect for swimming. At the head of the valley the road divides, heading either west towards Hardknott Pass or east to Wrynose Pass. But Duddon Valley is not seen at its best from a car; you simply miss too much of its beauty. Woods, fells, stepping stones and a magnificent river capture much of the very essence of the Lake District's appeal without the panoply of commercial development or overpopularity.

Discovering the wildlife
The course of the River Duddon, from high fell to sandy estuary, presents a microcosm of Lakeland wildlife. In terms of vegetation this is farmland in the lower valley giving way to coniferous woodland on the higher slopes and some mixed deciduous woodland on the lower slopes. There are also the open fells with sheep tracks on the middle slopes.
The birdlife reflects this change of habitat. The most dramatic bird likely to be seen is the buzzard, Lakeland's most common bird of prey. It feeds on small mammals, especially rabbits, and can often be seen over the open fells. Here, too, raven, carrion crow, meadow pipit and wheatear can be seen in summer. Mountain birdlife, always sparse, becomes almost non-existent in winter; it is also extremely limited in mature coniferous forests, as found at the head of the valley. A few goldcrests and tits do nest here, though, along with another bird of prey, the sparrowhawk. The birdlife is much more varied in areas of mixed or deciduous woodland in the lower valley. Here you will find wood and willow warblers, chiffchaff and blackcap, but again winter sees a reduced population as the woodland breeding birds leave to search for food elsewhere. The river itself attracts the dipper and grey wagtail which bob among the boulders. Sadly, otters are feared extinct, although there are plenty of foxes, red squirrel, badgers and — especially in winter — roe deer. ◇

Duddon Valley

Exploring the Duddon Valley can be as easy or as arduous as you choose. Rock climbers will head for Wallowbarrow Crag near Seathwaite while the more experienced hillwalkers will make for the fells at the head of the valley. Scafell Pike, at 3,206 feet the highest peak in England, lies northwest of Cockley Beck, although it is best approached from Wasdale Head. Walking anywhere on the high fells is a serious business, requiring proper kit and due respect for the elements. Even in summer the weather can change rapidly and a mild valley breeze can become a chilly gale. Experience should always therefore govern ambition.

Nevertheless there is much to enjoy in Duddon Valley for walkers with training shoes on their feet and T-shirts on their backs. The lack of a developed tourist industry, which contributes so much to the valley's appeal, means that it mostly lacks developed or waymarked trails of the kind found elsewhere in the Lake District. However there are plenty of paths clearly shown on the Ordnance Survey maps which can be used as the basis of circular and other routes round the valley. One advantage of the afforestation at the head of Duddon Valley is the provision by the Forestry Commission of one area with waymarked paths.

The Commission's car park at Hinning Close can be used as the base for a moderately easy six-mile walk as well as shorter circuits in the woods themselves. From the car park it is only a short distance to one of the valley's most famous (and most painted) landmarks — Birks Bridge. Here, where the river cuts through a narrow gorge is an idyllic picnic area. There is a riverside path heading south, but for the six-mile circuit cross the bridge and follow the path first for Birks and then via Grassguards to Seathwaite. The path will take you over open fells as well as the Forestry Commission land before returning to the river. Paths lead back via Turner Hall, Long House, and Tongue House before linking up with the river south of Birks Bridge. This six-mile route combines river, fell and forest in a beautiful stretch of the upper Duddon Valley.

A fairly easy five-mile circuit in the lower Duddon, again combining fells, forest and riverside, can be undertaken from Ulpha Bridge, partly using unclassified roads, via the ruins of Frith Hall and Mill How. The paths are shown on detailed Ordnance Survey maps.

Historic Duddon Valley

The nomenclature of the Duddon Valley, is a clue to the role of the Norsemen or Danes in clearing the fells. *Thwaite* is the old Norse word for clearing while *Frith* means woodland. However there are also Celtic echoes: Logan Beck comes from *Lagan* meaning a small hollow, while Penn Hill comes from the Celtic word for a hill, *penn*. One of the oldest remnants of man's settlement in the area is Swinside stone circle, two miles west of Duddon Bridge. It is not as spectacularly sited as the famous stone circles at Castlerigg and Long Meg, but it is more complete with 55 stones in a circle 85 feet across. ◇

Sparrowhawk

Above As its name suggests the sparrowhawk, a ferocious little falcon, feeds mainly on sparrows and other small birds. It nests in all types of woods. ◇

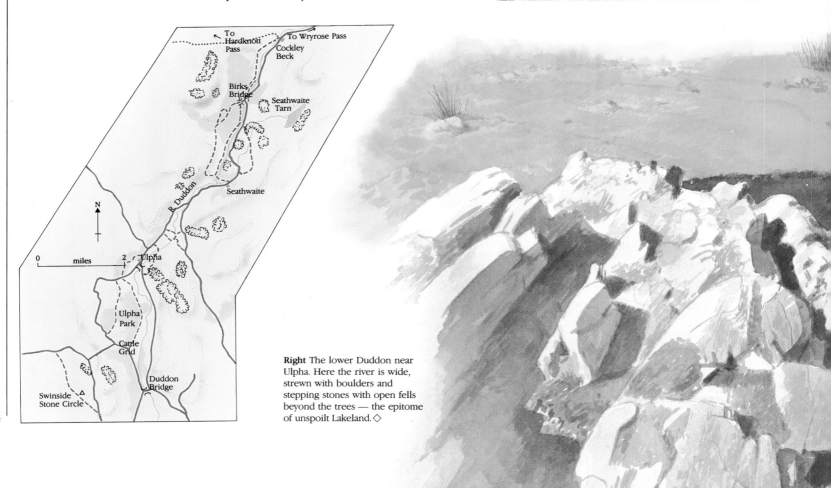

Right The lower Duddon near Ulpha. Here the river is wide, strewn with boulders and stepping stones with open fells beyond the trees — the epitome of unspoilt Lakeland. ◇

Swaledale Sheep

Herdwick Sheep

Above Birks Bridge stands where the Duddon cuts through a narrow gorge encircled by woodland. ◇

Above The most conspicuous mammals in Duddon Valley are sheep, mostly Herdwick and Swaledale.
The Herdwick is a smallish animal with a white face. Only the male has horns. As they grow older, their wool becomes lighter in colour. Herdwick sheep are found on the fells whereas the larger, less agile Swaledale is normally found in the valleys and plains. Both male (tup) and ewe Swaledale have dark faces and curved horns. Many Cumbrian shepherds still use an ancient method of counting their flocks: yan, tan and tether are Celtic words for one, two and three and so it goes on up to dick .. or ten. ◇

Worth a detour

Coniston A popular lake now plied during summer months by the NT-operated steam yacht, *Gondola.*
Hardknott Remains of a Roman fort in magnificent position near the summit of Hardknott Pass. 10 miles W of Ambleside.
Hill Top House where Bea-trix Potter wrote many of her books; some overcrowding. 2 miles S of Hawkshead. NT.
Wordsworth His birthplace at Cockermouth (NT) and two later homes (not NT) — Dove Cottage and Rydal Mount, both near Grasmere — contain many mementos of the poet.

Ben Lomond

Capercaillie

Above The capercaillie is the largest British gamebird, with the male not unlike a flying turkey. Once believed extinct, it is now quite common amid Scottish conifers.◇

Right Ben Lomond, where water, woodside and mountain complement each other to produce a landscape whose beauty belies its proximity to urban Scotland.◇

Rob Roy MacGregor

Above Rob Roy MacGregor and the National Trust for Scotland may not appear to have much in common, but both have owned part of Ben Lomond. Rob Roy, who was born in 1671 the son of a Highland chief, came to own the whole western flank of the mountain. He was outlawed after being bankrupted by his partner in cattle dealing, who absconded with £1,000. Rob Roy then lived by plundering the lands of his prosecutor, the Duke of Montrose, defying all efforts of king and army to crush him.◇

Right These neat cottages are at Luss, a fine viewpoint southwest from Ben Lomond on the western shore of Loch Lomond, the largest natural lake in Great Britain. ◇

76

Ben Lomond is Scotland's most southerly mountain over 3,000 feet: but its fame owes as much to the loch which stretches for 21 miles along its western flanks as to its 3,192-foot summit. Loch Lomond is Britain's largest expanse of inland water and also one of its most accessible beauty spots, with Glasgow barely 25 miles away. For two centuries, visitors have been drawn to its twisting shoreline beneath the mountain. Cruisers ply the loch during summer, yet it is still possible to leave the crowds behind on the eastern shore, north of Rowardennan, where the road ends.

The loch changes character from south to north: broad and open to the south, where its four-mile width is chequered by a dozen wooded islands, it gradually narrows until it cleaves the mountains like a fiord. Indeed, the loch was a true sea fiord at the close of the Ice Age. A huge glacier from the Rannoch ice cap had scooped out the rock basin in which the loch now lies. With the melting of the ice, sea levels rose and the

loch became a branch of the Firth of Clyde. Finally coastal lands, freed of their own weight of ice, rose so that the Vale of Leven silted up to leave the foot of Loch Lomond four miles from the Firth.

Ben Lomond itself has only recently been acquired by the National Trust for Scotland; previously it formed part of the Forestry Commission's neighbouring Queen Elizabeth Forest Park. Ease of access has made it probably Scotland's most popular mountain. Yet seen from the south, it does not impose itself on the landscape, but rises gently from the massive shoulder of the Ptarmigan peak. From Tarbet, east across the loch, its cone sharpens dramatically but the most graceful of its several profiles can be seen from Loch Ard in the Trossachs. Its twin tops are there apparent for the first time, deeply sculpted by its great eastern *corrie*. The summit is half a mile long, the upper end of a long ridge that curves nearly four miles down to Loch Lomond at Blairvockie Farm. This ridge offers the easiest ascent to the summit. It is a path which requires energy and sense rather than mountaineering skills.

The shores of Loch Lomond are richly wooded—mainly oak, rowan, birch, alder, beech, chestnut and larch. Scots pine is present in only small numbers. The banks are at their most colourful in spring and autumn, although in June bluebells haze the woodlands. The Forestry Commission owns nearly 20 square miles of conifer plantations around the loch, but the broad-leaved trees remain the prime feature of the 'bonnie banks', with splendid oakwoods around Sallochy. The diversity of woodland, allied to the changing colours of bracken and heather, means that each season has an allure of its own.

Discovering the wildlife

The wildlife of Loch Lomond is rich and diverse—one quarter of Britain's flowering species can be found here: and the range of habitat, from water and marsh and to mountain top, attracts 220 bird species. The loch itself holds not only the usual game fish—salmon and trout—but pike, eel, perch and powan. Birds around Ben Lomond include golden eagle, peregrine falcon and snow bunting. Woodland birds include collared dove, capercaillie and jay. On the water itself are red- and black-throated diver, merganser and cormorant. Osprey is a spring visitor while winter brings up to 2,000 geese to the wetlands around the Endrick River. The mammals most commonly seen are deer—red, roe and fallow—but Ben Lomond also has a herd of 100 feral goats.◇

Below Powan, the most numerous species of fish in Loch Lomond, looks like a herring, but is actually a member of the salmon family.◇

Powan

Short-eared Owl

Above The short-eared owl is a bird of mountains and moorland, especially near conifers, since these form a perfect habitat for its favourite prey, field voles.◇

Exploring the countryside

A road runs the length of Loch Lomond's western shore, but walkers have the northern half of the eastern bank to themselves. The hamlet of Rowardennan, where the eastern road ends, can be the base for an ascent of Ben Lomond or the start of a splendid walk along the loch. The path to the summit is four and a half miles. Wear boots and carry warm, waterproof clothing for there can be unexpected drops in temperature between shore and summit. The path is clear and not too demanding; an easy walking time to the top in summer is two and a half hours. The lochside walk is part of the long-distance West Highland Way from Milngavie near Glasgow to Fort William. North of Rowardennan it follows forestry tracks as well as footpaths and passes Rob Roy's Cave near Inversnaid, some seven miles north of Rowardennan. The route is well signposted and can also be followed for seven and a half miles south of Rowardennan as far as Balmaha, where it leaves the shore. On this stretch of the West Highland Way, you are never far from a parallel minor road, but both stretches offer varied scenery and easy going. At Balmaha, a two-mile walk can be undertaken to Conic Hill (1,175 feet) which gives views over the islands at the southern end of the loch. Two shorter forest walks also begin from Balmaha's car park and there are other walks through woodland and along the loch in the Sallochy woods, three and a half miles north. Boats can be hired at Balmaha to visit the island of Inchcailloch, where there is a nature trail on the Nature Conservancy Council's reserve.◇

Worth a detour
Balloch Castle Country park with gardens, nature trail and other paths along loch in grounds of castle built in 1808. At S end of loch off B854. Not NTS.
Loch Ard Forest Part of the Forestry Commission's vast Queen Elizabeth Forest Park which extends from the Trossachs to Ben Lomond. Many walks and picnic areas, including the 'Silver Ring', a 6-mile circuit through forest and alongside lochs starting from Aberfoyle.

Map labels: Ben Lomond, Loch Lomond, Queen Elizabeth Forest Park, Rowardennan, Dubh Loch, Sallochy, B837, A82, Luss, Conic Hill, Balmaha, B837, N, 0 miles 3

Glen Coe

Glen Coe would be famous for its scenery, even if it had never become infamous for its massacre. Yet the grim legacy of the slaughter in 1692 reinforces the impact of these glowering rocky mountains. A main road may now follow the valley, 100,000 tourists may visit the information centre each year, but these mountains can never be tamed. Leave the road or the riverside paths and you enter what, by British standards, is still a wilderness.

It is all the more spectacular for the suddenness with which it is approached. The road across the bleak expanse of Rannoch Moor descends abruptly into Glen Coe with mountains on either side soaring sheer to 3000 feet and more. Once these were as high as the Alps and, low though they may be in world terms, they remain mountains rather than hills. No trees grow on these slopes, only tufts of stubbly grass between the rocks. Although the lack of trees restricts the wildlife, the glen is the realm of those rare and monarchic creatures, the red deer and golden eagle as well as the elusive wildcat, which lives amid the screes above 1,000 feet. Glen Coe becomes broader towards the west with fields and clusters of trees softening the scenery as the bubbling River Coe reaches Loch Leven and Glencoe village.

Much of Glen Coe is now owned by the National Trust for Scotland which runs a visitor centre near Signal Rock. The glen appeals at different levels to different interests. Mountaineers head for Buachaille Etive Mór and some of the country's toughest rockfaces; experienced walkers likewise relish the challenge of Aonach Eagach's narrow ridge. These highest slopes of Glen Coe are no place for novices, who have neither the equipment nor the experience to match the terrain. However there are also routes which are less demanding, some of which head up passes away from the main valley. These require reasonable footwear and energy but even less arduous are the woodland walks for those who simply want to stop, stare, stroll and maybe picnic.

Japanese Larch

Red Deer

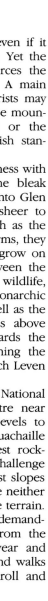

Right The 'Three Sisters' of Glen Coe tower like cliffs over the tiny River Coe in a valley gouged and deepened by huge glaciers. ◇

Exploring the countryside
Once much of lower Glen Coe was wooded but of this 'Caledonian Forest' of native Scots pine only a few fragments remain. Today's Glencoe Forest is a 20th-century creation, established by the Forestry Commission. Sitka spruce, Lodgepole pine, Japanese larch and Norway spruce are the most common species of conifer and the plantation roads provide easy walking around Glencoe village. One small tract of woodland lies near the NTS visitor centre from where trails lead to two knolls, Signal Rock and An Tor. Neither is particularly high or difficult to reach but each offers an excellent viewpoint. Signal Rock is traditionally believed to be the spot from where the signal was given to start the 1692 massacre. Each walk is approximately 1½ miles. The Lochan forest walk is a waymarked route among the woods north of Glencoe village bordering Loch Leven. The full trail is about 1¾ miles from a car park near Glencoe hospital, but a shorter route is possible round a small lake, the Lochan. ◇

Left Conifers such as Japanese larch have supplanted native Scots pine, but red deer still roam Glen Coe and Rannoch Moor in large herds. ◇

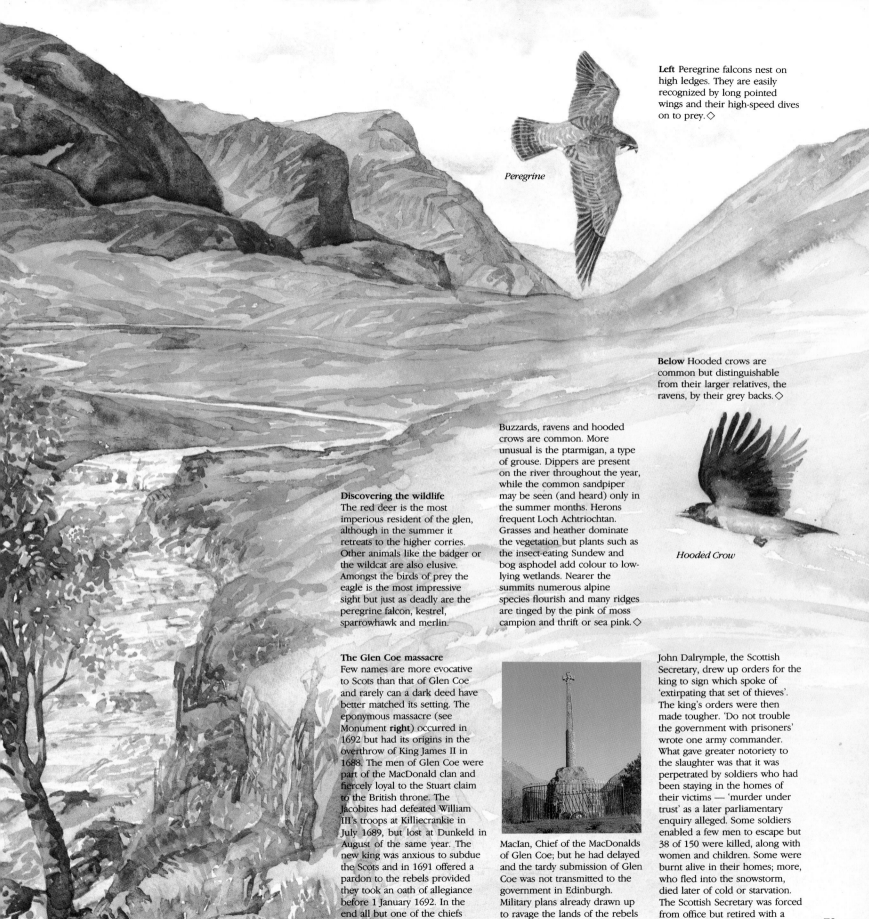

Left Peregrine falcons nest on high ledges. They are easily recognized by long pointed wings and their high-speed dives on to prey. ◇

Peregrine

Below Hooded crows are common but distinguishable from their larger relatives, the ravens, by their grey backs. ◇

Hooded Crow

Discovering the wildlife
The red deer is the most imperious resident of the glen, although in the summer it retreats to the higher corries. Other animals like the badger or the wildcat are also elusive. Amongst the birds of prey the eagle is the most impressive sight but just as deadly are the peregrine falcon, kestrel, sparrowhawk and merlin.

Buzzards, ravens and hooded crows are common. More unusual is the ptarmigan, a type of grouse. Dippers are present on the river throughout the year, while the common sandpiper may be seen (and heard) only in the summer months. Herons frequent Loch Achtriochtan. Grasses and heather dominate the vegetation but plants such as the insect-eating Sundew and bog asphodel add colour to low-lying wetlands. Nearer the summits numerous alpine species flourish and many ridges are tinged by the pink of moss campion and thrift or sea pink. ◇

The Glen Coe massacre
Few names are more evocative to Scots than that of Glen Coe and rarely can a dark deed have better matched its setting. The eponymous massacre (see Monument **right**) occurred in 1692 but had its origins in the overthrow of King James II in 1688. The men of Glen Coe were part of the MacDonald clan and fiercely loyal to the Stuart claim to the British throne. The Jacobites had defeated William III's troops at Killiecrankie in July 1689, but lost at Dunkeld in August of the same year. The new king was anxious to subdue the Scots and in 1691 offered a pardon to the rebels provided they took an oath of allegiance before 1 January 1692. In the end all but one of the chiefs made their peace, including

MacIan, Chief of the MacDonalds of Glen Coe; but he had delayed and the tardy submission of Glen Coe was not transmitted to the government in Edinburgh. Military plans already drawn up to ravage the lands of the rebels were brought into action. Sir

John Dalrymple, the Scottish Secretary, drew up orders for the king to sign which spoke of 'extirpating that set of thieves'. The king's orders were then made tougher. 'Do not trouble the government with prisoners' wrote one army commander. What gave greater notoriety to the slaughter was that it was perpetrated by soldiers who had been staying in the homes of their victims — 'murder under trust' as a later parliamentary enquiry alleged. Some soldiers enabled a few men to escape but 38 of 150 were killed, along with women and children. Some were burnt alive in their homes; more, who fled into the snowstorm, died later of cold or starvation. The Scottish Secretary was forced from office but retired with a pension and royal pardon. ◇

Glen Coe

Glen Coe is the second most-visited area owned by the National Trust for Scotland. Most visitors are content simply to admire the scenery from the main valley floor and few will be disappointed. But there are greater rewards for those able to head into the hills. The walks described below do not scale the heights and do not involve rock climbing, but as they do cover rough ground, sturdy walking boots are sensible. Warm and waterproof clothing is also advised and so, too, is a map. Pages 150–151 give more detailed advice about what to wear for serious hillwalking such as this, but the basic rules are simple: never overestimate your ability or equipment, never underestimate the mountains or the weather. However, as the four routes suggested here range from five to 12 miles they can be chosen to match varying degrees of equipment, experience and energy.

Coire Gabhail There are two translations of this Gaelic phrase — the Hidden Valley or place of concealment for stolen cattle. The path leaves the lay-by on the main road roughly three miles east of the NTS visitor centre and just west of Allt-na-Reich. It begins with a sharp descent and climb to and from the River Coe before following the line of the wooded Gabhail Burn to reach the flat valley floor of Coire Gabhail. This is ideal for picnics and is surrounded by mountains and often grazed by red deer. Return by the same route as it is a dead-end valley. Difficult in wet or icy conditions with some steep drops on the ascent. Distance: three miles.

Lairig Eilde or *Pass of the Hind* This footpath begins about one mile further east than the previous walk. It is signposted and follows an old bridle path to climb gently up the Eilde Valley with Beinn Fhada on the west side and Buachaille Etive Beag on the east. Red deer are common here, too, and occasionally a golden eagle may be seen. Return by the same route. Distance: 2½ miles to the summit of the pass.

Lairig Gartain or *Pass of Gartan* This path starts at a lay-by half a mile west of the gamekeeper's cottage at Altnafeadh. It rises gently to give superb views of Loch Etive, Glen Etive, Beinn Starav and Ben Cruachan. The path follows a stream and is invariably wet. Experienced walkers can cross the lower southern slopes of Stob Dubh above Dalness to return through Lairig Eilde (described above). Distance: nine miles by the circular route.

The Devil's Staircase Unlike the previous routes, this heads north of the main valley. It starts just west of the

Below Clachaig Gully, etched into the face of Sgorrnam Fiannaidh, was formed not by a river but by a fracture in the earth's surface. The geology of Glen Coe is complex, involving intense folding of rocks and prolonged volcanic activity. At one point, about 300 million years ago, a roughly circular area of land stretching from the present-day visitor centre to beyond Buachaille Etive Mór, subsided into the earth's crust. This 'cauldron subsidence' displaced the underlying molten magma, some of which was forced to the surface between the subsiding core and the surrounding rocks. Such a circular fracture in the crust is known as a *ring fault*. The Clachaig Gully and the deep groove in the hillside above the cottage beside Loch Achtriochtan are sections of this ring fault, clearly visible now after millions of years of erosion of shattered rocks in the line of the fault. The flat floor of the glen was formed in the Ice Ages when glaciers gouged U-shaped valleys leaving hanging valleys stranded high above the main valley floor. ◇

Right Buachaille Etive Mór, the Great Herdsman of Etive, stands guard over the head of Glen Coe at its junction with Glen Etive. ◇

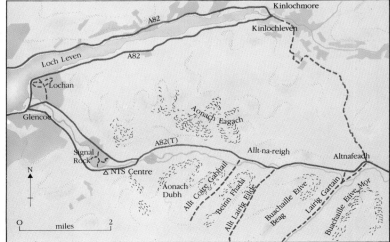

gamekeeper's cottage at Altnafeadh and is signposted to Kinlochleven. The track was the traditional route north but was improved in the 18th century to become one of Scotland's 'military roads'. It is well-defined and mostly good going. From a starting point at 1,000 feet, it climbs 800 feet to give panoramic views over the mountains and now forms part of the West Highland Way between the outskirts of Glasgow and Fort William. Distance one-way: six miles.

Ptarmigan

Above The ptarmigan is a type of grouse confined to the Scottish Highlands. In winter its plumage turns white, apart from its tail, as camouflage on snow-covered hills against predators. ◇

Tufted Hair Grass

Mat Grass

Deer Grass

Left and right Tufted hair grass grows in sturdy tussocks, whereas the slender spikelets of mat grass appear individually. Smooth-stemmed deer grass is rather an imposter, as it is really a sedge. ◇

Below Mountain everlasting is a perennial which flowers by streams in June and July. ◇

Mountain Everlasting

Worth a detour
Glenfinnan Here, at the head of Loch Shiel, Bonnie Prince Charlie raised his standard in the Jacobite rising of 1745. A simple monument marks the spot and an information centre tells the story of the abortive rebellion which took the self-proclaimed King Charles III to defeat at Culloden. Boats ply the loch in summer; a path follows the east bank. 18½ miles W of Fort William off the A830. NTS.
Falls of Lora More like rapids than a waterfall, but still impressive. At Connel under A828 bridge N of Oban.

Ben Lawers

Ben Lawers is Britain's ninth highest mountain. At 3,984 feet it dominates the Lawers Range, a group of six mountains on Tayside with seven peaks over 3,000 feet in height situated between Glen Lyon to the north and Loch Tay to the south. Yet it is renowned not for its height but as probably the best-known site in Britain for alpine and arctic flowers.

Most of the Scottish Highlands are covered by a layer of acidic soil. Rain falling on such soil itself becomes acidic and removes the nutrients and salts necessary for a wide range of flora. Ben Lawers in Perthshire is different because it is largely composed of various forms of *schists* — rock originally laid down under the sea and then forced back to the surface by earth movements which produced intense heat. The combination of the crumbly Ben Lawers schists and a severe mountain climate has produced an ideal habitat for plants on the upper slopes where the soils are often less acidic and rich in lime.

As a result, the upper slopes of the Ben Lawers Range are the home of an impressive array of mountain plants. In spring, the rocky outcrops produce a startling display of purple saxifrage, succeeded later in the season by several other, equally colourful species, including in July its close relative, the yellow mountain saxifrage. Elsewhere the abundant moss campion (aptly described by its alternative name of 'cushion pink') and mossy cyphel form extensive and colourful carpets interspersed with alpine lady's mantle (on the drier, grass slopes), meadow rue and sibbaldia. Mountain pansy scatters points of intense purple while wild thyme adds colour and aroma.

The boggy areas offer displays of bog asphodel and the two insectivorous plants, sundew and butterwort, while the wet springs, fed by water enriched by minerals dissolved from the rocks above, give rise to concen-

trations of interesting sedges and rushes. Russet sedge is particularly striking and dominant. More colourful species, such as the delicate Scottish asphodel and the succulent hairy stonecrop are also to be found around the richer springs. It is because of the exceptionally rich mountain flora of Ben Lawers that much of its southern slopes now form a national nature reserve managed jointly by the National Trust for Scotland and the Nature Conservancy Council. The flora also include several very uncommon species: the snow gentian, snow pearlwort and mountain sandwort are examples which can be seen in few other British sites while the bristle sedge is known only from the Lawers Range.

These species and habitats are found mainly at the higher altitudes, scattered over five mountains in the range. But several of the alpine species thrive equally well at lower altitudes, especially where the mountain burns have eroded their valleys through the glacial drift to expose the underlying rock. One such area,

Map OS map 51 in 1:50000 series

Alpine Meadow Rue

Above Alpine meadow rue in the Highlands is a smaller, neater version of its tall, bushy dampland relative, but has the same tiny yellow-stamened flowers. ◊

Right Mountain pansy, resplendent with flowers the size of a ten pence coin, is the largest wild pansy in Britain. The flowers may be yellow or violet. ◊

Ringlet Butterfly

Above The ringlet butterfly flies over grassy meadows and open woodland in high summer. Patterns vary, but the distinctive ringlet marking is constant. ◊

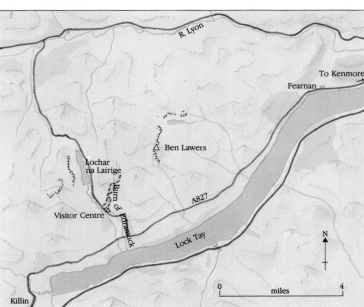

R. Lyon

To Kenmore →

Fearnan

Ben Lawers

Lochar na Lairige

Burn of Edramuck

Visitor Centre

A827

Loch Tay

N

Killin

0 — miles — 4

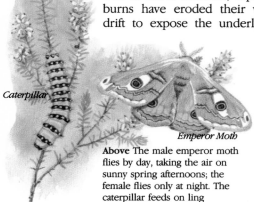

Caterpillar

Emperor Moth

Above The male emperor moth flies by day, taking the air on sunny spring afternoons; the female flies only at night. The caterpillar feeds on ling heather. ◊

Exploring the countryside
The Ben Lawers nature trail may be located on the lower slopes of the mountain, but the visitor is still more than 1,400 feet above sea level. Although the trail does not require the specialized mountain clothing or physical fitness necessary for the walk to the summit, stout footwear is still recommended. The route has been devised to include as many varied habitats as possible within easy reach of the car park; pausing to look at

Left There are higher mountains than Ben Lawers, but none has so many exotic alpine plants so readily accessible. ◇

Right Alpine lady's mantle is a low-growing perennial, producing frothy sprays of tiny green flowers and roundish leaves with silvery undersides. ◇

Left Purple saxifrage has tiny thyme-like leaves, and starry flowers which are the first sign of spring in the mountains. ◇

Purple Saxifrage

Mountain Pansy

Alpine Lady's Mantle

Yellow Mountain Saxifrage

Left Yellow mountain saxifrage, commoner than its marshland relative, blooms in high summer. Look out for the red spots on its narrow pointed leaves. ◇

Moss Campion

Short-tailed Vole

around the Edramucky Burn, has been chosen as the site of the nature trail so that visitors can see a selection of the mountain plants with minimum exertion — and without endangering the isolated populations of the rarest plants. A visitor centre is open in the summer.

Experienced hillwalkers, of course, will head for the summits and, as the highest peak for over 30 miles, Ben Lawers offers memorable views over the Scottish Highlands. Access to the nature reserve is from the Trust's car park on the minor road linking the A827 on Loch Tayside with Glen Lyon.

Right The short-tailed or field vole is a tiny but prolific rodent, seemingly dedicated to providing an endless food source for foxes and raptors. It lives in open woodland and hedgerows. ◇

the different locations will mean therefore that it can take up to two hours to complete the 1¼ mile circuit. The trail initially follows the main path to Ben Lawers, across a wet boggy area, then diverges from the summit path to follow a route crossing back and forth alongside the Edramucky Burn. At the top of the trail the path rejoins the track to Ben Lawers for the return journey to the car park. The trail provides an opportunity to see not only contrasting

features of landform and land use but also many species of mountain plants otherwise not readily accessible.

The fauna is generally less remarkable than the flora, with summer migrant birds such as the wheatear, meadow pipit and skylark the most conspicuous residents. Voles abound in the grassland but are seldom seen; lizards are also common but seen only as they dash for cover. Blackface sheep are much in evidence. ◇

Right Moss campion, rather a speciality of the region, is a luscious pincushion of tiny pointed leaves studded with bright rose pink flowers which bloom briefly in June and July. ◇

Worth a detour
Craigower A beacon hill with panoramic views over Perthshire. 1½ miles NW of Pitlochry off A924. NTS.
The Hermitage 50 acres of woodland along the deep gorge of the River Braan which take their name from a picturesque 18th-century folly overlooking a waterfall. Woodland walk. 2 miles W of Dunkeld. NTS.
Killiecrankie Famous wooded gorge, with its beauty little diminished by the main road through the pass to the Highlands. Towards the head of the pass is a viewpoint which impressed Queen Victoria in 1844. Not far away is the Soldier's Leap, a fearsome gap high above the swirling water which was jumped by a soldier fleeing the Jacobite army in the Battle of Killiecrankie of 1689. The battle itself took place on higher ground near Urrard, a mile north of the pass. A visitor centre recalls the battle as well as featuring the natural history of the area. 3 miles NW of Pitlochry. NTS.
Linn of Tummel Wooded walks along the banks of two rivers, the Tummel and the Garry, with a woodland walk and places for bathing or picnics. 2½ miles NW of Pitlochry. NTS.

Torridon

Map OS map 8 in Outdoor Leisure series

Queen Victoria

Above On 15 September 1873 Queen Victoria visited Torridon. She was, she said, most amazed: 'Soon the grand, wild, savage-looking but most beautiful and picturesque Glen of Torridon opened upon us, with the dark mural precipices of that most extraordinary mountain Liathach which the people pronounce Liarach. We were quite amazed as we drove below it. The mountains here rise so abruptly from their base that they seemed much higher than our Aberdeenshire mountains. Liarach is most peculiar from it being so dark and the rocks like terraces... or like fortifications and pillars — most curious.'◇

There are higher mountains in Scotland than those which overlook Loch Torridon, but none is more imposing. These peaks soar literally from sea level to heights well over 3,000 feet and comprise some of the oldest rocks on the face of the earth. Some of the toughest, too, as they have withstood 750 million years of erosion to produce the rugged outlines we see today. If it is this proximity of sea and mountains which offers pleasure to man, it is the same combination which provides sanctuary to some of Britain's rarest wildlife. Here you may see not only the golden eagle but also the sea eagle, not only the pine marten but also the wildcat.

Liathach, at 3,456 feet, is the highest of the Torridon peaks with its precipitous south face towering over the hamlet of Torridon itself. In fact Liathach is a series of seven separate peaks linked by more than five miles of ridges. These are narrow and jagged as frost erosion sends debris down the mountain to form broad aprons of screes. Liathach is gaelic for 'the grey one' and it could be argued plausibly that this refers to either these screes or the clouds which frequently shroud the summit. A more likely origin, however, is the hard, grey-white quartzite which is exposed at the higher reaches and which sparkles in summer sunshine.

The neighbouring mountains of Beinn Alligin and Beinn Eighe are scarcely less impressive. Beinn Eighe, to the east of Liathach, has an even more extensive white ridge of glistening quartzite and retains on its northern slopes towards Loch Maree a fragment of the erstwhile mighty Caledonian pine forest which once covered much of the Scottish Highlands.

The majesty of the mountains is enhanced by the comparative smallness of the villages which huddle at their base along the shores of Loch Torridon: Annat, Inveralligin, Fasag, Shieldaig and Diabaig are all attractive hamlets now benefiting from the new roads bringing tourists into a once impenetrable area. But life remains simple and, in winter, bleak. The land is too rocky and too infertile, the climate too windy and too cold to support anything but the most primitive agriculture. Some crofting is still practised, mainly based on hill sheep, and peat is still cut for fuel during May and June. It is the very simplicity of this life allied to the scenery which is so alluring to urban man. However, the mountains must be treated with respect: the ridges and peaks are among the most challenging climbs for mountaineers in Britain; and the clarity of a fine, sunny day can swiftly degenerate into storms and mists which would endanger inexperienced hillwalkers. It is a bonus, therefore, that so much can be enjoyed by car and by walking along the valleys and lochsides.

Heath Spotted Orchid

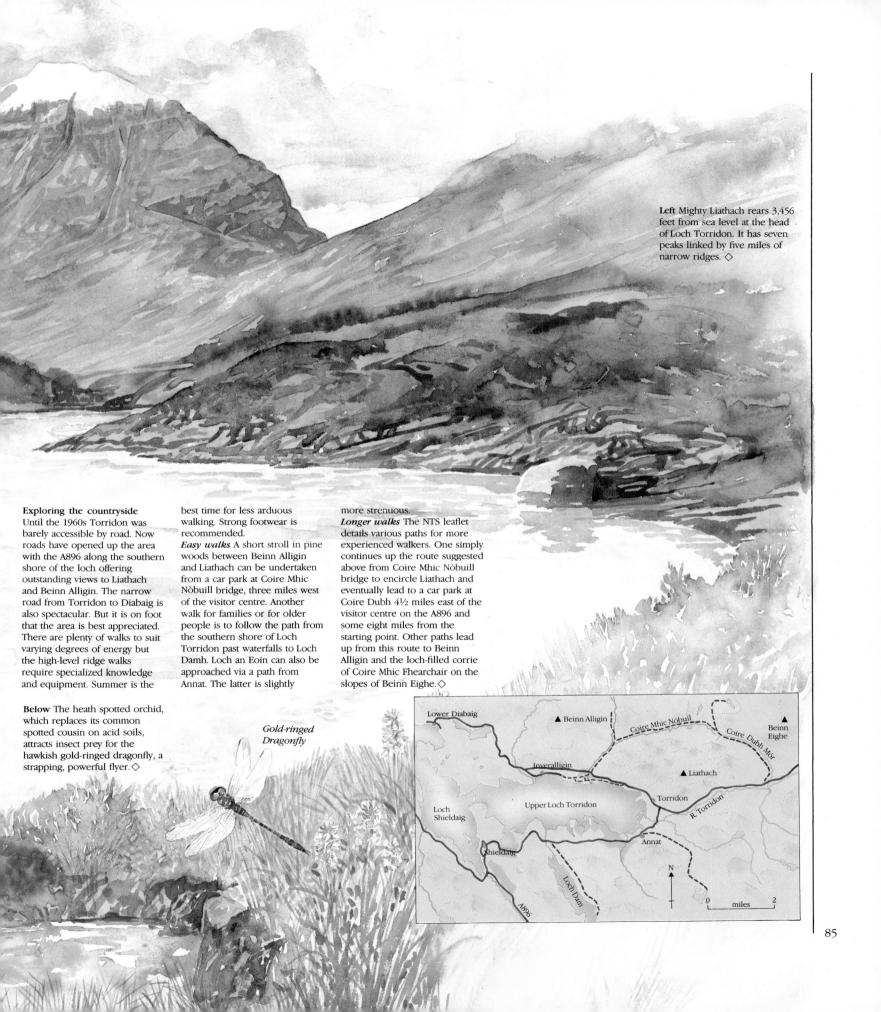

Left Mighty Liathach rears 3,456 feet from sea level at the head of Loch Torridon. It has seven peaks linked by five miles of narrow ridges. ◇

Exploring the countryside
Until the 1960s Torridon was barely accessible by road. Now roads have opened up the area with the A896 along the southern shore of the loch offering outstanding views to Liathach and Beinn Alligin. The narrow road from Torridon to Diabaig is also spectacular. But it is on foot that the area is best appreciated. There are plenty of walks to suit varying degrees of energy but the high-level ridge walks require specialized knowledge and equipment. Summer is the best time for less arduous walking. Strong footwear is recommended.

Easy walks A short stroll in pine woods between Beinn Alligin and Liathach can be undertaken from a car park at Coire Mhic Nòbuill bridge, three miles west of the visitor centre. Another walk for families or for older people is to follow the path from the southern shore of Loch Torridon past waterfalls to Loch Damh. Loch an Eoin can also be approached via a path from Annat. The latter is slightly more strenuous.

Longer walks The NTS leaflet details various paths for more experienced walkers. One simply continues up the route suggested above from Coire Mhic Nòbuill bridge to encircle Liathach and eventually lead to a car park at Coire Dubh 4½ miles east of the visitor centre on the A896 and some eight miles from the starting point. Other paths lead up from this route to Beinn Alligin and the loch-filled corrie of Coire Mhic Fhearchair on the slopes of Beinn Eighe. ◇

Below The heath spotted orchid, which replaces its common spotted cousin on acid soils, attracts insect prey for the hawkish gold-ringed dragonfly, a strapping, powerful flyer. ◇

Gold-ringed Dragonfly

Torridon

The Highlands of Scotland come closer than any area in Britain to remaining a wilderness. Yet their wild, seemingly desolate character supports a spectacular array of wildlife. Many of Britain's rarest animals and birds find refuge in the glens and corries of northwest Scotland. The area around Torridon is especially rich with mountains and lochs providing diverse and largely unspoilt habitats.

Animals, though, are notoriously difficult to observe as most sleep by day and hunt by night. The fox, pine marten, mountain hare, wildcat, stoat and weasel are among such elusive residents. Apart from sheep and some wild goats it is the red deer, Britain's largest living wild mammal, which is most likely to be seen and heard, too, especially in autumn as the roar of the stag echoes over the hills. This is the time of the rut when stags round up the hinds. The calves are born in May and June but because red deer often retreat to the higher corries during the summer it will be the hill-walker who sees them then.

The wildcat and mountain hare — hunter and hunted — are two mountain residents. Another is the ptarmigan which turns white in winter. This offers some protection against the birds of prey of whom the golden eagle is the most renowned (and feared). Other birds seen over the mountains are buzzards, peregrine falcons, red grouse and osprey but more than 100 species are listed in the NTS guide to Torridon.

Salmon can be seen on the River Balgie during July and August, while on the freshwater lochs black- and red-throated divers nest between April and August. Other birds which favour the waterside include the greenshank and oystercatcher. Most tantalizing of all, though, are the sea eagles: they occasionally visit Torridon; will they soon breed again?

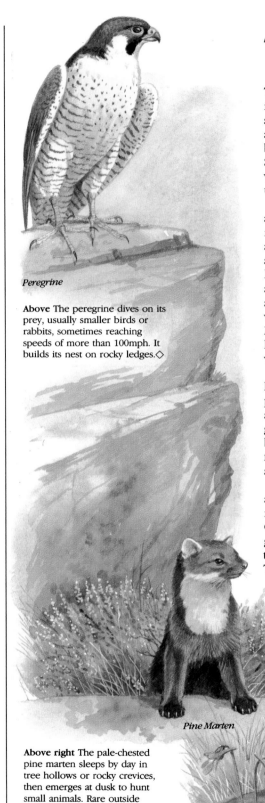

Peregrine

Above The peregrine dives on its prey, usually smaller birds or rabbits, sometimes reaching speeds of more than 100mph. It builds its nest on rocky ledges.◇

Pine Marten

Above right The pale-chested pine marten sleeps by day in tree hollows or rocky crevices, then emerges at dusk to hunt small animals. Rare outside Scotland.◇

Right Butterwort is an insect-eating plant found alongside ditches or roads. ◇

Butterwort

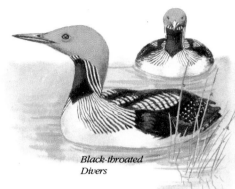

Black-throated Divers

Above The rare black-throated diver breeds near freshwater lochs. In winter, when its chest plumage turns white, it is more often found in coastal waters.◇

Below The red-throated diver loses its distinctive red plumage in winter, but can still be recognized by its smaller size and slightly uptilted bill.◇

Red-throated Divers

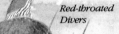

Left The mountain hare is also known as the blue hare because of its blue-grey summer fur. But in winter this fur turns white as protection in snowy landscapes. ◇

Mountain Hares

Right The wildcat hunts small animals such as voles by night; prey can include lambs or fawns.◇

Sea Eagle

Left The sea eagle, with its 8-foot wingspan and white tail, has recently been a rare visitor to Scotland. With luck, it may soon breed here again.◇

Below The salmon breeds in freshwater rivers to which it returns to spawn after up to four years at sea, often travelling thousands of miles to do so.◇

Salmon

The summits of the Torridon mountains have always been too high and too rugged to support vegetation. Now the lower slopes are also barren. It was not always so. Once these slopes formed part of the Great Wood of Caledon, the primeval northern pine forest which covered more than three million acres. Fire and the axe have destroyed the forest over the centuries leaving only fragments, such as that at Beinn Eighe nature reserve, or as stumps exposed by the erosion of peat bogs. A few Scots pine, along with silver birch and rowan, do survive but alongside the rocky watercourses of the valleys. The soil is poor and much of the lower land consists of bogs and heaths. Three heathers — cross-leafed, bell and ling — are common. So, too, are spotted orchids, lousewort, milkwort and bog asphodel whose flowers add colour to the moors in the summer. The insect-eating round-leaved sundew can be seen in peaty, boggy areas while another flytrap, butterwort, prefers damp green areas. The best time to see the Torridonian flora is between late May and early July; the best place to look (other than specifically for bog or water plants) is along the rock ledges where they are protected from grazing. The tiered cliffs of sandstone, with their water trickles and bands of limebearing rock, produce a particularly rich profusion of species ranging from alpine plants such as rose-root and saw-wort to meadow plants like globe flower and angelica to ferns, mosses and alpine grasses.

Above The pine-covered Shieldaig Island offers a stark contrast to the largely treeless landscapes of the mainland. The island is owned by the National Trust for Scotland, but there is no general access. Its name (and that of the attractive hamlet) derives from the Norse word, *Sildvik*, meaning 'Herring Bay'. One mile north of Shieldaig, where a bar of the ancient Lewisian gneiss rock crosses Loch Torridon, the promontory of Camas-ruadh offers a superb viewpoint towards Liathach.◇

Wildcat

Above The white sheen on the summit of Beinn Eighe is not snow but quartzite, one of the rocks which give Torridon its distinctive character. The other great influence on the landscape is glaciation although that is a mere flicker of geological time compared to the formation of the rocks themselves. The most common rock is the red-brown sandstone to which Torridon has given its name. This was formed 750 million years ago from sediments washed down from the even older Lewisian gneiss rock. The geological processes of successive millennia were as complex as they were long. Essentially, though, the sandstone thus established under the sea was in time raised to form a new land mass. The Lewisian gneiss itself survives, occasionally exposed as at a cutting on the highest point of the Inveralligin–Diabaig road. Earth movements also produced the 'caps' of white quartzite on Liathach and Beinn Eighe. They contain fossils of some of the earliest animals to live on earth. ◇

Worth a detour
Applecross Spectacular drive around remote peninsula, beginning at Shieldaig and returning via Kishorn.
Beinn Eighe Nature reserve on northern slopes overlooking Loch Maree. Highland wildlife, pine forest, nature trails and rock climbing. 4 miles W of Kinlochewe off A382.
Inverewe Semi-tropical garden north of Poolewe. NTS.

WATERSIDE

Whether it be on boats, fishing in the shallows or simply lazing on the banks, 'messing about on the river' has long been a favoured pastime. Rivers are full of movement, full of life. Like the sea their mood will vary, reflecting changes in the wind and weather, sometimes grey and sombre, other times bright and sparkling. The variety, as ever in the British Isles, is immense; even a single river passes through several distinct phases before joining the sea.

From its source in the hills, it often becomes a tumbling stream, bubbling over rocks crystal-clear beneath the surface. Sometimes, according to the rocks it encounters, it will carve deep gorges as it winds round spurs of hillsides. It is in the hills that a river is most likely to experience the most dramatic moment of its life—its transformation into a waterfall as it plunges over a ridge or lip of harder rock for possibly hundreds of feet.

As it reaches lower land, the river grows wider as other streams join, often swinging from side to side in great loops known as meanders. Finally, it joins the sea at a wide estuary, perhaps built up as a port or left undeveloped. Yet rivers are not the only form of waterside to be encountered in the British Isles.

There are lakes, natural and man-made. Often it is hard at first glance to distinguish one from another—the Norfolk Broads developed in hollows dug by man for peat, for instance. And tucked away in the woods of southeast England are tiny lakes, often not much larger than ponds, which were dug to store water for watermills attached to long-vanished iron foundries. More recently, much larger valleys in Wales and the Pennines have been flooded to provide water for the midlands and northern England.

Canals are manifestly made by man. The Romans built the first British canals but most of those still in existence date from the first stirrings of the industrial revolution. They brought watery landscapes to many parts of Britain which lacked rivers. In many European countries canals remain important industrial thoroughfares, but in Britain leisure has become the predominant use.

And then there are the areas where land and water seem to merge. Once much of England comprised such half-drowned landscapes, but drainage has enabled much to be reclaimed for agricultural use. Conservationists therefore jealously guard any remnants of old fenland, such as Wicken Fen (featured in this book) or around the Wash and Somerset Levels. For these areas are exceptionally rich in flora and fauna, making a home for species found nowhere else in Britain. The pleasures of such places, perhaps, require more knowledge than many other watersides, but with knowledge comes a greater respect and feeling for the matchless diversity of the British countryside.

There is no lack of variety in the watersides of the British Isles. Not all of it derives from nature alone; man has left his imprint in the form of lakes and canals. *Clockwise from right*: Henrhyd Falls, in South Wales, where the Nant Llech cascades 90 feet into a deep wooded ravine; the lake at Winkworth Arboretum in Surrey provides a serene haven for wild ducks; the salt marshes at Blakeney, on the North Norfolk coast, are a placid nether world where the boundaries between water and land are constantly changing; the mountain streams of Wales, here in the Elan Valley, are by contrast full of energy as they tumble over their rock-strewn course; Eilean Donnan castle, at the junction of three sea lochs in northwest Scotland, adds romance to the peerless natural beauty.

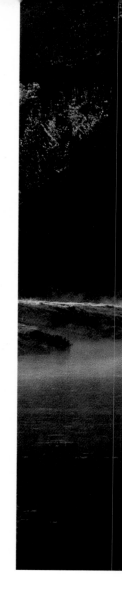

Loe Pool

Map OS map 203 in 1:50000 series

Below The seashore is never static. In parts of the United Kingdom it is reclaiming land from the sea, in others it is receding. It can also, as at Loe Pool, turn estuaries into lagoons by throwing up a spit or bar. Usually these are formed by what is known as longshore drift. Currents deposit shingle or sand along the line of the coast either on the beach itself or a short distance offshore at the point where waves break. Then, where the shoreline changes direction as at a bay or estuary, the currents cause the bank of shingle to drift into the open water, sometimes extending so far that it totally blocks the former bay or estuary.

One puzzle about the spit at Loe Pool is that it is mostly chalk and flint which cannot be found any closer than East Devon. For this reason it is argued that the spit was initially created by a series of dramatic storms. However it seems more likely that the storms simply speeded up the natural processes of the longshore drift. ◇

Geologists measure time in millions of years so it is always something of a surprise to discover that natural forces have reshaped the landscape within the last 600 or 700 years. Although the precise nature of these forces remains a matter of debate, the result has been the creation of Loe Pool, the largest natural freshwater lake in the West Country.

This was formed behind Loe Bar, a shingle spit or barrier which blocked the course of the River Cober to the sea on Mount's Bay. The small port of Helston, at the head of the Cober Estuary, eventually found itself marooned inland. Nor was this the end of Helston's problems: heavy rain regularly produced extensive flooding in the town as the river could not breach the bar. Trenches were dug in the bar to release the water, but the relief was only temporary. Shingle deposited by the currents soon restored the man-made breach and it

was not until the last 100 years that a culvert carved out of the rock has brought any feeling of security to Helston.

Nevertheless the average height of the water level is still ten feet above sea level and there is much marshy ground around the fringes of the lake. Loe Pool, or the Loe as it is often known, offers a quieter beauty than the cliffs and sandy bays for which Cornwall is best known. However, this is a quality which many will prize and naturalists will also relish the opportunity to see many freshwater species otherwise rare in the county.

For 200 years from 1770 the Loe and its surrounding woods and farmland were in the benign ownership of the Rogers family who lived at Penrose, the large house on the western side of the lake. In 1974 the Penrose estate was given to the National Trust which has fol-

(male) *(female)*

Tufted Ducks

Above The tufted duck is the most common British diving duck. It nests in colonies close to the water, often amid layers of rushes and grasses. ◇

Discovering the wildlife

In a county dominated by its 267 miles of coast, Loe Pool brings an element of diversity to the wildlife. Cornwall has few areas of freshwater and none larger than Loe Pool.

Where the River Cober enters the lake south of Helston there is a silted area where willow carr and reeds are host to birds such as reed warbler, moorhen and coots. A bird hide looks out on this area from the western side of the lake. These freshwater margins and marshes are also

where you are most likely to see herons which prey on the trout and eels in the lake. Other freshwater birds are pintail, goldeneye, pochard, tufted duck, teal, wigeon and shoveler. Closer to the bar these birds are joined by many species more commonly associated with estuaries and the seashore such as eider duck, spoonbill, whimbrel and various terns. The farmland and deciduous woodland around the Loe further adds to the variety of bird and plant life. ◇

Left The whimbrel is a summer visitor to the Loe and other coastal areas. It is similar to the curlew, but is smaller with a shorter bill and a pale streak on its head. ◇

Right The reed bunting is found most often in marshy fringes of freshwater. The cock, with its black head and white collar, is more distinctive than the female. ◇

Whimbrels

Spoonbill

Left Loe Pool is the West Country's largest freshwater lake. Once the tidal estuary of the River Cober, it is now cut off from the sea by a half-mile long shingle barrier. ◇

lowed faithfully the donor's wish to retain the tranquillity of the area. Boating and swimming are therefore not allowed, but four Trust car parks — two on either side of the Loe — give good access to the water's edge without threatening its peace.

A complete circuit of the Loe is about five miles long but it can become muddy after rain along the eastern bank so proper shoes should be worn. The paths are level, easy going and link up with the coastal footpath across the bar between Porthleven and the coves of the Lizard. The Trust has added some paths which are yet to appear on Ordnance Survey maps, but there are no waymarked nature trails to interpret the wildlife and no visitor centres to explain the area's history. The Loe remains an unspoilt area to be discovered for yourself, away from the crowds which in summer can clog Cornwall's better-known attractions.

Right The spoonbill uses its bill to scoop up small fish, water insects and plants as it wades through shallow estuaries. It no longer breeds in Britain but is a frequent summer visitor. ◇

Reed Bunting

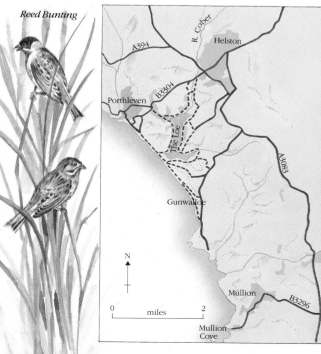

Below South of Loe Pool lie the cliffs and coves of the Lizard. The National Trust owns substantial portions of the peninsula and is making valiant efforts to maintain the quality of the landscape but places such as Kynance (seen here), Poldhu and Mullion Coves are too picturesque ever to be un-

crowded during the summer. Trust car parks are sited away from the shoreline and, as ever, anyone willing to abandon the car and take to his or her feet will leave most of the crowds behind. Polurrian Cove, for instance, cannot be approached by road and is consequently less crowded than its neighbours.

The coastal footpath south from Mullion Cove through the Lizard national nature reserve to Pedannack Head offers sweeping views over Mount's Bay. North of Mullion Cove is the Marconi Memorial marking the spot from where the first radio message was transmitted across the Atlantic Ocean in 1901. ◇

Worth a detour
Glendurgan Garden A valley garden with fine trees, shrubs and a water garden on the banks of the beautiful Helford River. There is also a maze. 4 miles SW of Falmouth near Mawnan Smith. NT.
Trelissick Gardens Large garden with park, woods and farmland. Woodland walks along the banks of the River Fal. 4 miles S of Truro off B3289. NT.
Penwith and Fowey See features on pages 12–15.

Upper Thames

Map OS map SU 29/39 in
1:25000 series

*Crack
Willow*

Above Crack willow is common
by rivers. It is similar to white
willow but has greener leaves,
straighter branches, a broader
crown and fragile twigs. ◇

Right The Thames, seen here
near Buscot, is still a stripling,
but river traffic is beginning with
motor cruisers gliding past its
tree-lined banks and meadows. ◇

The Thames is one of the world's great rivers, although
you might not guess so as it meanders gently through
the Oxfordshire meadows. At 210 miles the Thames is
a tiddler beside the 4,000 mile Amazon or 4,132 mile
Nile. However, greatness cannot be measured solely in
terms of size.

The River Thames still forms the spine of the capital
which was sited at the furthest point downstream at
which it could be bridged by the Romans. It has
brought in trade from an empire and transported
monarchs to their palaces; it has inspired songs and
poems; and it is an obligatory sight for visitors to
London. But there is a little-known Thames, far from
the mature river flowing sedately past the Houses of
Parliament, far even from the lush pastures of Henley
and Cliveden where oarsmen strain and statesmen have
strayed.

Lechlade is the highest navigable point of the
Thames. It is also the last town where a path follows
the river banks: one mile upstream it disappears
whereas downstream it is more or less intact for 134
miles to the London suburb of Putney. The Ramblers'
Association has suggested that this path be recognized
as an official long-distance footpath. However it is
around the National Trust village of Buscot, two miles
downstream from Lechlade, that this exploration of the
Upper Thames will concentrate.

Buscot, like neighbouring Kelmscot and indeed
Lechlade, did not grow alongside the river but stands a
short distance away, beyond some meadows. An im-
maculately-maintained lock (with fine stone cottages)
bypasses a large weir at Buscot but this does not dilute
the river's pastoral appeal. A path follows the river in
both directions from Buscot and walkers will soon
have the meadows very much to themselves, give or
take a few cows. Except near locks such as Buscot or
riverside pubs as at Radcot Bridge, you are likely to
encounter more people on the water than beside it;
this meandering stretch of the Thames is popular
among people who hire motor cruisers for boating
holidays.

Downstream the path leads first to the straggling
farming village of Kelmscot, where William Morris set
up court in the Elizabethan manor house and where he
is buried in the churchyard. This is just over two miles
from Buscot. Three more miles and you come to
Radcot Bridge where a pub overlooks an island
meadow straddled by a fine medieval bridge. Upstream
from Buscot, past the isolated church some half a mile
from the village, it is approximately two miles to
Lechlade where another church spire beckons from
across the water meadows. The path leaves the river
for half a mile downstream from St John's Lock, following a short stretch of the B4449 to or from the
Trout Inn and a path alongside a field bordered by
poplars.

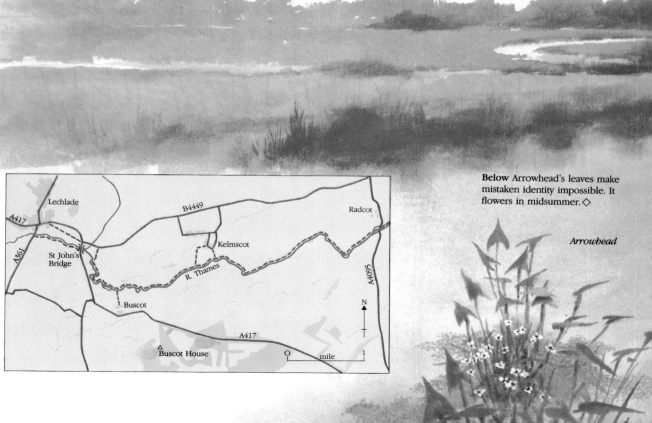

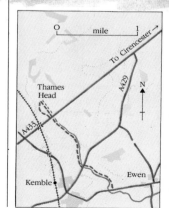

Below Arrowhead's leaves make
mistaken identity impossible. It
flowers in midsummer. ◇

Arrowhead

Old Father Thames

Above Old Father Thames presides over St John's Lock, the highest on the Thames one mile downstream from Lechlade. The statue traditionally marked the source of the river, but nowadays a less vandal-prone stone slab stands on this spot, known as Thames Head, southwest of

Cirencester. However, the Thames has no single indisputable or infallible source. It has been many years, for instance, since Thames Head produced water regularly. A more frequent source lies on the other side of the A433, near an old wind pump, although this can also be dry for weeks or months in hot summers.

Nevertheless the line of the infant Thames is unmistakable: a shallow bed curving around the edge of the field. Other hollows nearby reveal earlier courses, complete with the remains of stone bridges. The Thames is thus born of several springs whose activity reflects the varying levels of the water table from one season to another. ◇

Kelmscot House & William Morris

Above William Morris found inspiration in the peace of the riverside village which he made his home. The Elizabethan manor house at Kelmscot became a centre for the pre-Raphaelite movement of the late 19th century. Morris himself was much more than just a poet: designer, printer, pioneer socialist and writer of prose in which he espoused a dream

world unsullied by the poverty he fought politically. Morris is buried in Kelmscot churchyard and the manor house is open occasionally to the public. The Thames, has long inspired writers whether it be the 'sweet Thames! run softly' evoked by Spenser or the 'dank, defiled waters' Dickens saw in London. The tranquillity of the Thames led Shelley to produce one of his most mellow poems — about the churchyard at Lechlade where 'winds are still, or the dry church-tower grass knows not their gentle motions as they pass'. ◇

Yellow Flag

Sedge Warbler

Right Buscot Lock is the second highest on the Thames and one of the prettiest with immaculate stone cottages overlooking the lock and the adjoining weir. ◇

Left Yellow flag, a tall iris, was once prized for its medicinal properties – the root was believed to halt bleeding. It is common along freshwater margins as is reedmace, or false bulrush, whose winter spikes are beloved of flower arrangers. This is the home of the sedge warbler, which uses plant stems as 'scaffolding' for its nest. ◇

Reedmace

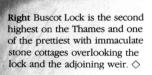

Worth a detour

Buscot House An 18th-century house with wooded parkland and water garden. 2 miles SE of Lechlade off A417. NT.
Chedworth Remains of a Roman villa. 3 miles NW of Fossebridge. NT.
Great Coxwell Stone-built

monastic barn dating from 13th century. 2 miles SW of Faringdon. NT.
Thames Walk A footpath from the source to Putney, in London, a distance of 156 miles. Booklet available from Ramblers' Association.

Waggoners' Wells

Map OS map SU 83/93 in 1:25000 series

Marsh Marigold

Wood Anemone

Above In early spring, the wood anemone, or windflower, spreads its large pale flowers over the woodland floor, while the chrome-yellow marsh marigold, or kingcup, clusters in marshy areas: in summer, it produces curved fruits. ◇

Summerden Cottage

Above Summerden cottage was built in 1893 as a holiday home, just below the lower lake. It now houses a National Trust warden in charge of fishing rights. ◇

Right Sluice gates were used to control the flow of water to furnaces further down the valley so that waterwheels had water when they needed it. ◇

96

Waggoners' Wells, a string of hidden and half-forgotten lakes, lie in a deep wooded valley less than a mile from the busy London to Portsmouth road near Hindhead. This is stockbroker country, close enough to London for affluent commuters yet far enough for daytrippers. How anywhere as beautiful as Waggoners' Wells can remain so tranquil and relatively undiscovered is the first of several surprises about these three lakes.

They are now owned by the National Trust, although some Trust books also ignore their existence in deference to the nearby Devil's Punchbowl. Most surprising of all, though, is the discovery that the lakes are man-made relics of the time when the Weald was the centre of England's first iron industry. The lakes are examples of 'hammer ponds' formed by damming the tiny stream which flows down the valley to become a tributary of the River Wey.

Sluice gates are the clues to an industrial past whose legacy is now enjoyed for recreation and wildlife. The great charm of Waggoners' Wells stems from the juxtaposition of natural woodland with the still green waters of the lakes. The slopes of the valley are quite steep — it is known as an 'incised valley' — and are covered by woodland, mostly oak and beech. There is no commercial cropping, so natural regeneration takes its course. Trees can thus be seen at all stages, from young saplings in small glades to full maturity. However, there is careful management, for instance, in coppicing the alders around the lower lake to encourage a marshy habitat for plants such as bulrushes and marsh marigold. Trees are occasionally lopped if they cut off light from plants below which need dappled shade in order to survive.

Waggoners' Wells is a place for all seasons and all times, where the light flickering through the trees is rarely constant. The autumn beeches are particularly striking, but in spring look for woodland flowers such as violet, anemone and wood sorrel as a subtle green

Right Dense woodland encircles the lakes of Waggoners' Wells, where the mineral glauconite has given the water a green tinge. ◇

Below The wood warbler is the largest and yellowest of Britain's warblers. Listen for its two songs — one long trill and a bell-like note, often combined. ◇

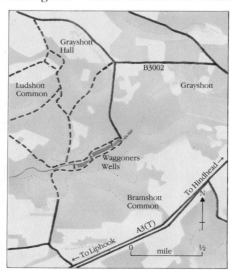

Wood Warbler

light filters through the branches. In winter, when the moon is higher, the intertwining of the bare branches forms a mosaic against the sky.

Woodland and water are two of the richest habitats for wildlife but the diversity here is further enhanced by proximity to the heathlands of Ludshott Common. Waggoners' Wells can be easily explored as paths encircle each of the lakes and they can be reached via a signposted minor road off the B3002. These paths link up with trails over Ludshott Common to the north and toward the Spaniard's Inn on the A3 to the south. NT leaflets are available describing not only some specific routes but also the wildlife likely to be seen.

The industrial past
The heyday of Waggoners' Wells as an industrial centre was during the 17th and early 18th centuries. But the history of iron-smelting in southeast England goes back to Roman times. The Romans had found iron ore in the Weald, then a densely-wooded plain. The trees provided the charcoal for smelting but the output was poor. Air is required to maintain the heat of the furnace and this could only be supplied by using hand bellows or siting the primitive furnace or 'bloomery' on a hill to exploit any natural wind. Impurities in the molten ore also had to be hammered out by hand. The industry was to be transformed by the discovery

Kingfisher

Water Forget-me-not

Left Water forget-me-not gives a blue border to the streams and lakes of Waggoners' Wells in the summer which is when the kingfisher **right** is also most easily seen. Kingfishers breed in burrows near fresh water but often winter near the seashore. ◇

Discovering the wildlife
More than 80 different birds have been sighted around the lakes of Waggoners' Wells and neighbouring Ludshott Common. This richness reflects the diversity of habitats: water, woodland and heathland. The woods around the lakes are predominantly beech and oak but rowan, larch, pussy willow, whitebeam, alder and wild cherry can also be seen. Wood sorrel, wood anemone, starwort and violets grow beneath the trees; marsh marigolds, water forget-me-nots and water lilies flourish beside (or on) the water. Over the water, there are kingfishers and moorhens while redstarts, wood warblers, grey wagtails and three types of woodpecker — green, great and lesser spotted — can be seen (and heard) in the woods.

Sparrowhawks fly up and down the valley looking for prey but the heathland of Ludshott Common attracts yellowhammer, stonechat, nightingale and various tits among many others. There are magnificent views over the open heathland where heather, gorse and bracken predominate. ◇

of water power which could turn a wheel to drive bellows or hammers. Furnaces could become bigger and output greater. However, as charcoal was still needed for fuel, the ideal iron-smelting area required a combination of trees, water and iron. The Weald still had the trees and enough iron, but water was a problem. Its streams were too small to provide enough power when it was needed. The solution was to dam some of the streams in order to retain water until it was needed. Often a string of ponds, as at Waggoners', was built, each with sluice gates so that water levels could be controlled. These artificial lakes are known as 'hammer' or 'furnace' ponds.

For almost 200 years the iron industry of the Weald flourished, churning out armaments in times of war and ornamental iron for the towns in times of peace. At Waggoners' — or Wakeners' Wells as they were also once known — it is likely that the ponds were developed and extended from fish ponds. But as late as the 18th century a furnace and cannon foundry at Fernhurst was using water from Waggoners'. However the Wealden industry was fatally undermined by the discovery of how to use coke rather than charcoal to fuel the furnaces. The industry shifted to the midlands and north, leaving the ponds and some placenames as the relics of the Weald's unlikely past. ◇

Right Sticklebacks are small, aggressive freshwater fish armed with three or more dorsal spines. Males defend their nests fiercely, fighting off all-comers, including other sticklebacks, who are prone to cannibalism. ◇

Stickleback

Worth a detour
Clandon Park An 18th-century house in parkland with fine furniture and marble hall. 3 miles E of Guildford on A247. NT.
Uppark A 17th-century house high on South Downs with remarkably untouched 18th-century furnishings. Landscaped garden. 5 miles SE of Petersfield. NT.
Winkworth Arboretum near Hascombe containing many rare trees. Excellent in spring and autumn. 2 miles SE of Godalming. NT.

Henrhyd Falls

Hawthorn

Above The hawthorn grows along the wooded gorge below Henrhyd Falls. A common thorny shrub or small tree, it produces white flowers in May or June and later a crop of crimson berries.◇

Pied Flycatcher

Redstart

Above right The pied flycatcher is not always as enterprising as its name, and will often eat lowlier insects and caterpillars. It nests in broadleaved woodland, but is not seen as often as the redstart, **above**, named for its vivid tail.◇

Right Cathedral Cave is part of the Dan-yr-Ogof caves north of Henrhyd. It is 160 feet long by 70 feet high and was formed as rivers forged underground passages in porous limestone. ◇

Henrhyd Falls, near Coelbren, is much more than just a waterfall. This National Trust property epitomizes many of the warring images and misconceptions that haunt South Wales. To some, the very mention of South Wales conjures up pictures of an environmental disaster area, littered with coal mines and the debris of heavy industry. But that image is fading fast: coal mining is now only a shadow of its former self and the valleys are steadfastly resuming the green cloak which once evoked so much Welsh lyricism.

Some industrial workings remain, of course, but increasingly they serve to highlight the surrounding natural beauty rather than to obliterate it. The panoramic view from above Henrhyd Falls illustrates the contrasting faces of South Wales: the forested slopes, national parkland and, admittedly, the industry are all evident. To the north, the view is dominated by the Black Mountain, a vast and largely empty highland region where even hardy Welsh sheep rarely venture. Serried ranks of conifers cover parts of the plateau to the east; and to the south, above the archetypal non-comformist chapel at Coelbren (no Welsh mining village was without at least one) a lunar landscape of open-cast mine workings fills the skyline.

Henrhyd Falls therefore lies on a great divide. In geological terms, this is explained as the line where the coal measures meet millstone grits; in socio-economic terms, it is the confluence of industrial and rural Wales. The falls themselves — a misnomer really, as there is only one proper waterfall — just squeeze inside the southern boundary of the Brecon Beacons national park. A steep, many-stepped and well-maintained footpath leads from the car park down into the basin of a thickly-wooded gorge.

The waters of the Nant Llech here take a shuddering plunge over a lip of rock into a pool 90 feet below. When in full spate, this unbroken drop is one of the most spectacular falls in Wales, so it is a tourist attraction which is enhanced rather than diminished by heavy rainfall. Yet even here there are clues to the other, industrial, face of South Wales; a thin seam of coal can be seen in the cliff face around the falls.

From the falls, the river winds its way through a deep sheltered gorge before joining the River Tawe one mile downstream. The Trust also owns the Craig-llech Woods, a narrow but profuse belt of woodland within the ravine. A footpath runs along the gorge through the deciduous woodland of ash, oak, hawthorn and hazel. Birds to look out for include tits, thrushes and blackbirds as well as pied flycatchers and redstarts. The path becomes increasingly indistinct so only the experienced should attempt the entire length.

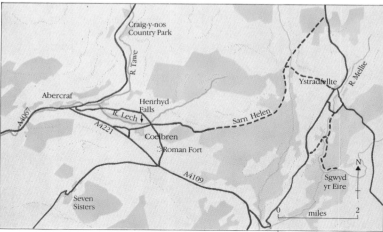

Opposite page Henrhyd Falls are half hidden by woodland so that the 90-foot drop of the Nant Llech cascading into a deep ravine bursts upon visitors with a spectacular roar.◇

Monkey-flower

Right Introduced to the British Isles in the early 19th century, monkey-flowers favour wet areas. The yellow flowers with red spots resemble small monkey faces.◇

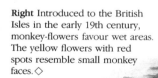

Exploring waterfall country

Henrhyd is on the doorstep of more falls, located in what has become known as the 'waterfall country' of South Wales in the valleys of the neighbouring Hepste and Mellte rivers. Here outcrops of millstone grit and carboniferous limestone have produced scenery which is in stark contrast to the rest of the Brecon Beacons further north. There are different degrees of hardness within millstone grit. As rivers flowed over the outcrops, often exposed by faulting, they eroded the softer rock more rapidly than the harder rock, thereby forming waterfalls. One section of the Mellte resembles a staircase, with no fewer than three major falls in a stretch less than a mile long.

The most celebrated single waterfall, pictured **above right**, is Sgwd-yr-Eira ('The Spout of Snow') on the Hepste, a tributary of the Mellte. Here the differential erosion has also produced a path *behind* the waterfall as the backwash of water has removed the softer shales.

The outcrops of the porous limestone have produced, by contrast, a waterless river. The Mellte disappears underground through a series of 'swallow

holes' south of Ystradfellte to reappear, briefly, at the mouth of Porth-yr-Ogof cave before finally emptying itself into a deep pool. The cave system produced by the river can be explored by potholers. Walkers can follow the Mellte south from Porth-yr-Ogof to the river's three waterfalls — Sgwd-yr-Eira on the Hepste is reached by a connecting path. The further south you go, the more difficult the terrain becomes, but the 2½ miles from Porth-yr-Ogof to the three falls on the Mellte follow a well-defined path so don't give up too easily. ◇

Walking the Roman road

The Romans constructed a camp on the outskirts of Coelbren. Scant remains of its border and ditches can be seen in the field beside the minor road leading into the village from the A4109. Part of the supporting network of roads built by the Romans can still be followed on foot. Head east from Henrhyd Falls along a narrow road. Within 1½ miles it enters a plantation where it becomes an unmade track. Park here and follow another track which skirts the edge of the forest in a northeasterly direction. This is the Sarn Helen Roman road which forges a direct pathway across the windswept moorland. The route is well-preserved for the four miles across the moors before it joins a metalled road north of Ystradfellte. Originally Sarn Helen would have connected the Roman base at Neath with their fort of Y Gaer at Brecon. ◇

Worth a detour

Aberdulais Falls A place of great beauty which also has historical importance as the birthplace of the Welsh metal industry. Now the subject of intensive restoration. 3 miles NE of Neath on A465. NT.

Craig-y-Nos A country park of 40 acres in the grounds of a sham 19th-century 'castle' once owned by the Italian-born opera singer Adelina Patti. It combines ornamental gardens (and lake) with meadows along the River Tawe. 2 miles north of Henrhyd on A4067.

Dan-yr-Ogof Claimed to be the largest showcave complex in western Europe open to the public. Two separate systems are open, but not all year. Also 2 miles north of Henrhyd Falls off A4067.

Stratford-upon-Avon Canal

Alder

Above The alder is a native tree common along watersides. It is conical when young but more open in shape when mature. ◇

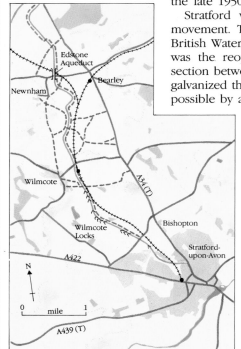

Above and left The maps show how Stratford-upon-Avon Canal fitted into the midlands network. Stratford opened in 1816, six months after its rival had already snaffled the profitable traffic. ◇

The West Midlands are crossed by no major river. The Avon, Severn and Trent skirt the edges of what is in reality a plateau, higher than these surrounding valleys. Apart from a few tributaries the diversity offered by watery landscapes, whether it be for wildlife or recreation, mostly comes from canals. The Midlands are the hub of a network of manmade waterways constructed in the late 18th century. And the Stratford-upon-Avon canal in many ways epitomizes the rise, fall and restoration of the canal movement.

The oldest canals are the Car Dyke and Fossdyke in East Anglia which were built by the Romans. In the 16th and 17th centuries various schemes were proposed to make stretches of river more navigable, including the Avon between Tewkesbury and Stratford. But 'canal mania' was a phenomenon of the late 18th century and it was a consequence of expanding trade, deteriorating roads and improving technology. Early canals had followed the contours but locks now allowed waterways to take more direct routes by changing gradients through a series of steps. Where even locks could not cope, new engineering skills enabled tunnels to be dug and aqueducts erected.

The Stratford-upon-Avon Canal was authorized in 1793 and completed in 1816. Neither of its two halves was particularly profitable; other canals offered too much competition even before first turnpikes and finally railways pushed the canal, like many others, to the point of death. The water silted up, lock gates decayed and were overgrown. By 1957 the only craft which could use the southern section was a canoe. But the fact that it did so thwarted a closure plan and by the late 1950s canals had found new champions.

Stratford was in the vanguard of the restoration movement. The northern section, now owned by the British Waterways Board, was the first to benefit but it was the reopening in 1964 of the 13-mile southern section between Kingswood Junction and Stratford that galvanized the movement nationally. It had been made possible by a combination of voluntary labour and the

National Trust which had acquired the southern section in 1959. It had been a mammoth undertaking. The descent from the Midlands plateau to the Avon involved 36 locks. Every gate but one was replaced, bridges were repaired, towpaths hacked clear. The canal is costly to maintain and the Trust, having rescued it, would like the British Waterways Board to take it over.

However, life has returned to the canal with narrow boats adding their distinctive colour to the Warwickshire countryside once more. Walkers can also enjoy a remarkable solitude close to tourist-crammed Stratford. Much of the towpath is overgrown, especially in summer, and ramblers will need sensible clothes to ward off the brambles. By far the easiest and most rewarding stretch is alongside Wilmcote Locks north of Bishopton road. A path leads from bridge 60, beyond the top lock, directly to Wilmcote from where other paths cut across country to Edstone Aqueduct.

Below The mute swan is anything but quiet if annoyed, when it hisses loudly. By far the most common British swan, it is found on canals, ponds and estuaries. ◇

Mute Swan

Damselfly

Emperor Dragonfly

Below Three groups of locks — 11 in total — provide a 'staircase' for the canal just south of Wilmcote. ◇

Right The canal basin at the very heart of Stratford-upon-Avon where the canal joins the Avon alongside the Stratford Memorial Theatre of the Royal Shakespeare Company. ◇

Moorhen

Nettles

Above left The banded agrion damselfly fluttering after food is itself prey to the emperor dragonfly, **left**, a giant with a 4-inch wingspan. Both are food for the moorhen, **above**, which thrives on any patch of water surrounded by protective vegetation such as nettles. ◇

Split Bridge

Above Canals have their own forms of architecture. This bridge, for instance, spans the water but not the towpath. In order for the towing rope to pass the bridge without the horse having to be unhitched, the two cantilevered cast iron sections of the bridge were specially built to leave a gap between — hence the name 'split bridge'. There are several such bridges to be seen on the Stratford-upon-Avon Canal. ◇

Mary Arden House

Above This half-timbered house was the family home of Mary Arden, Shakespeare's mother. It stands in the village of Wilmcote, three miles north of Stratford. It is typical of the half-timbered Elizabethan houses in which Shakespeare would have lived and been educated. Stratford's remoteness from industry has ensured that most buildings associated with Shakespeare have survived as well as the parish church in which he and his family are buried. Together with the Royal Shakespeare Theatre, they lure more foreign tourists than anywhere in Britain other than London and Edinburgh. Such is the power of the Shakespeare connection that nearby Charlecote Park is best known not for its deer park landscaped by Capability Brown or its 16th-century house but as the place where legend has it that young Will was caught poaching. Certainly his use of nature imagery reflects a boyhood familiar with the Avon meadows and hunting in the then extensive Forest of Arden. ◇

Glossary of canal terms

Bye-Weir	Channel that is used to conduct surplus water around a lock
Nearside	The side of the canal nearest to the towpath
Offside	The side of the canal opposite the towpath
Paddle	Movable shutter to allow water to pass into or out of a lock
Pound	A length of canal between two locks
Roving Bridge	Bridge where the towpath changes sides
Split Bridge	See picture and caption top right
Towpath	Path alongside a canal, originally used by horses for towing barges
Winding Hole	Indentation in canal bank to allow long boats to be turned
Windlass	Cranked handle for operating paddle gear, the mechanism for operating paddles

---

Worth a detour
Charlecote Park 16th-century house in deer park landscaped by Capability Brown. 4 miles E of Stratford. NT.
Hidcote Manor Famous garden, vulnerable to overcrowding. 4 miles NE of Chipping Campden off B4081. NT.
Packwood House Tudor house with yew garden. 2 miles E of Hockley Heath on A34. NT.

Wicken Fen

Wicken Fen represents the kind of land which once man sought to transform but now strives to protect. Set amidst what is now some of the most valuable farmland in Britain, Wicken Fen survives as a relic of the old undrained fenland with its almost forgotten crops and country lore. Fenland wildlife, which otherwise would have vanished, likewise survives and Wicken's rarity accords it great scientific importance as an open-air laboratory.

A fen is a waterlogged area where peat is accumulating but where the soil is not as acid as in bogs. Once fenland covered much of Cambridgeshire and Lincolnshire, but ever since Roman times there have been attempts to drain the fens and reclaim them for agriculture. The most significant work was done in the 17th century by the Dutch engineer, Cornelius Vermuyden. He cut two artificial channels known as the Bedford Rivers to carry the fen water more directly to the sea. Windmills and, later, steam engines were then used to pump water from the lowest-lying inner fens into these drainage channels.

The drained peat (and silt) proved highly fertile and today the fens produce a rich crop of cereals, potatoes and market garden produce. Wicken Fen was one of the few areas set aside to protect traditional crops of sedge — which was used for thatching — and peat-digging. Further agricultural expansion in the late 19th century threatened Wicken Fen again, but by then it had been discovered by Victorian naturalists for whom it was a valuable collecting site. Since 1899 much of the Fen has been protected by the National Trust. Wicken's reedbeds, sedge fields and lodes, as the drainage channels are known, shelter a variety of wetland habitats for plants and birds, and its droves, or old pathways, are rich in wild flowers and butterflies in summer.

Wicken appears wild and untouched but, in fact, is very carefully managed. Preserving what is now a unique ecological balance draws upon years of scientific study at the site. Sedge, the dominant plant species, must be cut every three to five years (as it was in the past for thatch) in order to maintain and encourage the rich community of herbaceous plants and variety of animal life. So, too, must the fen carr, or bushy scrub, which would otherwise progress into young trees. And so efficient has been the drainage of neighbouring farms that Wicken is now 10 feet higher than its surroundings; its own water level must therefore be constantly surveyed and maintained. Thus the variety of habitats — from open water through sedge fields and fen carr to fen woodland — retain their individuality while illustrating the natural succession of plants as the water table falls.

Wicken can appeal at many different levels. There will be lepidopterists who come to study its rare insects from spiders to butterflies. And there will be laymen, admiring if not always recognizing the summer flowers and winter birds and ever conscious that this is a glimpse into an almost-vanished world.

Map OS map 154 in 1:50000 series

Flowering Rush

Marsh Thistle

Common Comfrey

Above Marsh thistle, comfrey and flowering rush thrive along the droves or pathways of the Fen. July to August is the best time to see the flora here. ◇

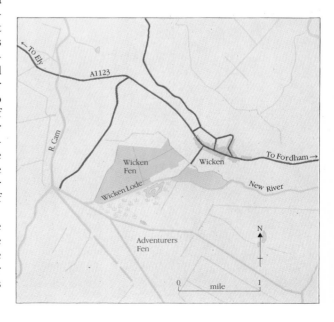

Below The limpid beauty of Wicken Fen: important as almost the last refuge of fenland wildlife yet alluring for its tranquillity. ◇

Right The snipe uses its long flexible bill to dig worms from the muddy, marshy areas where it breeds. The winter population is boosted by migrants from Europe. ◇

Snipe

Discovering the wildlife

Wicken Fen is the oldest nature reserve in Britain. It is also quite large, covering some 700 acres of water, sedge and woods. A two-mile circular nature trail around the most important parts of the fen starts from the visitor centre near the main entrance; a trail leaflet is available. The route passes a reconstructed windpump, flooded 'brickpits' — pools formed by old clay works— two bird hides, woodland and various droves or pathways. There is also a demonstration garden where the various species seen around the reserve are grown and labelled. Wicken Fen attracts about 200 species of birds including winter residents such as the hen harrier, redwing and great grey shrike. Two characteristic species of the fen carr are the bullfinch and long-tailed tit. Around the brickpits you can see the reed warbler and the less common sedge warbler, while lesser and great spotted woodpeckers haunt the woodland off Sedge Fen Drove. Skylarks are abundant in the more open areas. The Fen is even richer in butterflies: common species are the brimstone, peacock, orange-tip, red admiral, small tortoise-shell and green-veined white. However, if you exclude the somewhat specialist appeal of 212 different kinds of spiders, it is the flora for which Wicken is perhaps best known. Aquatic plants such as water-milfoil and bladderwort flourish among the water lilies in brickpits. The droves — ancient paths cleared to allow access to the Fens — are the best places to see the flowers such as ragged robin, yellow loosestrife, comfrey, marsh thistle and marsh orchid. ◇

Bearded Tit

Peacock Butterfly

Red Admiral Butterfly

Above Wicken Fen's abundant and varied flora attracts many butterflies, especially the red admiral and peacock. Look out for them along the droves and the open ditches. ◇

Left Windpumps were once common on fenland, but now only this one remains. 'Mills' such as this were used to pump water from the low-lying fens up into rivers or drainage channels which were often at higher levels. ◇

Reed Warbler

Left The bearded tit is not a tit at all but an elegant expatriate, the sole European member of the babbler family. ◇

Above The reed warbler is a summer visitor to England. Very similar to the marsh warbler, but with a softer, churring song like two pebbles rubbing together. ◇

◇◇◇

Worth a detour
Anglesey Abbey 17th-century house on site of former abbey with fine paintings, statuary in garden. In Lode 6 miles NE of Cambridge. NT.
Ickworth Sumptuous house with rotunda plus classical gardens, woods. In Horringer, 3 miles SW of Bury St Edmunds. NT.
Wimpole Hall Superb 18th-century mansion in parkland. Home Farm has many rare breeds. 8 miles SW of Cambridge. NT.

◇◇◇

Western Lakes

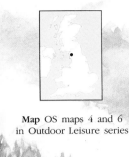

Map OS maps 4 and 6
in Outdoor Leisure series

Above Ennerdale is Lakeland at
its least crowded — seven miles
of water, forest and fells with a
sense of solitude enhanced by
being the only major lake
without a road on either side. ◇

Right Look carefully and you will
see climbers, dwarfed by the
scale of this Lakeland peak
known as the Pillar (2,927 feet)
which lies between Wast Water
and Ennerdale. ◇

Ennerdale Water and Wast Water are the least crowded
of the major lakes, but this is not due to any lack of
natural beauty. Indeed, in terms of scenery as well as
solitude, these valleys more than match anything the
Lake District can offer. It is lack of access which keeps
the crowds at bay since the lakes can be approached by
car only from the west.

This remoteness from central Lakeland is further
enhanced in Ennerdale, which is the only one of the 16
lakes without a road on either side. The valley is thus
the preserve of walkers, whether they be sturdy fell-
walkers making for the peaks at the head of the valley
or less ambitious ramblers attracted by forest trails and
picnic sites. Much of the fellside around Ennerdale is
owned by the National Trust, although the valley floor
and the northern slopes around the lake are largely
given over to Forestry Commission plantations. The
regimented lines of the pre-war plantations have since
been somewhat softened by allowing treelines to
follow the contours more sympathetically. This new
sensitivity by the Forestry Commission has been ac-
companied by the provision of many more footpaths.

The lake itself is a reservoir and there was a controversial plan to raise the water level still further. However, largely due to the Trust's ownership of the lake
shore, the idea has been abandoned. At the head of the
valley some of Lakeland's most formidable summits
soar above the conifers and controversy.

Exploring the countryside

Ennerdale is well-endowed with waymarked trails in addition to 16 miles of forest roads which are open to the public. The paths above the treeline should only be followed by walkers equipped for fellwalking.

The starting place for many — whatever their ambition — will be Bowness Knott, southeast of the hamlet of Croasdale. Here the Forestry Commission has provided a lakeside picnic area with superb views across the water toward the near-vertical wall of Crag Fell.

Lakeside walk A complete circuit is seven miles and includes some rough ground. However, it requires sturdy boots rather than fellwalking expertise. A forest road provides part of the route and it also goes through a rare stretch of broadleaved woodland. Side Wood, as it is known, lies near the head of the lake on the southern shore; it is owned by the National Trust and scheduled as a Site of Special Scientific Interest. The southern shore is rugged but could be avoided if walkers retrace their steps.

Forest walks Many people will devise their own routes from the many miles of paths available, but there are also two waymarked trails. Smithy Beck trail is the easiest: a one- or two-mile ramble along the lakeside and then a short climb into the forest. The Nine Becks trail leads into the heart of Ennerdale and takes its name from the streams which tumble into the River Liza. It includes some rough, steep ground but is a good alternative when bad weather makes the upper fells dangerous. ◇

Discovering the wildlife

The Forestry Commission has long been sensitive to charges that its coniferous kingdoms are devoid of wildlife. Not true, it says, pointing to the increasing numbers of roe deer, badgers and red squirrels to be found in Ennerdale Forest. But apart from the squirrel, these are shy creatures and the forests do lack the bird and plant life of the broadleaved woodland. In Ennerdale this perhaps matters less than elsewhere since the presence of water attracts birds such as the mallard to the lake and the dipper and grey wagtail to the streams. And there are marsh plants such as meadow sweet and valerian.

The forest itself does contain some Scots pine, the one native conifer, but this is outnumbered by spruces and larches. Norway spruce — best known as the Christmas tree — and Sitka spruce are most common. There are also a few sycamore and some holly trees which provide a habitat for the rare holly blue butterfly. ◇

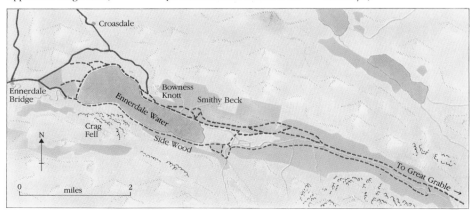

Map labels: Croasdale · Ennerdale Bridge · Bowness Knott · Smithy Beck · Ennerdale Water · Crag Fell · Side Wood · To Great Gable · N · 0 miles 2

Scots Pine

Above Scots pine is the only native British pine and can be easily distinguished from its imported brethren by its less regularly conical profile. ◇

Western Lakes

Unless you are a mountaineer, Wast Water can only be approached from the west: a relative remoteness which accords to Wasdale, as it does to Ennerdale, some relief from the infamous Lakeland traffic jams. However mountaineers are one group you are almost certain to see around Wasdale Head for here rock climbing, as a sport, began. It was an appropriate birthplace for England's first climbing club since looming over Wast Water is Scafell Pike, England's highest mountain at 3,206 feet above sea level. Scafell Pike is just one of several imposing peaks which encircle Wasdale Head; another is Great Gable which, flanked by Kirkfell and Lingmell, will be familiar to many people as the emblem of the Lake District national park.

Everything about Wasdale is on the grand scale since beneath the highest mountain is England's deepest lake: 262 feet deep with the famous Wasdale screes shelving into the water at an angle of 45 degrees. These screes fan out along the southeastern shore of Wast Water, often rising 600 feet or more to the high fells beyond. Frost and wind are continuing to erode the screes which were first formed when ice undermined the pre-glacial fellside.

Much of the land around Wasdale is owned by the National Trust. A road follows the northern shore as far as Wasdale Head while paths at both ends of the lake enable walkers as well as climbers to explore the dramatic, if desolate, beauty of the valley.

Merganser

Above Merganser, a stylish, streamlined, fast-flying duck which breeds on freshwater lakes and winters on the coast. Its narrow bill has serrated edges to grip slippery fish. ◇

Tormentil

Above Tormentil grows on the stabler lower slopes of the Wasdale screes where harebell, parsley fern and club moss also thrive on the acidity. ◇

William Wordsworth

Above To many people William Wordsworth and the Lakes are synonymous; and certainly knowledge of one does aid the other. The Lakes were a source of inspiration to Wordsworth as well as his home.
He was born in Cockermouth in 1770, the son of a lawyer affluent enough to afford an education at Hawkshead Grammar School as well as Cambridge. He and his sister Dorothy lived in the West Country for a time but returned

in 1799 to settle initially at Dove Cottage near Grasmere. This is the place most associated with Wordsworth; he was at the height of his powers as a poet and this reputation lured the other 'Lakeland poets', Coleridge and Southey, to the Lakes.
By the time Wordsworth had moved to his final home, Rydal Mount, he had become something of a tourist attraction himself. Yet the man who wrote the first guide to the Lake

District professed a hatred of tourism that led him to lead the fight against plans to build a railway to Windermere. He died in 1850 and is buried in the churchyard at Grasmere.

Right Several of Wordsworth's houses, such as Dove Cottage, are open to the public. The sights which inspired his poetry remain little disturbed by the visitors following in his footsteps. ◇

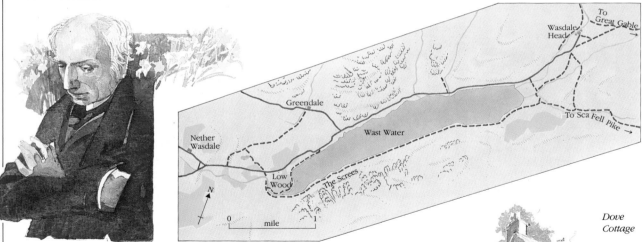

Exploring the countryside
Wasdale Head is climbing country. It provides a good if arduous base for the ascent of Great Gable and the easiest approach to Scafell Pike. Even the 'easy' route past the Brackenclose climbing hut is serious hillwalking, requiring proper clothing and settled weather.
However, it is possible to stroll in the shadow of these great peaks with neither great experience nor special equipment. Several paths will allow walkers to devise their own circuits between the hamlet of Wasdale Head, the lakeside and the farm at Burnthwaite. Two waymarked routes can be found at the other end of Wast Water. These start near Netherwasdale and have been laid out by the Cumbria Trust for Nature Conservation through a variety of habitats including lakeside, pasture, bog and screes. One of the attractions of the trails — which are 2½ and 3½ miles long — is that they provide an excellent introduction to the wildlife of the valley. Ironically, the lake itself is too pure to have sufficient nutrients for many species of fish to breed, but it does attract several birds into the valley. Mergansers and mallards will be seen on the lake in summer while dipper and grey wagtail abound on the streams and around the lake sides. The broadleaved woods near Netherwasdale attract redstarts and wood warblers, among others, while high above patrol the birds of prey such as buzzards, ravens and kestrels. ◇

Dove Cottage

Above Wast Water is a place for superlatives: England's deepest lake at 262 feet deep at the foot of England's highest mountain, the 3,206 foot summit of Scafell Pike. Here you see Wast Water's screes. ◇

Right Wast Water with Great Gable in the centre flanked by Kirkfell and Lingmell at its head presents the majestic and wild heart of the Lake District's mountains. ◇

Worth a detour

Cockermouth Georgian house in the High Street which was the birthplace of William Wordsworth. NT.

Ravenglass Once a port, now a tourist attraction as the terminus of a narrow gauge railway and nearby Muncaster Castle overlooking the Esk Estuary.

Wordsworth Apart from Cockermouth the best-known houses are Dove Cottage and Rydal Mount, near Grasmere. Further afield is Gowbarrow Park, where in 1804 he saw his 'host of golden daffodils', north of Ullswater near Aira Force waterfall.

Grey Mare's Tail

Map: OS map 79 in 1:50000 series

Two Scottish writers are linked to the Grey Mare's Tail. The waterfall was named after the Grey Mare in Robert Burns's poem, *Tam O'Shanter*, but Burns is more associated with Ayrshire and Galloway. The writer most closely linked with these Border hills is Sir Walter Scott (1771–1832), **below**. He lived at Abbotsford, near Melrose, for 20 years from where he visited Grey Mare's Tail several times. He is buried at Dryburgh Abbey.◇

Walter Scott

The Scottish Lowlands are often neglected as Scots head for the lakes and resorts of England while the English speed through on their way to the Highlands and Islands of northern Scotland. But the Lowlands are certainly not lacking in drama and they are not even particularly low, especially by English standards. The hills may lack the rugged grandeur of their northern counterparts but many peaks exceed 2,000 feet. Among them is White Coomb, 2,696 feet in the Moffat Hills which overlooks one of Scotland's highest waterfalls — Grey Mare's Tail. Both are owned by the National Trust for Scotland.

The spectacular waterfall was named after the Grey Mare in Robert Burns's *Tam O'Shanter*. It formed as a result of glacial activity which left the Tail Burn (or stream) 'hanging' 200 feet above the valley of the larger Moffat Water. It lies just five minutes walk off the A708 road between Moffat and Selkirk, some ten miles northeast of Moffat. The Trust has erected an information display at the main car park which explains the geology and natural history of the area. And there is much more to see than simply the waterfall, impressive though it is.

A short distance (although a sharp climb) beyond the Tail is a 'hidden' loch which can only be reached on foot. Loch Skeen is about three-quarters of a mile long and overlooked on two sides by rocky outcrops and steep screes. It, too, reflects the impact of ice upon the Moffat Hills for it was dammed at its outflow by a *moraine* of rocky debris dumped by the ice sheets and glaciers as they retreated.

Wildlife in the area ranges from alpine plants to a herd of feral goats. The former are best seen in June and July but the goats which roam the grassy slopes near the waterfall are less seasonal. The most common mammal, though, is the sheep and the treeless landscape is typical of an area which has been heavily grazed for centuries. Although trees are mostly confined to inaccessible rocky ledges, the area is surprisingly rich in birdlife.

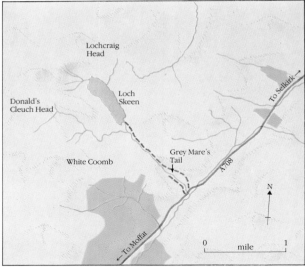

Below Grey Mare's Tail is a perfect example of a 'hanging valley'. In the Ice Ages, glaciers occupied the valleys of both the Tail Burn and Moffat Water. These glaciers deepened the valleys as they progressed slowly southward. But the larger glacier of Moffatdale had greater power and thus lowered this main valley substantially more than the tributary valleys.

When the ice retreated these tributary valleys, such as that now occupied by the Tail Burn, were left 'hanging' on the side of the larger valley and the waterfall is the result. In this case the work of glaciers was aided by the presence of a geological fault from St Mary's Loch to Moffat; the sheltered rock in the fault-line was more easily eroded by the main glacier.◇

The Ice Age valley

The 'hanging valley' today

Right The hills around the waterfall are mostly covered by heather, acid grassland and peat bogs, but are home to the flourishing herd of feral goats. The vegetation around White Coomb includes alpines such as lady's mantle, saw-wort and bistort, rock rose, northern bedstraw, globe flower and mossy saxifrage. Most of the common upland birds can be seen, and around the Tail Burn wren, grey wagtail and dipper all breed. You may spot a kestrel, but the local short-eared owl and peregrine are more elusive. ◇

Far right The waterfall takes its name from the Grey Mare in Robert Burns's *Tam O'Shanter*. The 'tail' is this spectacular 200 foot drop towards Moffat Water. ◇

Rock Rose

Globe Flower

Mossy Saxifrage

Kestrel

Feral Goats

Above Loch Skeen is reached by one of the two footpaths which begin from the car parks for the Grey Mare's Tail. It lies only 1½ miles from the car park but the path is steep, so allow anything between 45–60 minutes each way. The path can also be boggy further up the hill so it is best tackled by walkers with some energy and strong footwear. A rough path around the loch itself takes about an hour.

Short walk Family groups will probably choose the left-hand of the two paths from the car park. It is the only safe route to get near the waterfall and takes about ten minutes each way. But do keep to the path: the cliffs and grassy slopes are extremely dangerous.

Hill walk The path to Loch Skeen can be a good starting point for experienced walkers wishing to explore the hills. No paths exist beyond the loch, and conditions are very variable, but the tops of Lochcraig Head, Firthybrig Head, Donald's Cleuch Head and White Coomb can all be combined in a circular walk around the loch. ◇

Worth a detour

Priorwood Garden NTS garden and orchard next to Melrose Abbey. Special feature — flowers grown suitable for drying.

Carlyle's birthplace In Ecclefechan, 5½ miles SE of Lockerbie. Contains mementos of Thomas Carlyle's work as writer, historian and social reformer. NTS.

Abbotsford House The home of Sir Walter Scott, 2 miles W of Melrose. The Border country provided the inspiration for many of Scott's novels and ballads and his house is still largely as he left it. Not NTS.

Sea Lochs of Western Scotland

Map OS maps 24 and 33 in 1:50000 series.

Above The snow-capped peaks of the Five Sisters of Kintail soar above Loch Duich, dwarfing the waterside castle of Eilean Donnan. ◇

The sea lochs of the Western Highlands do not lack drama. Eagles soar above mountainous peaks such as the Five Sisters of Kintail, towering over Loch Duich; moorland burns plunge 370 feet as at the Falls of Glomach; narrow straits of swirling tides separate the mainland from the alluring island of Skye; and fortifications from prehistoric to Jacobean times bear testimony to man's struggle to subdue — and survive — this Highland wilderness.

The sea lochs probe deeply into the Highlands so that the mountains often rise sheer from the water. Much of the tortuous coastline, especially south from Loch Alsh, remains inaccessible except by boat; much of the land is populated only by some of Britain's wildest and rarest animals or birds. Only the peninsula bounded by lochs Duich, Alsh and Carron has modern roads on all sides, although it was the railway which first made Kyle of Lochalsh into the gateway to Skye. Previously the main crossing point had been at Kyle Rhea — swum by highland cattle en route to mainland markets — but now this has a ferry in summer only. Skye has been an island for barely 10,000 years —

since the sea level rose after the last Ice Age — and a magnet for visitors for a century. Yet the mainland offers landscapes which are just as spectacular, perhaps more so, and certainly with far fewer crowds.

It is an area with a surprising variety of scenery. Ancient oak and birch woods lie side by side with modern conifer plantations; cultivated strips of croft land mix with barren moorland; palm trees bloom just a few miles from rare alpine plants in high mountain corries. The contrasting features can all be found within two large areas owned by the National Trust for Scotland — Balmacara around the headland of the Lochalsh Peninsula and Kintail at the head of Loch Duich. Walking these areas is the best way to savour the magnificence of the mountains, although rugged Kintail requires energy to match the rewards.

However, motorists are not denied all the best views. The old military road over Ratagan Pass between Shiel Bridge and Kyle Rhea, for instance, offers superb views both towards Skye and back to the Five Sisters. And Eilean Donnan castle, at the junction of three sea lochs, is picturesque whatever the viewpoint.

110

Discovering the wildlife

The proximity of sea to mountain ensures a greater diversity of wildlife than is found in many Highland areas. However, it is still the rarity of species that attracts most attention — birds such as the golden eagle or the ptarmigan, for instance, and animals like the wildcat and pine marten. These rarest species are also the most elusive or more likely to be confined to the higher levels. Red deer also retreat to the high corries in summer, although roe deer can be seen in the woods. Here badgers are also found while on the seashore otters are even more evident.

Birdlife varies from buzzards, eagles, ravens, crows and ring ousels to the common birds of sea and river: cormorant, gulls, teal, mallard and dipper, and some not so common birds such as the red- and black- throated divers which breed on freshwater mountain lochs. The woodland around Kyle of Lochalsh is yet another habitat for birds and flowers, but again the most unusual plants are on the higher slopes. These include alpine meadow rue, moss campion, several saxifrages, dwarf willow, marsh marigold and mountain azalea. The corries of Ben Attow and the Five Sisters display a good variety of mountain species but wet areas along streams are also rich in flora. ◇

Above Eilean Donnan castle was built in the 13th century on an island at the junction of three lochs. Once a ruin, it has been restored to become Scotland's most picturesque castle. ◇

Exploring the countryside

Kintail offers walks to suit most degrees of experience and energy. It is dominated by the magnificent outline of the Five Sisters. No one should be deluded by their grassy slopes; the gradients are steep and the countryside rugged.

In all Kintail has nine peaks over 3,000 feet and there are other famous mountains nearby, such as the Saddle across Glen Shiel from the Five Sisters. But in summer there are also several walks which could be tackled by walkers with some energy and appropriate clothes.

The easiest walks are along the glens. A stroll alongside the meandering River Croe, for instance, in Glen Lichd will convey more grandeur than could ever be glimpsed through a car window. More experienced (or energetic) walkers can continue up this glen from Morvich until the path links with others, returning either past Loch a'Bhealaich or the slopes of Ben Attow — the 'long mountain' with more than four miles of undulating summit. Other routes lead to Glen Affric as well as the Falls of Glomach. Scenically, the best views are obtained by walking from east to west so that the sea lochs are kept in sight. Always allow an hour for every two miles and add an hour for each 1,000 feet to be climbed. ◇

Above The dolphin swims in schools and is best known for its acrobatics in the water. ◇

Common Dolphin

Below The porpoise leaps less often and otherwise can be distinguished from a dolphin by its blunter head and smaller fin. ◇

Common Porpoise

Sea Lochs of Western Scotland

The Lochalsh Peninsula is bounded by water yet never far from land. Skye is barely a quarter of a mile away, the peninsulas of Applecross, Loch Carron and Glenelg little further. However, unlike these neighbouring peninsulas, Lochalsh has been opened up by modern communications: a railway hugs the northern shore alongside Loch Carron, roads encircle the peninsula, and busy ferries shuttle to and from Kyle of Lochalsh.

Kyle has become the gateway to Skye which means that at times it is also a place of noise and congestion. But you do not have to go far to escape the traffic fumes. Even the rocky knoll above Kyle itself affords a splendid view across the narrows of Kyle Akin (*kyle* is Gaelic for 'narrow place') towards the Cuillin Hills of Skye. The juxtaposition of land and water makes this a peninsula of spectacular views which compensate for any lack of height compared to inland Kintail.

Much of the peninsula is owned by the National Trust for Scotland as part of its Balmacara estate. It is a gentle landscape, where small fishing and crofting townships such as Plockton were established at the time of the Highland clearances. Its sheltered shores, warmed by the north Atlantic drift, enable trees to flourish and semi-tropical plants to be introduced in gardens such as those of Lochalsh House two miles east of Kyle. A small NTS visitor centre here includes displays about the area's wildlife and history and there are woodland walks with views over Loch Alsh toward the straits of Kyle Rhea. The visitor centre is unmanned but in summer information about other walks within the Balmacara estate is available from a reception centre near the car park.

Walking here is less demanding than in nearby Kintail with Auchertyre Hill the highest summit at 1,484 feet. This can be reached from Balmacara via a forest track through Coille-Mhor – the big wood. Other woodland walks can be found south of Stromeferry on the northern shore of the peninsula and at Ard Point on the southern shore. Rarely is the sea out of sight but gentler still are the walks along the shore around Drumbuie or between Plockton and Duncraig. Go at dusk and experience the awe-inspiring sunsets.

Broch dun Telve

Above Broch dun Telve in Glenn Beag is an example of a fortified home unique to Scotland, dating from the Iron Age and amazingly still 32 feet high. ◇

Right Roe deer are smaller than red deer, averaging just two feet when mature. This, allied to a preference for woodland and undergrowth, makes these shy animals rather elusive. ◇

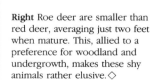

Roe Deer

Left *Glomach* is Gaelic for forbidding or fearsome. Few who have seen the Falls of Glomach would think they have been poorly christened. It is not only the height, although the total drop of 370 feet puts the falls among the highest in Britain. It is equally the location, high in a wild mountain glen. Although there is no easy route to the falls, they can be reached with energy rather than mountaineering skills — and the remoteness adds to their appeal. The falls can be approached from either above or below. The only guaranteed access throughout the year is from above, because the lower route may be closed during the deer-stalking season in August and September. However, one of the two higher routes is confined to National Trust land which is always open. To reach this, head north then northeast from Morvich on Loch Duich to the Forestry Commission car park at Dorusduain. From here there are

two paths. The one on NTS land twists southeast only along Glen Chòinneachain before climbing the Bealach an Sgàirne pass to reach Loch a'Bhealaich. This is the largest of the small lochs which feed the falls. The path, as such, disappears but by following the water downstream (or north) you eventually reach the falls. The shortness of the mountain burn does not prepare you for the suddenness of its descent, plunging sheer for 300 feet before hitting a ledge and splitting into several chutes. Even now it is difficult to gauge its full extent as the rocks and spray mask its fall from all but rock climbers. A shorter route leads back to Dorusduain, initially as a steep climb towards the pass of Bealach na Sròine before a steady descent across open moorland and finally through conifers. This is the alternative (and signposted) route from the car park. Allow at least seven hours for the full circuit and dress appropriately. ◇

Above Cattle graze contentedly along the shore, palm trees flutter on the main street, yachts cluster in the bay — Plockton offers a placid contrast to the more dramatic seascapes and mountains nearby. Laid out as a 'model village' in the last century, Plockton flourished as a fishing port. Nowadays it lures tourists by land and sea. ◇

Left The shrubs and trees of Lochalsh garden near Balmacara are nurtured by the protective effect of the north Atlantic drift on Scotland's west coast. ◇

Worth a detour

Affric Classic highland glen with important relic of old Caledonian pine forest.
Forest walks Access for experienced walkers via NTS Kintail property or by car via A831 W of Drumnadrochit on Loch Ness.
Strome Castle Ruins of a medieval castle destroyed in 1602. 4½ miles SW of Lochcarron off A896. NTS.

Corrieshalloch Gorge

Birch

Above The common birch is often known as the silver birch because of its white trunk. It grows rapidly when young and at greater heights than most other trees.◇

Corrieshalloch Gorge is one of Scotland's more accessible natural attractions. Indeed, only its site in the northwest Highlands renders it remote. But although the gorge is passed by two roads, you have to leave your car to appreciate fully the splendour of the wooded slopes and, at the head of the gorge, one of Scotland's finest waterfalls.

The River Droma flows toward Loch Broom through a conventional U-shaped valley of the Ice Age before plummeting, suddenly, 150 feet into the narrow and densely-wooded Corrieshalloch Gorge. The Falls of Measach are part of a mile-long stretch of the gorge now owned by the National Trust for Scotland. The gorge, which in places is 200 feet deep, is rich in wildlife with a particularly wide variety of trees. The combination of woodland, water and the neighbouring peaks nurtures birdlife which ranges from eagles and buzzards to wagtails and woodpeckers. It is no surprise, therefore, that a national nature reserve covering 13 acres of the gorge has been established here by the Nature Conservancy Council.

The gorge can be approached from either a car park one mile north of the Braemore Road junction on the A835 or another, a little further south, on the A832 on the opposite side of the gorge. A path leads from the former to a viewing platform which provides a dramatic panorama of both the gorge and the falls. Only two people at a time can squeeze onto the viewing platform but whether in summer, when the trees and mosses are at their lushest, or in winter, when melting snow produces cascades of water down the sides of the gorge, it rarely disappoints. A well-fenced and relatively flat path leads to a suspension bridge across the gorge which offers a closer view of the falls themselves. Another path leads from this 50-foot-long bridge to the car park on the A832.

Left The River Droma, tumbling down the narrow cleft of the Falls of Measach seems too small to have carved such a gorge. In fact, the gorge was formed some 13,000 years ago, at the end of the last Ice Age. As the ice melted, it produced huge torrents which poured down valleys, cutting them far deeper than would have occurred simply through the work of non-glacial river water. ◇

Left Loch Broom is the longest sea loch of Scotland's northern Highlands. It penetrates almost 20 miles into the hills and has on its northern shore the busy fishing port of Ullapool. Here, the white houses are grouped together on a terrace some 40 feet above the sea. This was once a river delta formed at the mouth of Glen Achall by glacial deposits, but has since been raised above the present level of the sea by a series of geological changes which have 'uplifted' the land since the last Ice Age. Further evidence of these changes can be seen in a number of 'raised beaches' which occur around the edges of Loch Broom. ◇

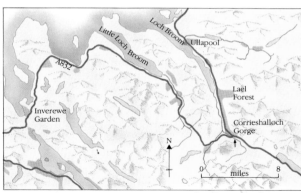

Left Inverewe is on the same latitude as Siberia, but you would not think so at this garden run by the National Trust for Scotland on the shore of Loch Ewe. The warming effect of the north Atlantic drift allied to a 'shelter belt' of evergreen trees enables plants from many nations to thrive. ◇

Discovering the wildlife

The steep slopes of the ravine are densely wooded. Among the native species birch, larch, Scots fir and copper beech are the most evident but rowan, hazel, bird cherry and wych elm are also present. The lower ledges are dominated by ferns while high humidity and lack of sunlight at the base of the gorge encourages a rich flora of mosses and liverworts. The gorge thus offers a wide variety of habitats for birds: woods, water and mountains. So eagles, buzzards and falcons can be spotted soaring high over the mountains that surround the gorge, while in the ravine itself there are wagtails, wheatears, woodcock, snipe, thrush, green woodpeckers, robins, long-tailed (and other) tits, as well as cuckoos and siskins. ◇

Woodcock

Snipe

Left Woodcock and snipe have sensitive bills which probe the mud for larvae and worms. The upper bill tip 'hinges' so that prey can be grasped without opening the entire bill. ◇

Right Otters have become relatively scarce in southern Britain, but they thrive on the protected banks of Corrieshalloch Gorge. Stoats and voles can also be seen, while on the higher slopes there are pine martens, hares, foxes and both red and roe deer. There are also feral and wild goats. Trout swim in the waters of the Droma itself while salmon and sea trout get up to a mile downstream. ◇

Otter

◇◇◇

Worth a detour

Walks The countryside around Corrieshalloch is essentially for walkers with experience of rugged terrain and accustomed to using compasses, since few paths exist on the hills. One exception is Lael Forest at the head of Loch Broom where the Forestry Commission has laid out a series of short trails.

Drives The A832 on the southern side of the gorge can be the starting point for a splendid drive to Inverewe on the coast. The distance to Inverewe is 39 miles. To avoid retracing your route continue on the A832, past Gairloch to Loch Maree. Here Beinn Eighe nature reserve has a short trail and picnic area. The A832 heads east along the Bran Valley until meeting the A835, which takes you back to Corrieshalloch Gorge and Ullapool.

◇◇◇

Strangford Lough

Ballycopeland Windmill

Above Only one working windmill survives from the days when grain was the basis of this area's prosperity. It is at Ballycopeland, near Millisle, on the northern Ards peninsula. ◇

Above Grey Abbey was one of three monasteries founded by the Cistercians toward the end of the 12th century. Extensive ruins remain here and also at Inch Abbey, but less is to be seen of the third at Comber. ◇

Strangford Lough is both an escape and an enigma, a magnet for yachtsmen and birdwatchers, a maze of inlets and islands with a shoreline 150 miles long. At one end turbulent tidal currents from the sea thrash through an entrance barely half a mile wide; at the other, low tide exposes acres of mudflats near the market town of Newtownards. The lough is almost 21 miles long yet separated from the Irish Sea only by the long, spindly arm of the Ards Peninsula. Depending upon the time of day, the tides, a trick of the light, this vast sea-fed lough can display a multitude of faces or moods; no matter how deeply you may penetrate its winding shore, there always remains the suspicion that other secrets are waiting to be discovered.

The lough owes its name to Viking invaders whose *Strang Fjord* meant 'violent inlet'. Every day some 400 million tons of water rush through the rocky channel which separates the open lough from the sea. These 'Narrows', guarded by the salty harbour villages of Portaferry and Strangford, are altogether more rugged than the placid shores of the middle and upper lough. The great mudflats at the upper or northern end are bordered by strips of reclaimed land, while the middle area is dominated by numerous small hills known as *drumlins*. These are mounds of sediment left by glaciers as the ice melted, many forming tiny islands within the lough. Apart from Scrabo Hill north of the lough, this is a low-lying landscape utterly different to the sea lochs of western Scotland; here, nowhere is more than a few hundred feet above sea level.

Here, too, human life is in some ways less evident than wildlife. There is some fishing, but farming dominates the landscape so that the shoreline appears largely undeveloped, apart from a few sailing clubs along the western shore, and a handful of villages such as Grey Abbey and Whiterock. Although Belfast is within commuting distance, there is a timeless tranquillity about Strangford Lough that has resisted commercialization. By far the busiest lives, in and around the lough, are led by the birds, with species from the Arctic in winter and from the tropics in summer. In all, more than 130 species of birds have been seen here—and with a road following the eastern shore it is one of the easiest and most rewarding places to go bird watching in the United Kingdom.

The National Trust owns or manages most of the 150 miles of foreshore of the lough, together with a number of its 70 islands. It is currently developing a major programme of interpretation of the lough and its wildlife. This will build upon the success of a scheme launched in 1966 to protect the many species of wildfowl and help preserve its unspoilt character.

The sense of space — and mystery — evoked by this relative wildness has become its most potent appeal, but the lough was not always a place of escape or solitude. Nowhere in Northern Ireland has a richer history and its shores still reveal evidence of a turbulent past; from prehistoric times to St Patrick, from the Normans to Cromwell, man has left his mark on Strangford Lough.

Left Strangford village stands at the gateway to the lough opposite Portaferry. In the 18th century it became a thriving port for the corn trade, and many fine houses date from this time. ◇

The monastic tradition
Strangford Lough may appear largely unspoilt, but for 7,000 years man has hunted and cultivated its shores and fished its waters. There are prehistoric remains at Millin Bay, near Portaferry, in the south, and also at Scrabo Hill in the north. But the most interesting period is probably early christianity. St Patrick himself first landed in Ireland in AD 432 at the point where the River Slaney flows into the lough. At Saul, near Downpatrick, a replica of an early church marks the supposed spot of Patrick's first sermon to the Irish people. The relative isolation of the lough offered a safe retreat to the monks of Nendrum who set up a sanctuary on Mahee Island which is linked to the mainland by a causeway. The monastery was destroyed by Norseman in 974 but impressive remains can still be seen. So, too, can the remains of the three great Cistercian monasteries at Inch Abbey, Grey Abbey and Comber. At about the same time the Normans built castles at Audleystown and Kilclief. ◇

Brent Goose

Golden Plover

Black-tailed Godwit

Above Islandmore off the western shore of Strangford Lough is one of seventy islands dotted around the lough, some of which appear and disappear with each tide. ◇

Left The tortuous shoreline of the lough presents a wide range of habitats. Great swathes of eel grass sprout from the mudflats to provide pasture for the many wildfowl which winter there. Among these are pale-bellied Brent geese, shelduck, whooper swans, pintails, mallards and wigeons. Other inhabitants, feeding on worms and small shellfish, are waders such as golden plover and black-tailed godwit. ◇

Strangford Lough

Lapwing

Above Lapwings are adaptable waders, at home in fresh water or on the shore and equally happy eating grass and worms or seaweed and molluscs. Their plangent 'pee-wit' gives them their other name. ◇

Below Castle Ward, overlooking the Lough's southern shore, is half Gothic and half classical— the bizarre but splendid result of a disagreement between the peer and his wife, who built the house in the 18th century. ◇

It is possible, in theory, to walk the entire 150-mile foreshore of Strangford Lough. However, you would need waterproof boots and detailed knowledge of the tides, since there are no designated or waymarked trails along the waterside. Despite this, the lough is easy and rewarding to explore whether it be by road along the eastern shore or on foot; walkers can plan their own itineraries to match their own energy and interests.

Many will wish to see the birds for which the lough is renowned. Four hides have been established and many other observation points are available; wherever you are, the best time to see birds is two or three hours before high tide when they are being driven closer to the shore

There are four national nature reserves which demonstrate that there is more to Strangford Lough than birds alone. Three are in the south on either side of the lough's rocky gateway to the sea. To the west is Killard Point, where dunes shelter a variety of wild flowers. Nearby, at Cloghy Rocks, and across the Narrows at Granagh Bay nature reserve, common seals breed during June and July. The fourth reserve is at Ardkeen, about four miles north of Portaferry.

Beyond Granagh Bay a lovely walk leads from Bar Hall Bay around Ballyquintin Point. In winter this headland can be lashed by violent sea storms — there is even a whirlpool near Granagh Bay. Summer walkers will find a balmier scene of poppies, foxgloves and herbs among the lush grasses. Part of the path to Ballyquintin Point crosses private land, so remember the country code.

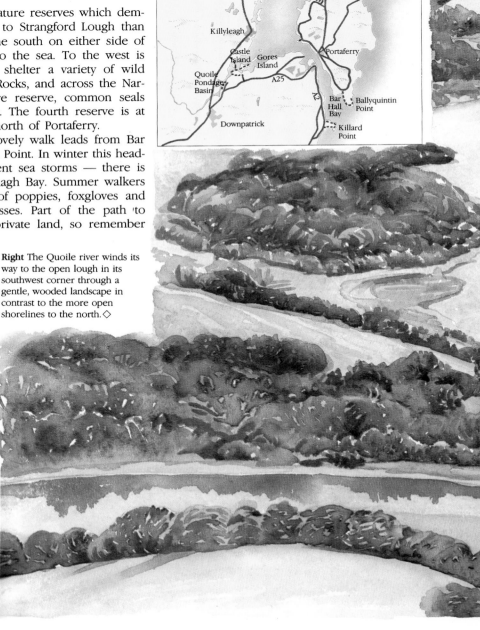

Right The Quoile river winds its way to the open lough in its southwest corner through a gentle, wooded landscape in contrast to the more open shorelines to the north. ◇

Below Mallards nest on islands in Strangford Lough, laying eggs between March and May. They often have two broods. ◇

Mallards

118

Exploring the islands

Strangford Lough is dotted by islands, many of which you can walk to across causeways. One of these is Long Island, off the western shore north of Ardmillan. It is a wild, remote landscape, truly unspoilt since it is reached only by skirting the mudflats. Ahead are the boney fingers of Reagh Island and Mahee Island, jutting into the Lough. The view here is fully 180 degrees, excellent for birdwatching or simply getting away from it all. But the walk is very muddy, even when sticking as close as possible to the shore. Always beware of the mudflats, especially those separating Long Island from Wood Island: the mud won't stand your weight. There are two Castle Islands. The most southerly of the two is linked to the mainland by a causeway. Other causeways then lead from here to the smaller Hare and Gores islands; these are sometimes impassable. What is most remarkable, however, is the contrast either side of the main causeway between Strangford Lough and the Quoile Pondage. To the northeast is the sea; to the southwest is the freshwater landscape of the Quoile River. This survives because of a barrage built off Hare Island to protect the market town of Downpatrick from flooding. Remains of the old docks may still be seen. There is a nature reserve at Quoile Pondage Basin and pleasant walks along the river banks. ◇

Where to see birds

There are four hides and several observation points in addition to numerous other places suitable for watching birds.
Best in Autumn and early winter (Oct–Dec) Castle Espie hide, Reagh Island hide, Gashouse hide at Mt Stewart, Grey Abbey (2 car parks), Newtownards embankment.
Best in winter (Dec–Mar) Eagleson hide at Castle Ward, Gransha Point, Gibbs Island, Tully Hill lay-by on the W side of the Narrows south of Strangford village.
Summer Strangford village quay for views of terns nesting on Swan Island.
Good all year Ballyhenry Island, Quoile Pondage. ◇

Right Whooper swans, named after their distinctive call, are noisy winter visitors. They do not breed here, but non-breeding juveniles may stop over for the summer. ◇

Whooper Swans

Exploring Gransha Point

Gransha Point penetrates deeply into the waters of the lough, only becoming covered by the sea at the highest of tides. At its furthest point, though, you seem surrounded by water with views as far as Newtownards to the north and Quoile to the south. In winter the muddy track to the causeway dissolves to a quagmire, so leave your car behind. ◇

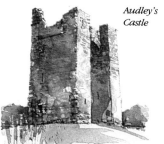

Audley's Castle

Above Tower houses such as Audley's Castle are a legacy from the 15th and 16th centuries. More common than the grand castles built at the time, they served much the same purpose of enabling landowners to protect family and possessions. ◇

Exploring the eastern shore

The waterside road north from Portaferry on the eastern shore is one of the most scenic drives around the lough. It gives uninterrupted views across the water to Castle Ward and the surrounding wooded landscape with its houses and old farm buildings. At any point you can leave the car and walk — either along the shore or across to Ballyhenry Island. The road cuts inland briefly before rejoining the lough at the Dorn, an intricate series of bays, mudflats and islands. Here you can walk round Ballywallon and Phersons islands or for miles along the winding foreshore to the promontory of Ardkeen with its ruined castle. ◇

Worth a detour

Castle Ward 18th-century house, half Gothic and half classical style. Parkland overlooking the lough. 7 miles NE of Downpatrick. NT.
Mount Stewart Another 18th-century house but more famous as one of Ireland's greatest gardens. 5 miles SE of Newtownards. NT.
Rowallane Garden created from rocky landscape with rare trees and shrubs. 1 mile S of Saintfield. NT.

WOODSIDE

Woods appear to be an integral part of the British countryside. There are the woodlands themselves—ancient forests of oak, beech and yew as well as modern conifer plantations. There are the watersides lined with alder and willow trees, and there are the wooded hedgerows, copses and groves providing a framework for the open fields. Yet this is one of the least wooded countries in Europe: woodland covers approximately 15 per cent of the British Isles.

In little more than 10,000 years the woods have come and largely gone. As the climate improved after the last Ice Age, vegetation tentatively re-established itself on the frozen tundra-like wastes. Scots pine, juniper, dwarf birch and willow were among the pioneers, to be followed, as temperatures rose, by oak, hazel, ash and elm. These latter trees gradually became predominant, except in Scotland where the Great Wood of Caledon blanketed more than three million acres of land with Scots pine.

Successive invasions added to the richness of our woodlands. The Romans brought walnut and sweet chestnut, while other species, such as the sycamore and horse chestnut, were established in the Middle Ages. But the woods were under attack—from man. From the Stone Age onward we have been clearing woods to make room for agriculture or to use the timber for shelter or fuel. For many centuries, wood was fundamental to our ancestors' way of life and as such it was developed with care. The broadleaved woodland displayed a remarkable capacity to develop new shoots so a system of management known as *coppicing* developed, whereby various types of trees were cut on rotation to provide raw materials. Later generations were less conscientious and woods were flattened wholesale to make way for industrial Britain. Hedgerows were also erased to make larger, more cost-effective fields. And with the disappearance of the trees went the teeming wildlife of long-established woodland. Where trees have been planted they have mostly been conifers, since their rapid growth makes them a more profitable timber crop.

In recent years, there have been attempts to plant conifers with more subtlety, so they present a less uniform and regimented appearance. These woods are developing some wildlife, although this cannot compare in richness to that of a naturally-regenerating broadleaved or deciduous woodland. Yet in one sense the new coniferous forests do represent an echo of the past: they are increasingly being used for recreation with waymarked trails and picnic areas. The recreational use of ancient forests was more lordly. Many were maintained as royal hunting grounds and copses were often planted to provide breeding grounds for deer. Relics of ancient forests survive and these are now being protected as much for their wildlife as the beauty they contribute to the countryside as a whole.

Once most of Britain was covered by trees. Many woodlands have been cleared by man to provide timber for shelter and room for agriculture, but enough remain to add colour and seasonal change to the landscape. *Below*: The golden shower of autumn leaves transforms the woods at Hardcastle Crags into a surreal setting.

Clockwise from right: The New Forest is the largest remaining tract of former royal hunting forest in Britain, with open heaths as well as glades, such as the one seen here near the Ornamental Drive; broadleaved woodland gives Rydal Water, in the Lake District, a more homely appearance than many of the larger conifer-surrounded lakes; the woods of Ebbor Gorge are rich in ferns, mosses and fungi with a dense canopy of deciduous trees; Winkworth Arboretum brings together many rare trees and shrubs so that these Surrey hills are never without colour.

Teign Valley

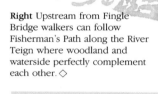

Raven

Above The all-black raven is
Britain's largest crow, nesting on
ledges on moorland, mountains
or seacliffs. Sometimes known as
the vultures of sheep country,
ravens are also renowned for
aerial acrobatics. ◇

Rivers flow off the granite upland of Dartmoor to all
points of the compass, hurrying down to lowland
Devon through deep-cut valleys clothed in trees. The
River Teign is in one of the lushest of these valleys and
although one of the most accessible, is largely unexplored. Paths follow the river, on one side or the other,
for a meandering seven miles between Dogmarsh
Bridge on the A382 and Steps Bridge on the B3212.

Although there are commercial conifer plantations, it
is the oak woodland which is dominant. It is perhaps at
its best in the spring when the trees come into leaf at
slightly different times to produce an attractive mosaic
of colour; in autumn, too, there is differential shading
as the leaves darken. The slopes were always too steep
for cultivation but traditionally provided fencing,
firewood and charcoal for local people. Now, however,
large tracts of the woods are being conserved by the
National Trust simply for their beauty. This involves
removing the poorer trees which, by allowing more
light to penetrate, will also improve the natural regeneration of the woodland.

The largest area of Trust land forms part of the
Castle Drogo estate at the western gateway to the
valley. Less conspicuous, but with better claims to
former defensive purposes, are three Iron Age hill forts
which overlook the valley — Cranbrook, Prestonbury
and Wooston Castles. Cranbrook in particular offers
one of the finest viewpoints on northeast Dartmoor
from its 1,105-foot summit to the south of the River
Teign above the latterday beauty spot of Fingle Bridge.
Hills and woods, riverside and castles thus complement
each other in this remarkably unspoilt valley.

Right Upstream from Fingle
Bridge walkers can follow
Fisherman's Path along the River
Teign where woodland and
waterside perfectly complement
each other. ◇

Hazel

Above The hazel is a shrub which
forms a small tree in wooded
areas but is also common in
hedgerows. The male flowers of
hanging catkins appear from
January to March. ◇

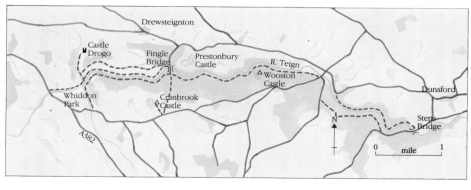

Above Castle Drogo, once
dismissed as an architectural
aberration or folly, is
increasingly regarded as a
masterpiece of 20th-century
building. It was designed by Sir
Edwin Lutyens and completed in
1930, 19 years after building had
commenced and was probably
the last castle to be built in
Britain. It was the home of Julius
Drewe, a Victorian grocer, who
nonetheless showed admirable
military sense by siting his castle
on a commanding bluff. ◇

124

Exploring the countryside

The most popular walk within the Teign Valley links Castle Drogo with Fingle Bridge, a narrow 16th-century bridge where a minor road ends at the heart of the valley. Two paths run upstream along the north bank from here: the high-level Hunters' Path and the riverside Fisherman's Path. They can be combined to make a delightful four-mile circuit. Deer are often seen, descendants of the denizens of a deer park which once surrounded Whiddon Park House on the south bank opposite Castle Drogo. Ravens nest on the crags of Sharp Tor but the bird most often seen on the river is the dipper.

A path continues downstream from Fingle Bridge, past the ruins of an old watermill, alongside the river as far as Clifford Bridge, where a small caravan site provides a reminder of 20th-century tourism. The path then briefly leaves the river, crosses to the left bank and follows a quiet road before scurrying back into the woods for the last lap to Steps Bridge. This stretch of the valley is particularly popular in the spring when wild daffodils bloom in great profusion from March to mid-April. It is managed by the Devon Trust for Nature Conservation which asks visitors not to pick any flowers.

At Steps Bridge, between Easter and October, an information centre is provided by the Dartmoor national park authority. The National Trust also plans to develop a new network of paths south of the river at Steps Bridge.

Other paths lead to the hills or viewpoints such as the Iron Age hill forts overlooking the valley. Cranbrook Castle is reached off a track south from Fingle Bridge which was once the main route between Drewsteignton and Moretonhampstead; the track gives an idea of what roads (and travel) were like 150 years ago. ◇

Dipper

Above The dipper is found on fast-flowing streams, bobbing from stone to stone, or standing midstream, searching for food. ◇

Mink

Right The mink sometimes seen along rivers will probably be escapees from fur-farms now living in the wild preying on fish and waterfowl. ◇

Wild Daffodils

Left The wild daffodils which flourish along the Teign near Steps Bridge can be distinguished from those cultivated for florists by their darker yellow 'trumpet'. ◇

Worth a detour

Castle Drogo Lutyens' magnificent castle overlooking the Teign Valley. 1 mile SW of Drewsteignton. NT.

Church House, Widecombe-in-the-Moor A building dating back to the 16th century which has been variously a brewhouse and the village school in a well-known village in the centre of Dartmoor. Part of it now houses a NT information centre.

Parke Over 200 acres of parkland in the wooded valley of the River Bovey with riverside and woodland paths plus a collection of rare farm animal breeds. W of Bovey Tracey. NT.

Ebbor Gorge

Map OS map 182 in 1:50000 series plus trail leaflet

Ebbor Gorge is a narrow ravine etched deeply into the southwest face of the Mendips. So narrow is it, that in places only one person at a time can clamber between its cliff-like sides. So dense is the canopy of trees that it all but masks the gorge from view, bestowing a secretive air utterly different to nearby Cheddar Gorge.

Ebbor, like Cheddar, is a gorge without a river but unlike its more famous neighbour, Ebbor can only be explored on foot. The lack of commercial exploitation has enabled a far wider range of wildlife to thrive and Ebbor is now a national nature reserve leased by the National Trust to the Nature Conservancy Council. Two trails lead into the gorge, one of which turns into a scramble up the head of the gorge itself; this route is longer (although still only 1½ miles) and more arduous, but it is infinitely more rewarding. Most of the path follows dense woodland, largely ash and oak, and this offers welcome shade on the 500-foot climb to the top of the gorge. The height becomes apparent when the trail leads to a rocky crag overlooking not only the gorge but the vast expanse of the Somerset plain to Glastonbury and beyond.

The contrast between hills and plain is dramatic and must have been more so before many of the wetlands of the Somerset Levels were drained. Settlement today is concentrated along the foothills of the Mendips where the subterranean rivers emerge from their passages through the porous limestone of the hills. Towns such as Wells, Axbridge and Cheddar have historic pasts but they are relatively recent arrivals in archaeological terms. High on the 1,000-foot plateau of the Mendips, near the village of Priddy, are numerous prehistoric barrows or burial mounds while near Charterhouse is the outline of a small amphitheatre. This is a relic, along with the bumps and hollows of disturbed ground, of Roman lead mining in the Mendips.

However, the earliest evidence of man comes from the gorges themselves. Fragments of bones and tools from Stone Age times have been found in the caves which pockmark the bare limestone walls of gorges such as Ebbor. So, too, have bones of animals now extinct in England such as reindeer, lemmings, bears and wolves. The caves of Ebbor are smaller than those of Cheddar and Wookey — and too dangerous to enter — but their natural state evokes an accurate impression of how our ancestors first colonized this land.

Hornbeam

Above The hornbeam has a smooth grey bark and oval leaves similar to beech trees, but is a type of birch. Look for its gnarled and crooked trunk with a buttressed base. ◇

Formation of Ebbor Gorge
The making of Ebbor Gorge goes back at least five million years. As a general rule, a stream running off a plateau would form an ordinary river valley: but the Mendips are composed of limestone, a rock which has both vertical and horizontal faults; more important still, limestone is porous and when rainwater absorbs carbon dioxide from the atmosphere it forms a weak carbonic acid. Gradually, the acidic water wears away the limestone, honeycombing it with *swallow holes* into which the streams plunge and tumble. Once underground, the water would continue to erode the fault-lines of the limestone until it met an impermeable rock and was forced back onto the surface. Where the water first went underground, the stream would have continued to cut backwards until it uncovered another weakness in the limestone. It would then disappear down a swallow hole to forge a new series of underground caves. This process went on at Ebbor over millions of years so that the gorge became longer and the caves larger. Then, during the Ice Age, the ground became frozen and impermeable. This meant that the water could no longer disappear underground and once again ran along the surface. It thus began to erode a conventional river valley, but the down-cutting eventually broke through what were previously the roofs of the underground cave systems. These systems were exposed to the surface to form the gorge we see today. ◇

Stage one: acidic water flows along the faults of the limestone carving a subterranean cavern system. ◇

Stage two: the roof of the underground caves collapse or are eroded leaving the walls and floor to form a gorge. ◇

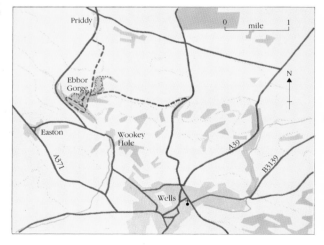

Badger

Right The badger is a woodland animal, common yet reclusive, appearing only at dusk from underground *setts*—mounds of disturbed ground concealing elaborate tunnels. Footprints are more likely to be seen than the animal itself. ◇

Jay

Right The jay is the most colourful member of the crow family. It breeds in woodland, preferring the denser centre where it preys on eggs and nestlings. In autumn it hoards acorns; many are forgotten and seed new oaks. ◇

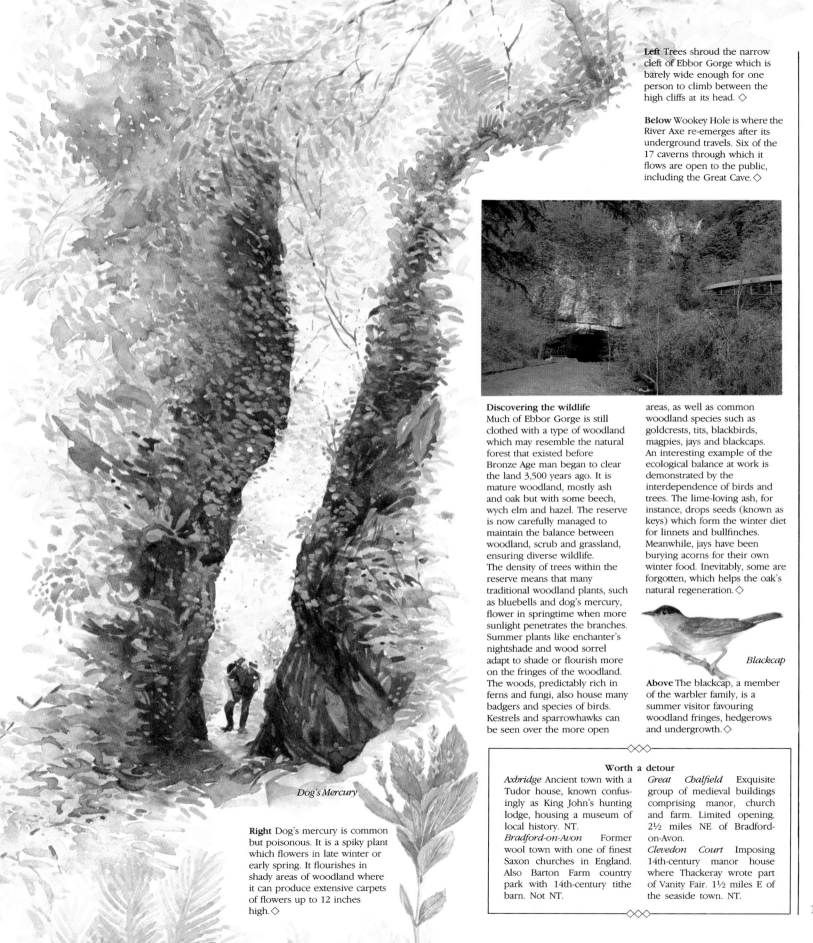

Left Trees shroud the narrow cleft of Ebbor Gorge which is barely wide enough for one person to climb between the high cliffs at its head. ◇

Below Wookey Hole is where the River Axe re-emerges after its underground travels. Six of the 17 caverns through which it flows are open to the public, including the Great Cave. ◇

Discovering the wildlife

Much of Ebbor Gorge is still clothed with a type of woodland which may resemble the natural forest that existed before Bronze Age man began to clear the land 3,500 years ago. It is mature woodland, mostly ash and oak but with some beech, wych elm and hazel. The reserve is now carefully managed to maintain the balance between woodland, scrub and grassland, ensuring diverse wildlife.

The density of trees within the reserve means that many traditional woodland plants, such as bluebells and dog's mercury, flower in springtime when more sunlight penetrates the branches. Summer plants like enchanter's nightshade and wood sorrel adapt to shade or flourish more on the fringes of the woodland. The woods, predictably rich in ferns and fungi, also house many badgers and species of birds. Kestrels and sparrowhawks can be seen over the more open areas, as well as common woodland species such as goldcrests, tits, blackbirds, magpies, jays and blackcaps. An interesting example of the ecological balance at work is demonstrated by the interdependence of birds and trees. The lime-loving ash, for instance, drops seeds (known as keys) which form the winter diet for linnets and bullfinches. Meanwhile, jays have been burying acorns for their own winter food. Inevitably, some are forgotten, which helps the oak's natural regeneration. ◇

Blackcap

Above The blackcap, a member of the warbler family, is a summer visitor favouring woodland fringes, hedgerows and undergrowth. ◇

Dog's Mercury

Right Dog's mercury is common but poisonous. It is a spiky plant which flowers in late winter or early spring. It flourishes in shady areas of woodland where it can produce extensive carpets of flowers up to 12 inches high. ◇

Worth a detour

Axbridge Ancient town with a Tudor house, known confusingly as King John's hunting lodge, housing a museum of local history. NT.

Bradford-on-Avon Former wool town with one of finest Saxon churches in England. Also Barton Farm country park with 14th-century tithe barn. Not NT.

Great Chalfield Exquisite group of medieval buildings comprising manor, church and farm. Limited opening. 2½ miles NE of Bradford-on-Avon.

Clevedon Court Imposing 14th-century manor house where Thackeray wrote part of Vanity Fair. 1½ miles E of the seaside town. NT.

Black Down

Sweet Chestnut

There is a feeling of solitude about Black Down that is surprising for anywhere in southeast England. For a start, it is higher than it appears — at 919 feet, the second highest hill in the region. The dense woodland, heather and gorse are in stark contrast to the patchwork of fields below. Almost as unexpected as this relative wildness, barely an hour's drive from London, is the lack of visitors walking along its sunken paths.

Yet there is nowhere in southeast England that does not bear the imprint of man upon the landscape, however unspoilt it may now appear. Black Down, on the western edge of the Weald, is no exception. A walk around its sandy, secretive paths reveals evidence, from the Stone Age onwards, of man's activities. For the last 40 years this influence has taken the form of management by the National Trust, partly for amenity, partly for timber. Previously the hill had been largely scrubland, used for grazing sheep. Now it is heavily wooded with Scots pine predominant and oak spreading. However, there are still extensive stretches of heather and gorse, often preserved as firebreaks but coincidentally producing magnificent views over the Weald.

Left Sweet chestnut was planted on Black Down for coppicing to make stakes and fencing. However the nuts themselves form a more accessible harvest. ◇

There are several such viewpoints along the route of a 1½-mile nature trail which begins from either of the two car parks off Tennyson's Lane south of Haslemere. To the south the chalk downs are clearly visible with the clump of trees on Chanctonbury Ring jutting above the smooth outline of the hills. Mostly, though, it is the traditional pattern of field, hedgerow and woodland which you see from viewpoints such as the Temple of the Winds, once the site of a summer house used by Lord Alfred Tennyson.

Farms have been established since the Middle Ages, generally below the 'spring line' where the permeable sandstone of Black Down itself meets the underlying clay. But there have been rural industries, too, such as the 16th- and 17th-century glassworks and iron smelting which today linger only as the names of fields or lanes. Even further back in time is a plateau which was a mesolithic site where 8,000 years ago Stone Age man worked flints into hunting tools. Nearby a sunken track is still known by the ancient Celtic name of Pen-y-Bos.

Later excavations of sand and stone for building materials have mostly been obliterated by the spread of trees, but the many droveways which crossed Black Down can be used to provide a variety of walks. However the nature trail — with its explanatory leaflet which is available from the Trust — is the best introduction to one of the south's least-known uplands.

Linnet (male)

Ling Heather

Linnet (female)

Right Linnets are typical of the open heathland birds which nest among the gorse and heather of Black Down. The red-flecked male linnet is more distinctive than the brown and grey female. ◇

Left Ling is the commonest form of the seven species of heather found in Britain. It produces a carpet of pale purple between July and October. ◇

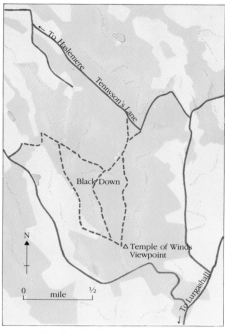

Below Conifers, heather and gorse are more redolent of northern moors than stockbroker country, but Black Down near Haslemere is an exception to the manicured image of southern downland. ◇

Above The Temple of the Winds was once the site of a summer house owned by Tennyson. How it acquired its romantic name nobody seems to know, but it certainly offers the hill's most dramatic viewpoint. ◇

Below left The tiny goldcrest is Britain's smallest bird, averaging only 3½ inches when mature. It is also one of the few regularly found among conifers such as the Scots pine, now naturally regenerating on Black Down. The male's crest is more golden than that of the yellowish female. ◇

Alfred Tennyson

Above The tree-shrouded lane leading to Black Down takes its name from Alfred Tennyson. He was already Poet Laureate when he first visited the Down with his wife in 1867. They were looking for somewhere to build and were captivated by the view over the Weald. 'It wants nothing but a great river looping through the midst of it,' said Tennyson. He wrote of the 'purple distance' he saw from the hill as he taught his grandchildren the names of birds and plants. For his last 25 years he spent half the year here, writing at a summer house on the site now called the Temple of the Winds. ◇

Below Butterflies such as the small tortoiseshell are more common around the wetter hollows of the Down while the orange-tip is found around the birch trees from March. ◇

Goldcrest

Small Tortoiseshell Butterfly

Orange-tip Butterfly

Bell Heather

Left Bell heather is a darker shade than ling and flowers a month earlier. It is also found on heathland, but is slightly taller than ling and takes its name from its bell-shaped flowers. ◇

Discovering the wildlife
The wildlife of Black Down owes its character primarily to the coarse, acid sandstone. This drains rapidly to produce the moorland vegetation of heathers, gorse and bracken. Since the end of sheep-grazing, however, the natural progression from scrub to woodland has begun with birch the first colonizer. Scots pine is now predominant although oak may yet supercede it. The fairly dense pine does not offer a varied habitat so the number of bird species is small. On the open heathland, linnets nest in the gorse while meadow pipits are common in the autumn. Green and great spotted woodpeckers can be seen on the wooded slopes where other common birds include goldcrest, various tits and redpolls. Summer visitors include willow warblers, chiffchaffs and, near beeches, wood warblers. The bog pools have their own distinctive flora but the wetter hollows of the southern slopes are the best place for wild flowers and butterflies. ◇

Worth a detour
Nymans Notable Wealden garden with many rare and beautiful plants, shrubs and trees. 4½ miles S of Crawley off M23/A23. NT.
Petworth Splendid late 17th-century house with important collection of paintings, furniture. Set in 700 acre deer park. 5½ miles E of Midhurst. NT.
Witley Common Three nature trails around the common and woodland with visitor centre. 1 mile SW of Milford. NT.
Waggoners' Wells. See feature on page 96–97.

129

Ashridge

Beech

Above The beech produces
open vistas, as plants cannot
grow beneath its dense, leafy
canopy. ◇

The Chilterns are the closest countryside to north and west London. On a sunny weekend, with cars clogging the approaches to the Bridgewater Monument, motorists may feel that Ashridge looks distinctly on a well-beaten track. Yet stray no more than a quarter of a mile from the car parks and you will find 4,000 acres of Trust property, largely unexplored. the size of Ashridge estate, which enables it to swallow up visitors, is one of its attractions; another is the wide variety of landscape and therefore wildlife, that the area displays within a few miles.

The Chilterns are chalk country; indeed *chilt* is Saxon for chalk. But apart from the northernmost hills, such as Ivinghoe Beacon, Ashridge does not present the image of grassy, sheep-grazed hills most associated with chalk. Ashridge marks the northern limit of a 40-mile stretch of woodland which covers the hills. Thus, in close proximity, can be seen two of the most distinctive forms of English countryside. Wide avenues between beech and oak trees lead to panoramic views over the escarpment, and leafy glades give way to open downland.

This diversity is due mostly to the existence of a thin cover of clay-with-flints on top of the chalk plateau, whereas the chalk is uncovered on the northern hills and at the escarpment. It is also due, to a lesser extent, to the impact of man on the landscape. Chalkland left to itself would eventually revert to woodland via intermediate scrubland stages. It is constant grazing which retains the grass cover not only of the outlying hills but also the tracts of common land above Aldbury which

were cleared in the Middle Ages. However, the soil is too shallow for much agriculture — and too dry. Chalk is a porous rock and supports few streams.

Yet there are valleys. The Coombe, which is located just south of the Beacon, is a classic example of what is called a 'dry valley'. It must have been formed by a stream, perhaps when the Ice Age froze the ground to make it impermeable or when the depth of the water saturation underground was at a higher level. Whatever the origin, such valleys are an intrinsic element in Ashridge's appeal.

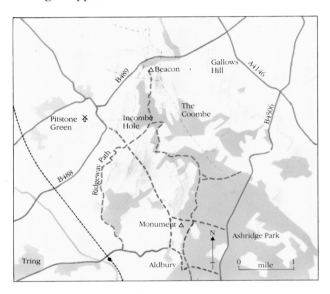

Exploring the countryside Ashridge contains one of the oldest and one of the newest forms of routeway: the 3,000-year-old Icknield Way and a nature trail. The Icknield Way is incorporated into the long-distance Ridgeway Path which begins (or ends) at Ivinghoe Beacon. Originally it extended as far as the flint mines of Grime's Graves in Norfolk and tended to follow a lower 'spring line'. The Ridgeway path runs for 85 miles before ending near Avebury. The Ashridge nature trail is much

more modest: a 1½-mile circuit starting near the monument. But the real joy of Ashridge is that you do not need to follow specific waymarked routes. Virtually the entire 4,000 acres is open for public access. Only the escarpment paths are steep but take care (and a map) if you go deep into the woods. However, one broad avenue, perhaps another ancient trackway, hugs the escarpment giving fine views, especially above Incombe Hole and Duncombe Farm. Also visit Ivinghoe Beacon and Steps Hill. ◇

Above and right The view shows the wooded escarpment north of the monument with farmland below and the barer chalk hills toward Ivinghoe Beacon. ◇

Right The great tit, with a repertoire of over 80 calls, announces spring from the tree-tops; the blue tit, tirelessly raising a brood of 10 to 13, barely has time to cheep. Yellow archangel and the wood pimpernel both thrive in stiff woodland soil. ◇

Great Tit

Blue Tit

Left 'Bridgewater's column', a 108-foot high monument to the Canal Duke, Francis, 3rd Duke of Bridgewater. It was he who initiated the canal boom of the 18th century, commissioning a ten-mile canal to link the collieries on his estate at Worsley to the industrial centres of Salford and Manchester. He also owned Ashridge House. The 172 steps to the top of the monument can be climbed at summer weekends. ◇

Bridgewater Monument

Left The village of Aldbury has sheltered under the Chiltern escarpment since Saxon times, although its much-photographed stocks and whipping-post near the pond and green are a restored version of Victoriana. ◇

Left Pitstone Windmill dates from 1671 and is the oldest post mill in Britain. In a post mill the entire body of the mill turns on a central post so that its sails can capture any available wind. ◇

Below Blackbirds were once simple woodlanders: now most of them live in suburbia. ◇

Blackbird

Yellow Archangel

Wood Pimpernel

Discovering the wildlife
The diversity of habitats at Ashridge ensures a rich wildlife. The northern downland attracts skylarks and meadow pipits and also linnet and dunnock who prefer the mixed habitat of scrub. The willow warbler likes the relics of common land, whereas the wren, blackbird and chaffinch thrive in denser woods. Tree sparrows, green woodpeckers and the blue and great tits are numerous. Woodland flora is richest around the oak trees. Look for the less familiar wood sorrel and wood pimpernel. Abundant butterflies include the meadow brown, small heath and dark green fritillary. On a larger scale, fallow deer can often be seen. ◇

Worth a detour
Ashridge House Early 18th-century house, now a management centre but occasionally open. Fine garden by Repton open summer weekends. 3½ miles N of Berkhamsted.
Ascott 19th-century house with outstanding art collection and furniture. 2 miles SW of Leighton Buzzard. NT.
Hughenden Manor Home of Disraeli, contains many of his possessions. 1½ miles N of High Wycombe off A4128. N.T.
Pitstone Windmill Open summer Sundays; see text above left and map. NT.

Croft

Map OS map SO46 in 1:25000 series or 137 in 1:50000 series

Sweet Chestnut

Above The sweet chestnut was brought to Britain by the Romans. It flowers in June or July, with dangling, cream male catkins first to appear. Look also for its long leaves and incised mature bark.◇

Right The present Croft Castle is a mixture of battlements and country house with an 18th-century interior housed within walls and towers dating from the era of the Marcher Lords in the 14th and 15th centuries.◇

In the northwest corner of Herefordshire lies the estate around Croft Castle. This 1,350 acres is now owned by the National Trust, but it is still occupied as it has been – for all but a break of 170 years – since Norman times, by the Croft family. This is a landscape where history lies thick on the ground, for those with eyes to read it. Just a mile to the north of the present Croft Castle, which owes nothing architecturally to its Norman foundation, is Croft Ambrey hill fort. This Iron Age hill fort, set on a commanding position on a limestone ridge, now looks out over a tranquil border landscape of wooded hills which enfold pockets of fertile farmland.

But to the northwest, the ruins of Wigmore Castle, standing in romantic detachment above the present village of Wigmore, are a reminder that this was once the province of powerful Lords Marchers. However, it is

not only the memories of great battles and struggles for border supremacy that make this landscape so redolent of the past. The scene is still one of narrow lanes connecting isolated villages and hamlets where timber-framed vernacular architecture predominates. Attempts have been made in earlier times to develop the area. Wigmore was once a borough and so, even more improbably, was Richards Castle, founded by Richard le Scrob, a neighbour of the earliest Crofts. Today only an earthwork, behind the solid church with its unusual detached tower, reminds visitors of the castle's existence.

The Croft estate itself, between Richards Castle to the northeast and the village of Croft, provides other echoes of past economies. Take either of two narrow dead-end lanes and you will emerge on the lower edge of Bircher Common. Cottages line the southern and eastern edges and a few even occupy island sites—a classic example of development through squatting and the gradual encroachment on the margin of common land.

The estate and the wider area of Mortimer Forest offer excellent walking in all seasons. The best way to sample the delights of this forgotten corner of the Welsh Marches is to begin at the Croft Castle car park which is available at all times, whether or not the castle is open. An estate plan located in the car park indicates three waymarked walls of between one and three miles but OS maps will enable the more ambitious to devise longer circuits; a map of the estate is also available from the castle during opening hours. Most walkers will probably want to go up the slope to Croft Ambrey. From behind the castle a track leads through

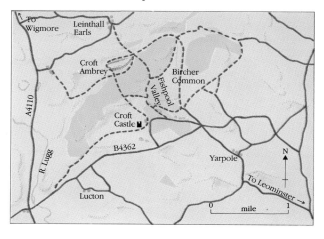

Exploring the woodlands

The woodlands of the Croft estate, owned by the National Trust since 1957, are mostly leased to the Forestry Commission to form part of its Mortimer Forest. This is named after Ralph de Mortimer of Wigmore who fought with William at the Battle of Hastings and was given the old Saxon hunting forests as a reward. Woodland management was first undertaken, albeit unwittingly, by the Iron Age occupants of Croft Ambrey. They required timber for their huts and defences, as well as needing to clear land to grow food crops. The trees then would have been oak, ash, birch and cherry with alder on wetter ground. The deciduous woodlands still support fine specimens of these native trees, but subsequent colonists and landscapers have added others. Three hundred or more years ago two avenues of sweet chestnuts were laid out west and north of Croft Castle. Avenues are a distinctive aspect of Croft; there are avenues of oak, beech and lime while on the ridge below the hill fort is a line of hornbeams. The parkland immediately around the castle shows signs of typical 18th- and early 19th-century treatment, with newly discovered species such as redwoods and deodar cedar. Today the economic demand is for softwoods with Douglas fir the most important tree of the Mortimer Forest.◇

the lesser of Croft's two great avenues of sweet or Spanish chestnuts; a path through conifers then leads to the open land around the hill fort.

Here the ramparts may be walked as they were by the sentries of old. For a direct return to the car park along a different route, drop down from the east end of the ramparts through the forestry plantation to the lovely Fishpool Valley. The ponds here were originally dammed to add variety to the menu, but no fishing is allowed today.

A longer circuit would take in Bircher Common, reached by continuing eastward along the ridge from Croft Ambrey or by following the main track down the east side of Fishpool Valley. Either path leads to the splendid tract of common land across which you may wander as freely as the commoner's livestock in this timeless border landscape.

Below The hawfinch is Britain's largest finch with a massive bill (for its size) which it uses to crack open fruit stones. It gets its name from the hawthorn berries on which it also feeds.◇

Hawfinch

Fallow Deer

Above The fallow deer is not native, but is now our commonest woodland deer, growing to three feet tall. Look for the flattened antlers on the male or buck.◇

Discovering the wildlife

The wildlife is as varied as you would expect of countryside that still preserves a range of habitats—agricultural land that retains a higher than usual proportion of hedgerows and old orchards, parkland and coniferous and deciduous woods. But a few creatures are worth a special mention. The largest forest mammal is the fallow deer. Today the guardians of the ancient hunting forests, the Forestry Commission, still manage the descendants of the fallow deer herds, but not for sport. Roe and red deer that used to roam the area are now here extinct, but the main fallow herd is maintained at something over 200 animals. It is usually in the woodland to the east of Croft, above Ludlow. Look out for the long-coated variety of fallow deer which is thought to be unique to Mortimer Forest. Among the woodland birdlife an uncommon summer visitor is the pied flycatcher which enjoys the combination of open woodland and waterside provided by the Fishpool Valley. In the winter, hornbeam trees along the avenue by the hill fort attract flocks of hawfinches which feed upon the drooping bunches of winged seeds.◇

Worth a detour
Berrington Hall Late 18th-century house with grounds landscaped by Capability Brown. 3 miles N of Leominster on W side of A49. NT.
Bradnor Hill 340 acres of common land near Welsh border. Half a mile NW of Kington. NT.
Brilley Three typical Marches farms above the valley of the River Arrow offer good walking country. (One farmhouse occasionally open.) 4 miles SW of Kington between A4111/A438. NT.

Churnet Valley

Staffordshire is not synonymous with natural beauty in the manner of Devon or even neighbouring Derbyshire. And in the heart of the Potteries it is hard to imagine that somewhere as peaceful as the Churnet Valley could be barely 12 miles away. Yet this largely undiscovered valley eludes the crowds which jam the busy roads to Dovedale or Alton a short distance away and belies the county's rather dour and industrialized image.

Churnet means 'river of many windings' and throughout its course it meanders along a tortuous route. The Churnet rises north of Leek and flows for 20 miles before joining the River Dove near Uttoxeter. The size of the valley indicates that the present-day river must be but a shadow of its former self. Certainly it was too narrow and too twisty to offer much of a waterway for traffic. This led to the construction of a canal which once followed much of its course but which now goes no further south than Froghall. Once, too, the river was followed by a railway. This has survived to go a little further than the canal, but only to Oakamoor to serve the nearby quarries.

Industry has always been part of the life of the Churnet Valley. Ironically, the most attractive stretch of the valley from around Oakamoor to Alton owes much to this unpromising forefather. The old railway has become a footpath, an old colliery part of a nature reserve. A riverside picnic area has replaced an old copper factory at Oakamoor. Mill ponds remain hidden in Dimmingsdale, a tributary valley of great beauty near Alton. The spectacular gardens of Alton Towers, with rare trees and shrubs jostling for attention amid pagodas and fountains, are similarly a triumph for man over nature. They were created in what was previously a bare valley and deservedly won fame a century before theme parks had been invented. The Churnet is not as long as the nearby Manifold and Dove, but it deserves to be just as well known.

Map OS map 119 in 1:50000 series or SK04 in 1:25000 series

Field Maple

Above The field maple is more often a hedgerow shrub, but can grow to a bushy tree. It is Britain's only native maple.◇

Swift

Above The swift is a late and brief summer visitor, screeching loudly on summer evenings. It is found in town and country. ◇

Song Thrush

Above right Gentle in disposition, the song thrush has a spotted breast and melodic song, almost always sung on a high branch. ◇

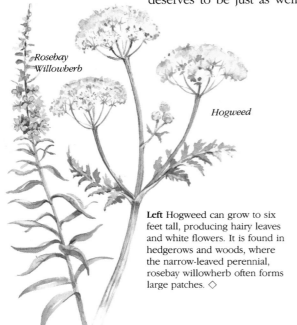

Rosebay Willowherb

Hogweed

Left Hogweed can grow to six feet tall, producing hairy leaves and white flowers. It is found in hedgerows and woods, where the narrow-leaved perennial, rosebay willowherb often forms large patches. ◇

Discovering the wildlife

The Churnet Valley is mostly an area of woodland with only the valley floor used for pasture. Both types of land use can be seen within the 300 acres of the National Trust's Hawksmoor nature reserve; the entrance is off the B5417 one mile west of Oakamoor. Four trails lead through the reserve but because it is not heavily used, some stretches are overgrown. The pathways within Gibridding Wood and beyond the railway are most difficult. However the stretch from the gates of the reserve to Eastwall Farm at its centre is sufficient to sample the range of wildlife; it makes a circuit of about 2½ miles but if you want to avoid steep climbs, stick to the main track to the farm rather than the route in the trail guide. The slopes are predominantly deciduous woodland; even where the Forestry Commission has planted trees there have been red oak, maple and beech as well as conifers such as European larch and Norway spruce. The natural woodland of the valley is sessile oak although in places this, like the glades of birch, is being engulfed by the naturally-regenerating sycamore. The woods house the customary woodland flowers but bilberry and bracken are also common. Foxes, badgers, hares, stoats and weasels live in the reserve but are rarely seen by day. Birds are more numerous with over 60 breeding species identified within Hawksmoor. Among them are the blue tit, chaffinch, wren, swift, dunnock, woodcock and various warblers and thrushes nesting in the broadleaved woodland. Fewer birds are found amid the conifers but they include the goldcrest and coal tit. The watery habitats of the farm ponds and the river tend to attract mallards and moorhens while the open pasture is the place to spot skylark, lapwing and curlew.

Hawksmoor has not always been totally rural. Eastwall Farm was the site of a medieval iron smelting furnace and coal was dug in Gibridding Wood in the 19th century. The embankment of the tramway which took coal to the canal still forms a grassy mound across the river meadows.◇

Above Alton Castle stands on a rocky precipice on the opposite side of the valley to Alton Towers. Both were built in the 19th century. One now houses a school, the other a theme park. ◇

Left The Churnet Valley is shown looking north from within the National Trust's Hawksmoor nature reserve towards Froghall. The wide valley suggests that the river was once much larger. ◇

Below The trackway of the old Churnet Valley railway has been converted into a path for easy walking (and bumpy cycling) south of Oakamoor. It is most attractive approaching Alton. ◇

Worth a detour
Cheddleton Two watermills have been preserved beside the Caldon Canal. Open some weekends. 3 miles S of Leek. Not NT.
Little Moreton Hall Half-timbered 16th-century house surrounded by moat. 4 miles SW of Congleton off A34. N.T.
Shugborough Country house from 17th–18th centuries with extensive gardens. 5½ miles SE of Stafford on A513. NT.
Ilam Hall see pages 64–67 for description of Hall and Manifold Valley.

Exploring the valley

The Churnet Valley is at its most spectacular and accessible in the 2½ miles between Oakamoor and Alton. Yet this is a stretch where man has done much to mould the landscape. A minor road hugs the steeply wooded slopes but a better bet for exploration and enjoyment is the trackway of the former Churnet Valley railway. This has been converted into a path, starting just south of Oakamoor beyond the overgrown platforms. It continues as far as Denstone but the most attractive stretch is the two miles to Alton where Augustus Pugin, the Victorian architect, designed the Italianate station to match the turrets of Alton Castle. That tourism is not a recent phenomenon at Alton is shown by the length and number of platforms built on this branch line for the excursion trains to see the gardens at Alton Towers. Much of the rail track followed an even earlier route — the now mostly abandoned Froghall to Uttoxeter Canal. Halfway between Oakamoor and Alton is Lord's Bridge from where a path leads to a side valley called Dimmingsdale. This leads off the minor road near a pink building known as the Ramblers' Retreat and can be used to construct marvellous circular walks based on either Oakamoor or Alton. The stream of Dimmingsdale was dammed in four places to create ponds for first a smelting mill and then a corn mill, now being restored. The ponds now create an atmosphere of great beauty and tranquillity deep in deciduous woodland. ◇

Hardcastle Crags

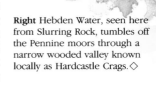

Map OS map 21 in Outdoor Leisure series

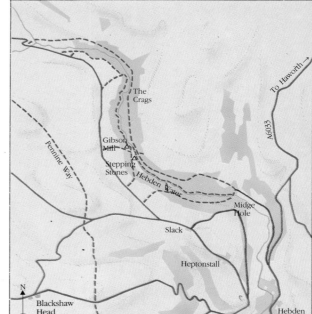

Hardcastle Crags is the name given to a stretch of Hebden Water as it tumbles toward the River Calder in the central Pennines. It is an area which, although locally well known, has so far failed to win wider renown. Perhaps this is because it does not conform to the tourist notion of Yorkshire: densely-wooded banks by the fast-flowing stream are in stark contrast not only with the industrial image of West Yorkshire but also the moorland mood suggested by the presence of a few miles to the north of the Brontë village of Haworth.

Calderdale is one of a number of valleys cut by rivers flowing eastward through the hills. This has made it an important route across the Pennines since prehistoric times; turnpikes succeeded packhorse trails, railways followed canals. The waters of the dales also came to be used by man to power mills in the nascent cotton and wool industries. The dales are more wooded and, in the wider ones, more cultivated than the uplands. Tributary valleys or *cloughs* such as Hebden Water are too narrow to support significant agriculture or population, although a 19th-century cotton mill does survive there in an idyllic rural setting.

The crags themselves — two rocky mounds halfway up the Hebden valley — are neither particularly remarkable nor unusual. The Pennines are comprised of millstone grit, thick beds of coarse rock, which frequently forms outcrops of bare rock on valley slopes. Mostly, though, the millstone grit produces a broad plateau of barren moorland. No trees grow here and although the uplands were originally centres for prehistoric settlement there is little cultivation either. Heather moors, with gorse and bracken, predominate below 1,200 feet with peaty tracts known as *mosses* to be found above that height.

There is a grandeur about these uplands that is both daunting and impressive. Yet it makes the contrast offered by the waters of Hardcastle Crags all the more attractive. The wildlife, too, is much more varied, with dozens of bird species nesting in the woods and an even larger array of plants. Paths along the valley make this a more accessible form of beauty than that of the uplands, although the inevitable corollary is less peace and solitude. The Pennines abound in contrasts — wooded valleys and bleak moors, unspoilt countryside and early industry — and nowhere more so than around Hebden Water.

Right Hebden Water, seen here from Slurring Rock, tumbles off the Pennine moors through a narrow wooded valley known locally as Hardcastle Crags. ◇

Left This ruined church tower presides over the hilltop village of Heptonstall above Hebden Dale. The lower masonry dates back to the 13th century; the upper portion and windows were added in the 15th century. Nearby is a 19th-century church. ◇

Sycamore

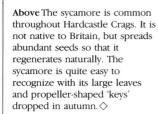

Above The sycamore is common throughout Hardcastle Crags. It is not native to Britain, but spreads abundant seeds so that it regenerates naturally. The sycamore is quite easy to recognize with its large leaves and propeller-shaped 'keys' dropped in autumn. ◇

136

Far right Heptonstall is perched on a hill above Hebden Water: an outstanding monument to a pre-industrial age. The houses reflect the days when textiles were made by hand. ◇

Right Some weavers (or their families) were also farmers; others gathered together to work in cottages which were built with long upper windows to allow the maximum possible light.
But the handloom was outdated first by the development of water power and then by steam. Both inventions shifted the focus of the textile industry down the hillside to towns situated near fast-flowing streams, such as Hebden Bridge which grew as its neighbour declined. ◇

137

Hardcastle Crags

Most visitors to Hardcastle Crags explore the southern end of the valley where car parks at Midge Hole, 1¾ miles north of Hebden Bridge, give easy access to the valley. Some come simply to picnic or sunbathe, but many follow a delightful two-mile nature trail along the banks and through the woods. Slurring Rock trail, as it is known, is a circular route along the northern bank of Hebden Water through mostly oak and ash woodland, much of which is owned by the National Trust. The route includes one steep climb and strong footwear is advised, as conditions can become muddy after wet weather. Eighteen marker posts along the way indicate places or species of particular interest which are also described in a helpful trail leaflet published by the Calderdale Council.

Although the trail as such is confined to the north bank, stepping stones lead across to a flat meadow called 'The Holme' and there are good paths on each side of the water to Gibson Mill. The trail itself leaves the riverside at the stepping stones and climbs toward the road above the valley's eastern side. Slurring Rock, at 800 feet, is at the highest point of the walk and from here the trail returns by way of an old packhorse track.

This packhorse route is among a number of paths which can be used to devise different or longer circuits not only through this more southerly and popular stretch of Hebden Water but also the less-visited upper reaches. Another access point is a Trust car park near Greenwood Lee above Heptonstall. Paths from here lead down the western bank towards 19th-century Gibson Mill.

Below The coal tit flickers about the trees in a constant blur searching for food. **Below right** The green woodpecker, a less dedicated 'drummer' than its fellows, is partial to ants. ◇

Coal Tit

Below The stepping stones that cross Hebden Water are also known locally as *hippins*. They lead to a low meadow called 'The Holme' — a Norse word meaning island or low-lying land close to water. It is now owned by a Yorkshire Scout association. ◇

Discovering the wildlife

The woodland of Hardcastle Crags is mostly deciduous, although a coniferous plantation includes Scots pine and European larch. In the woods of the valleys, the oak and ash predominate with good stands of pine, sycamore and beech. Willow and alder favour the damper valley floor while birch is plentiful on higher slopes where soil is thinner. Bilberry colonizes paths on upper slopes. The green woodpecker can be heard in the woods along with the willow warbler in spring and blackbirds, thrushes and magpies. Grey wagtails and dippers naturally like the wetter places as do plants such as wood sorrel, nipplewort and pink claytonia which flower in early summer. Another damp-loving plant is the Himalayan balsam which can be found here. Red and grey squirrels both live in the woods. ◇

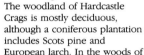
Indian Balsam

Left Indian balsam, or policeman's helmet, is a sturdy plant growing up to six feet tall. It patrols the riverside, often in force. ◇

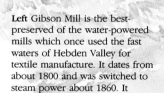

Left Gibson Mill is the best-preserved of the water-powered mills which once used the fast waters of Hebden Valley for textile manufacture. It dates from about 1800 and was switched to steam power about 1860. It closed 40 or so years later. ◇

Lady Fern

Green Woodpecker

Above Betwixt and between: the lush woodland of Hardcastle Crags is in stark contrast to bleak Pennine moorland and the industrial Calder Valley. ◇

Wood Sorrel

Left Lady fern, with its daintily divided leaves, is widespread on acid soils and in damp areas. Like most ferns, it carries its spores on the underside of its fronds. ◇

Above Wood sorrel is common throughout woodlands and on hedge banks, displaying its delicate, pale veined flowers, which grow singly, against a backdrop of trefoil leaves. ◇

Above Haworth lies eight miles north of Hebden Bridge. Not even the crowds and souvenir shops can totally dispel the atmosphere which must have existed when the Brontës lived in the parsonage there. Still more redolent are the moors themselves. The sisters' favourite walk was reputedly two miles to a small waterfall now known as Brontë Falls; the path is signposted from West Lane at the top of the village. ◇

Worth a detour

East Riddlesden Hall Late 17th-century manor with medieval tithe barn and small formal garden. 1 mile NE of Keighley off A650. NT.

Shibden Hall West Yorkshire Folk Museum features hill farming and cottage industry. ¼ mile SE of Halifax on A58. Not NT.

Blackstone Edge Finest section of exposed Roman road surviving in Britain. 1 mile E of Littleborough on A58, then by signposted path.

Nostell Priory Palladian house with gardens and lake. Fine furniture 6 miles SE of Wakefield off A638. NT.

Arnside

Map OS map SD 37/47
in 1:25000 series

Whitebeam

Above The grey undersides of the leaves of the whitebeam give it a silvery appearance, reinforced by clusters of white flowers in May and June. ◇

Tawny Owl

Fox

South of the Lake District, separated from the national park by Morecambe Bay, lies the perfect antidote to the crowds of a Lakeland summer. Arnside and Silverdale lack the wildness and scale of the geological upheavals to the north but they contain more than enough gems of their own to repay the discerning explorer. Within 30 square miles tucked between Morecambe Bay and the A6 are a rocky coastline, limestone pavements, saltmarshes, country lanes, wooded hillsides and a well-signposted network of footpaths and bridleways.

The scenery is dominated by the Kent Estuary as it opens into the shifting sands of Morecambe Bay. A viaduct cuts across the estuary, carrying the railway to Cartmel roughly parallel to a highway across the sands once used by stage coaches. This low tide route is dangerous not only because of the tides but also the constantly changing course of the Kent. In recent years this has shifted towards Arnside with destructive effects on the saltmarshes. The narrowness of the Kent channel also creates a fast-running 'bore' or tidal wave just before high tide: a siren warns of its approach and you are advised to heed the warning.

Arnside was once a small port with its own boat-building yard. The shifting channel and the coming of the railway changed all that and today it is chiefly a retirement town, existing on what tourism may come its way. Behind the solid grey houses stands imposing Arnside Knott. The summit of this wooded, limestone hill — 522 feet above sea level — affords splendid

views across the bay to the distant Lakeland fells.

To the south of Arnside lies the other half of the officially designated Area of Outstanding Natural Beauty: Silverdale. The small village is overlooked by Eaves Wood, a coppice woodland again with fine views and again largely owned by the National Trust. The contrasts of estuary and woodland, seashore and bare limestone, make Arnside and Silverdale especially rich in a wide range of wildlife, so that their combined attractions more than bear comparison with their illustrious neighbour across the bay.

Left Tawny or brown owl, the commonest and most familiar European owl, distinguished by its lack of ear tufts. Plumage is greyish, more rarely brown.

Right Arnside tower is a fortified house known in the north as a pele tower; now a ruin, it was built in the 14th century but partly rebuilt 250 years later. ◇

Left The fox finds natural cover on the wooded slopes of Eaves Wood and Arnside Knott, but is rarely seen during daytime. ◇

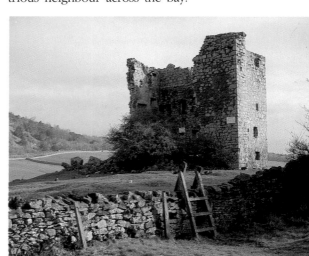

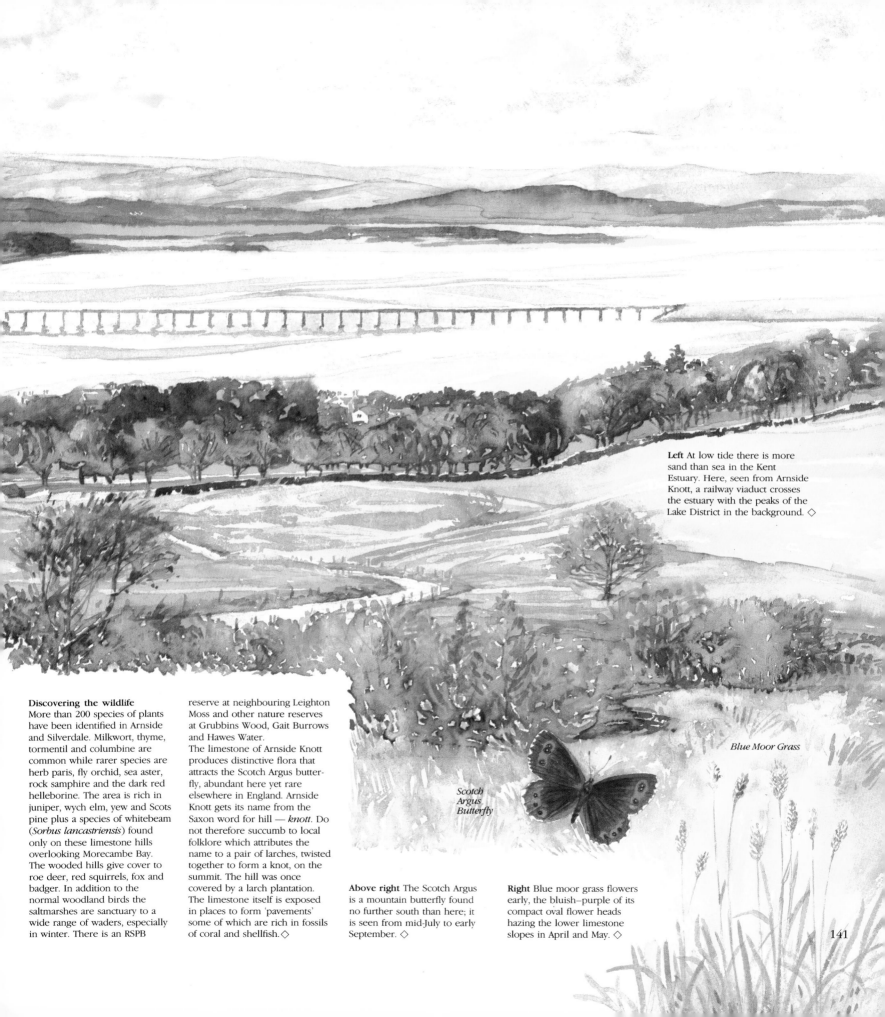

Left At low tide there is more sand than sea in the Kent Estuary. Here, seen from Arnside Knott, a railway viaduct crosses the estuary with the peaks of the Lake District in the background. ◇

Blue Moor Grass

Scotch Argus Butterfly

Discovering the wildlife

More than 200 species of plants have been identified in Arnside and Silverdale. Milkwort, thyme, tormentil and columbine are common while rarer species are herb paris, fly orchid, sea aster, rock samphire and the dark red helleborine. The area is rich in juniper, wych elm, yew and Scots pine plus a species of whitebeam (*Sorbus lancastriensis*) found only on these limestone hills overlooking Morecambe Bay. The wooded hills give cover to roe deer, red squirrels, fox and badger. In addition to the normal woodland birds the saltmarshes are sanctuary to a wide range of waders, especially in winter. There is an RSPB reserve at neighbouring Leighton Moss and other nature reserves at Grubbins Wood, Gait Burrows and Hawes Water.

The limestone of Arnside Knott produces distinctive flora that attracts the Scotch Argus butterfly, abundant here yet rare elsewhere in England. Arnside Knott gets its name from the Saxon word for hill — *knott*. Do not therefore succumb to local folklore which attributes the name to a pair of larches, twisted together to form a knot, on the summit. The hill was once covered by a larch plantation. The limestone itself is exposed in places to form 'pavements' some of which are rich in fossils of coral and shellfish. ◇

Above right The Scotch Argus is a mountain butterfly found no further south than here; it is seen from mid-July to early September. ◇

Right Blue moor grass flowers early, the bluish–purple of its compact oval flower heads hazing the lower limestone slopes in April and May. ◇

Arnside

Arnside and Silverdale are ripe for exploration. There are innumerable footpaths, mostly well signposted and some incorporated into waymarked nature trails for which the National Trust has produced excellent leaflets (available locally).

Coastal Walk At low tide it is possible to make a five-mile circuit from Arnside south along the shore to Arnside Point and Park Point before heading back via the Knott from Far Arnside. Some of the woods immediately southwest of Arnside are privately owned which is why the walk is only possible at low tide. The shingle sections can be something of a scramble but south of New Barns Farm there is a path along the edge of 40-foot cliffs giving extensive views over the estuary. The route in fact switches from cliff to foreshore until Far Arnside where a sign points the way back to "Arnside via Knott". On top of the hill is a toposcope identifying the Lakeland peaks visible across the bay or, looking west, towards Ingleborough.

Hilltop walk A six-mile walk combines Arnside Knott, Arnside Tower and the Pepperpot on Castlebarrow Hill above Silverdale. There are so many paths between the village of Arnside and the Knott that you can choose whether to approach the hill from its western or eastern slopes. Either way the summit itself is reached only by detouring from the tracks which follow the lower (and gentler) contours. Overlooking the valley between the Knott and Castlebarrow Hill is Arnside Tower, a pele tower or fortified house dating from the 14th century: an impressive ruin but now too dangerous to explore closely, as well as being on private ground. Also take care when exploring south of the Tower in Eaves Wood and adjoining Castlebarrow Hill. Here sections of the limestone are exposed as pavement containing deep fissures, known locally as *grikes*, which can be dangerous — particularly in wooded areas where moss and plants mask the cracks. The Pepperpot itself is a monument on the highest point of Castlebarrow Hill with excellent views across Morecambe Bay. Walkers with energy still to spare could then head eastward into Eaves Wood; otherwise retrace your steps to the Tower and then back to Arnside skirting the opposite side of the Knott.

Nature walks The National Trust has devised trails within Eaves Wood and round Arnside Knott. The walk around Eaves Wood includes the Pepperpot viewpoint described above. It starts from a car park east of Silverdale and is two miles in length, although a short cut is also signposted. There are three walks waymarked round Arnside Knott, all beginning from the car park on the minor road known as Saul's Drive which runs west of the hill.

Wych Elm

Above Wych elm has a broader crown than other elms and its bark, at least in older trees, is rougher. It appears to be more widespread these days because it was more resistant to the Dutch Elm disease epidemic which swept the country in the 1970s. ◇

Left Eaves Wood is a hilly area of ancient coppice woodland south of Arnside Knott. The name Eaves is derived from medieval meanings of *efes* for the edge of a wood or wood on a hillside. ◇

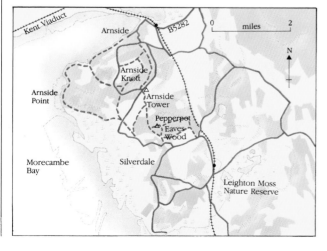

Exploring the countryside

At low tide nearly 50 square miles of sand or mud are exposed in Morecambe Bay. The shifting sands and high tide 'bore' makes the bay a dangerous place to explore. Yet once there was a daily coach service across the sands between Hest Bank, just north of Morecambe, and Kent's Bank, just south of Grange-over-Sands. Professional guides still take parties along this route to Furness but it should not be attempted without knowledge of the sandbanks, tides and currents. A siren sounds 15 and 30 minutes before the bore is due as the tide races in. ◇

Common Wild Thyme

Milkwort

Above Wild thyme produces tight clusters of purple-tinged pink flowers, between June and September. You will find it on dry grassland and heaths. ◇

Above Common milkwort is identified by the shape of its leaves and flowers since its colour can vary from blue, pink, purple, white or a mixture. ◇

Left Eaves Wood, north of Silverdale village, is an ancient woodland with oak predominant but also yews which are characteristic of shallow soils in limestone areas. ◇

Above Mammals are more elusive than birds and shy of humans. Often they only emerge at dusk so tracks are the most likely clues to their presence. ◇

Chiffchaff

The Pepperpot

Above The chiffchaff is an active and sturdy warbler, often the first to arrive back at the breeding grounds. It lives in woods, preferring higher trees. ◇

Above The Pepperpot crowns the summit of Eaves Wood. This rather odd stone obelisk was erected to commemorate the Diamond Jubilee of Queen Victoria in 1897. ◇

Worth a detour

Cartmel Attractive town with 12th-century cathedral-like priory church .and NT-owned 14th-century gatehouse.

Fell Foot Park Country park with access to the southern shore of Windermere. Near Newby Bridge. NT.

Leighton Moss A bird reserve where dense reed-beds shelter bitterns in their more northerly nesting habitat. Many other species include rare ospreys and marsh harriers. Also one of the few places you may see an otter in England. Between the villages of Silverdale and Yealand Redmayne. RSPB.

Sizergh Castle A 14th-century pele tower is the oldest part of the castle but there is also a Tudor wing with perhaps the best Elizabethan woodcarving in England. Large rock garden 3½ miles S of Kendal off A6/A591. NT.

North York Moors

Map OS maps 26 and 27 in Outdoor Leisure series

In late summer, the plateau of the North York Moors is covered by a sea of purple so extensive that it is easy to believe that here is the largest tract of heather in the country. However, no other national park has quite so much diversity in such a compact area. The moorland is incised by lush dales, some farmed but many now planted with conifers which, although threatening the heather, offer new outlets for recreation. The plateau itself does not seem particularly high, but this is deceptive: not so much at, say, bleak Urra Moor, 1,490 feet above sea level, as at the western and northern fringes where the hills rear from the plains in a sharp escarpment. This escarpment eventually reaches the coast south of Whitby to form rugged cliffs indented by tiny

coves where picturesque harbours like Robin Hood's Bay cling precariously to the shore.

The National Trust owns comparatively little of the North York Moors. Yet in terms of quality the Trust's land-ownings are strong, notably the weird sculptures of Bridestones Moor above Dalby Forest and the spectacular coastline at Ravenscar. This brief introduction to the 533 square miles of the national park will focus on these two areas plus the many walks now possible through the extensive Forestry Commission plantations. These range from short strolls to long treks of more than 10 miles, but the waymarking is generally good and leaflets are often available.

Forestry and agriculture are the main forms of occupation and both have been regarded warily by naturalists as a 'threat' to the heather-clad moors. Yet there has always been some woodland on and around these uplands. Even after cultivation had removed some trees from the dales and lower slopes, enough remained to form extensive hunting forests in Norman times. On the plateau itself, it was the deterioration of already poor soil which gradually saw heather replace the natural wood cover. In the dales and along the foothills there is some mixed woodland but mostly the infertile soils of higher ground can only support conifers. The Scots pine is among the many species now planted.

The combination of forest, moorland, farmland and coast produces a considerable range of wildlife. Add to this a legacy of outstanding monastic ruins, castles and stream-bisected villages and you have an area that, for all its diversity, has a character all its own.

Sitka Spruce

Above Sitka spruce grows well on poor moorland soil but is sensitive to late spring frosts. It is easily distinguished from the more common Norway spruce by its greyer bark and blue-green needles that are silvery underneath. The ripe cones are curiously soft and springy to the touch.◇

Red Grouse

Right The red grouse is a bird of the moors, feeding almost entirely on ling — the commonest form of heather. Unlike other members of the grouse family, it is only found in Britain and Ireland. The pheasant nests in woods but as a gamebird is also reared for the autumn shooting season.◇

Merlin

Above The merlin is Britain's smallest falcon, with the male little larger than a blackbird, yet it hunts creatures its own size in its moorland habitat.◇

Left No two Bridestones are the same: some are pedestals with broad tops perched precariously on narrow bases; others are pitted with caves; some crouch like cliffs below the heather-clad plateau. In fact, they were all parts of cliffs but erosion has removed the softer rocks to leave just isolated, and intriguing outcrops. And weathering continues to shrink the base of the outcrops which are formed of layered sandstone. In time this erosion along the weaker layers and faults of the rock will destroy the Bridestones, but happily not in our lifetime. There are two clusters of these extraordinarily-shaped outcrops: the Low Bridestones and the High Bridestones. This applies more to their locations either side of a small ravine (known locally as a *griff*) rather than any difference in height. In shape and origin they are not dissimilar to the Brimham Rocks near Ripon, but their impact is enhanced by a much greater isolation: you have to walk a mile to reach the first of the Bridestones. A three-mile trail leads to the Bridestones from the Dalby Forest drive just west of Staindale Water; leaflets are available at the forest visitor centre.◇

Above Discovering Newtondale by train has a romantic appeal for many, since it can involve riding steam trains operated by the North York Moors Railway between Pickering in the south and Grosmont in the north. The line was planned by George Stephenson, inventor of the *Rocket*, and opened in 1836. ◇

Pheasant

Exploring the countryside
There are many places in this book which can be seen only on foot. Newtondale is the first place which can be visited by railway. It is a steep-sided gorge which winds northward from Pickering to form the most dramatic valley in the entire North York Moors national park. It carves through the heart of the moors, often several hundred feet below the heather and gorse of the moorland. In the north, below Fen Bog, there are towering cliffs exposing rocks 150 million years old. Yet the gorge is believed to have been created within perhaps no more than 20 years. This occurred at the end of the last Ice Age around 10,000 years·ago. Massive ice sheets formed a huge lake in Eskdale as the snow and ice melted. Then, when even this lake was unable to contain the melting ice, the water overflowed south across the moors towards the Vale of Pickering. Within ten or 20 years Newtondale had been formed — 14 miles long and up to 400 feet deep. But the gorge we see today has only been created in the last 50 years. Until then the slopes were bare and used for sheep pasture; now they form part of the Forestry Commission's coniferous plantations. There are several enjoyable walks through the forest.◇

North York Moors

The plantations of the Forestry Commission have been planted with timber and not recreation in mind, yet just as many people now explore the forests as the moors. Indeed, in terms of access and safety, the forests may be more suitable for less experienced walkers. The moorland section of the Cleveland Way, for instance, is rugged going, especially in poor weather.

The Cleveland Way skirts the western and northern flanks of the moors before following the coast towards Scarborough — a distance of 93 miles which fully conveys the range of scenery offered by the national park. Not all rambling need be so daunting, however. In all there are more than a thousand miles of public paths and many have been used to create waymarked trails. These are some areas where trails can be found.

Dalby Forest A private road through this forest north of Thornton Dale forms a forest drive for which a toll is charged. Several trails lead off the drive, including the one to the Bridestones described earlier. Other walks range from one to seven miles, although you can always simply picnic alongside the placid Staindale Lake.

Falling Foss There is a small area of forest in the north of the national park south of Whitby and here there are two contrasting trails. One leads to the Falling Foss waterfall while another, called the May Beck trail, shows different forms of land use such as agriculture, forestry and game conservation.

Newtondale A special halt has been built north of Levisham to give access to the woods of Cropton Forest and Newtondale itself. Three trails lead from the halt ranging from a gentle 2⅓ miles to a seven-mile trek which includes a dramatic view across the gorge from Needle Point. Check train times in advance.

Sutton Bank Unlike the areas described above, this is an area of open hill country. Many people simply park their cars at this point on the crest of the Hambleton Hills and admire a panoramic view. However, it can also be the starting point for two walks: the Garbutt Wood nature trail heads north of the A170, while the Kilburn White Horse walk begins half a mile to the south of the hill.

Leaflets for all these walks are available from the various information centres operated by the national park or Forestry Commission, although some of these may be closed in winter. The geological trail along the Trust-owned coast at Ravenscar is described separately.

Water Mint

Above left Water mint grows alongside streams, such as Dovedale Griff below the Bridestones, and can sometimes be found in the water itself.◇

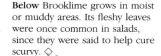

Below Brooklime grows in moist or muddy areas. Its fleshy leaves were once common in salads, since they were said to help cure scurvy. ◇

Brooklime

Right Wheeldale Moor southwest of Goathland boasts one of the best stretches of Roman road still visible anywhere in Britain: not just the familiar raised mound cutting straight across country but culverts, kerbstones and foundations 16 feet wide survive here. It follows up to 16 miles of remote moorland near the hamlet of Hunt House, and originally was part of the Roman road from Malton to Whitby, which is sometimes called Wade's Causeway. ◇

Exploring Ravenscar

Nature trails have become quite common in the last ten years or so, but Ravenscar has the first and possibly still the only geological trail in the country. Much of the shoreline here is owned by the National Trust and there are panoramic views north towards Robin Hood's Bay. But the particular appeal of the trail is that a major geological fault occurs here and has exposed different kinds and ages of rocks. These are clearly visible, not only as nature left them alongside a narrow gorge leading to the coast, but also where man created quarries. The trail is divided into two sections. The easier, high-level section covers 2½ miles to and from the quarries; a further two miles leads down to the rock-strewn foreshore and involves a very steep climb back. The Trust has a small centre explaining the geology and an excellent leaflet describes the trails in detail.◇

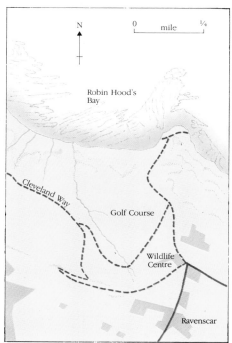

Left Tucked in a fold of the hills northwest of Helmsley is Rievaulx Abbey, the finest ecclesiastical ruin in Britain. The nave and transepts which survive from the 12th century represent the earliest large church built by the Cistercians in England; the choir, added in the next century, is even more sublime. Rievaulx has an austere beauty that fully complements its setting. ◇

Worth a detour

Gilling Castle Behind an 18th-century frontage is what is widely regarded as the finest Elizabethan chamber in England. Now a school, so opening is limited. 4 miles SW of Helmsley. Not NT.

Mount Grace Priory The most important Carthusian remains in England dating from the 14th century. 6 miles NE of Northallerton off A19. NT.

Nunnington Hall Large manor house dating from 16th century, but mostly 17th century, on banks of the River Rye. 4½ miles SE of Helmsley. NT.

Rievaulx Terrace Grassy terrace overlooking the abbey with a classical temple at each end. 2½ m NW of Helmsley. NT.

Allen Banks

The town of Allendale claims to be the geographical centre of Britain. Although this claim is echoed in nearby Hexham, what cannot be disputed is that this southernmost corner of Northumberland is also the northern outpost of the Pennines. To the north, beyond the South Tyne valley and Hadrian's Wall, green uplands rise in waves towards the Scottish border. The area largely featured here lies north of the town of Allendale where the two parallel valleys of East and West Allendale meet to form the wooded gorge of Allen Banks which harbours many miles of exhilarating walks among its steep banks and crags. The best access point is the National Trust car park and picnic area at Ridley Hall on a minor road off the A69 three miles west of Haydon Bridge.

The Allen finally joins the South Tyne east of Bardon Mill. Although its twin upper valleys give no clue of the headlong rush through the 250-foot high gorge to come, they are by no means without appeal. The two Allendales are similar, never more than four miles apart with moors between and on either side rising to 1,800 feet. Stone farmhouses appear austere in their isolation but the landscape is softened by 'shelter belts' of trees and hedgerows in the lower valleys. On the higher slopes, though, there are the more familiar stone walls of Pennine country. Many of these were built in the 18th and 19th centuries when men combined farming with work in the then flourishing lead mines. Ruined workings identify old centres of industry in what now seems a totally rural setting. One legacy of those days is a network of miners' and packhorse trails which can still be followed across the moors and through the valleys of this bypassed corner of the Pennines.

Map OS map 87 in 1:50000 series

Juniper

Above Juniper is a versatile evergreen of the cypress family that can grow as a small tree or a shrub. Its berries are used to flavour gin and liqueurs and various meat dishes, especially venison.◇

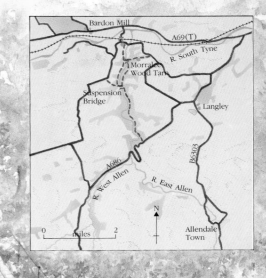

Exploring the countryside

Paths follow both banks of the Allen for much of its course in the gorge. Notices at the NT car park at adjoining Ridley Hall show the paths clearly, but there is no waymarking or signposting along the way. It is fairly easy, however, to devise circular routes that combine river, woodland and views over open country. Heading south from the car park on the western bank there is a choice of paths: a lower route along the river bank and a higher path which climbs into beech woodland offering superb views over the valley and parkland of Ridley Hall. The upper path passes Briarswood Banks nature reserve before

joining the lower route just north of the suspension bridge near Plankey Mill Farm. This offers a convenient point to turn back on the eastern bank. At first, though, you have to head up a road but soon a field path leads back to the river near bushes of broom and, in summer, a mass of wild flowers. Where the river winds into the gorge, opposite Raven Crag, the path climbs into deciduous woods where ferns and mosses thrive. Rhododendrons add colour here in early summer. Eventually the path descends to river level where a second suspension bridge leads to the west bank

and back to the car park. This circuit is about three miles but walkers can devise several alternatives. One leads up the steep eastern bank from the northerly suspension bridge to Moralee Wood tarn. Some gradients are steep and there are stone steps which can be slippery, as well as muddy ground in wet weather. Strong footwear is therefore advised. ◇

Below Rhododendron, an evergreen shrub, grows in acid soil. The goosander, largest of the mergansers, nests in tree hollows.◇

Rhododendron

Goosander

Left A suspension bridge slung across Allendale near Plankey Mill Farm links paths through the thickly wooded gorge south of the Allen's confluence with the Tyne.◇

Below Moralee Wood Tarn is man-made but that does not dim its beauty. It is set amid young larch, Scots pine and banks of rhododendrons. In summer it is white with waterlilies. Among the birds attracted to the tarn are mallard and the occasional heron. Access is by footpaths from the northern suspension bridge at Allen Banks or from the Langley road to the east.◇

Left Hadrian's Wall lies barely two-miles north of Allen Banks — and the stretch here is among the best-preserved of its entire 73-mile length. The NT owns 3½ miles of the wall including the fort and museum at Housesteads and several mile-castles. The wall is by far the most dramatic monument to Roman Britain, especially as it exploited a ridge of volcanic rock known as the Whin Sill to make the defences even more formidable. Even today it is a daunting, if beautiful, place.◇

Below The leaves and flowers of wild pansies are variable; they bloom all through summer.
Below right The wood mouse is the unenviable star of the small carnivore's food chain.◇

Wild Pansies

Discovering the wildlife
The purple mountain pansy prospers in the river meadows of Allen Banks during June. In spring the white starlike flowers of wild garlic abound — a sure sign of long-established woodland. Although beech are dominant, many other species can be seen including the comparatively rare juniper. Other trees include the oak, birch, ash, hawthorn and elder. Look out, too, for the red squirrel.◇

Industrial Allen Banks
The limekiln at Stag Hill is a reminder that the apparently unspoilt moorland above Allendale was once the centre of industry. Lead mining in the Pennines goes back to Roman times, but it was the activity of the 18th and 19th centuries which left its mark on this landscape. In addition to relics such as old chimneys, quarries and kilns, chapels and schools have industrial origins.◇

Wood Mouse

Worth a detour
Hadrian's Wall Large NT holdings near Housesteads — see above.
Wylam Cottage of George Stephenson, local hero and inventor of railways. Access via riverside path ½ mile E of Wylam, off A69. NT.
Hexham A Saxon crypt survives in the mostly 13th-century priory church. Other buildings of note include 14th-century prison. Not NT.

There are 120,000 miles of public right of way in Great Britain, more than in any country of comparable size. Most are footpaths but there are also bridleways which are legally available for horses as well as walkers. Every now and then, disputes arise about paths which have been obstructed or overgrown. The Ramblers' Association plays an active role in not only maintaining access but also developing new routes. The Scottish Rights of Way Society plays a similar role north of the border.

In addition to this vast network of rights of way there are also 'permitted' routes where landowners allow access although they have no legal obligation to do so; examples of these in this book can be found along the Stratford-upon-Avon canal and in the Vale of Edale. Such permitted paths may be more overgrown than footpaths or bridlepaths which are rights of way. There are also vast tracts of common land which allow unrestricted access and many nature and forest trails which offer shorter routes.

The many walks suggested in this book range from simple waymarked circuits to sections of long-distance footpaths. For the shorter lowland walks, whether through woodland or open countryside, training shoes and T-shirts will be fine in the summer. But for more rugged country, stronger footwear is essential and waterproof clothing should be carried, if not worn. The weather can be hazardous in the uplands at any time of the year; the temperature drops one degree Fahrenheit for every 300 feet climbed, a stiff breeze in the valley becomes an icy gale on the summit, rain becomes heavier.

More detailed advice is given below but the basic rule is never to allow enthusiasm to overtake ability or experience. Allow an hour for every 2½ miles plus an extra half-hour for every 700 feet climbed. If this seems slow, just wait until you tackle clumps of heather, long grass, loose stones and scree slopes for the first time. Properly clothed and equipped you can walk in most parts of Britain for most of the year, but the cautionary words about the weather are even more applicable during the winter. Walking offers an intimacy with the countryside that is denied to motorists, but it also involves responsibilities. The country code should become as integral a part of a rambler's kit as a backpack and boots.

The country code
◇ Guard against all risks of fires
◇ Fasten all gates
◇ Keep dogs under proper control
◇ Keep to paths across farmland
◇ Avoid damaging fences, hedges and walls
◇ Leave no litter
◇ Safeguard water supplies
◇ Protect wildlife, wild plants and trees*
◇ Go carefully on country roads
◇ Respect the life of the countryside

* Wild life is best seen, not collected. To pick flowers will spoil other people's enjoyment and reduce the chances of natural repollination. It is also an offence under the 1981 Wildlife and Countryside Act to uproot any wild flower. As one National Trust warden put it: 'Take only photographs, leave only footprints'.

What to wear
The majority of the walks suggested in this book can be tackled without special equipment. However nearly all of them would be made more comfortable by good footwear, essential for more rugged walks.

Boots should be waterproof with thick rubber soles to absorb the shock of stone-strewn paths. The best boots come with one-piece leather uppers, an outside tongue and interior padding. Comfort is the key so always break in new boots gradually. Make sure that there is room for two pairs of socks—a thin pair next to the skin and a thick pair over them.

After the boots, the jacket is the next most important item. Anyone planning to walk frequently will find it worthwhile to buy an anorak; most have hoods for bad weather and large pockets for maps. For really wet weather a 'cagoule' is ideal. This is a knee-length anorak, usually made of nylon and completely waterproof. The one drawback with cagoules is that condensation builds up within them, so choose models with long zips. Waterproof over-trousers are also sensible if you plan to walk any distance during unsettled weather. Even in summer long grass can be moist from dew or a heavy shower.

Otherwise it is usually possible to use your normal clothing, although jeans are not recommended for anything more than a low-level summer stroll; they are too thin to provide much warmth. The variable nature of the British climate means that ramblers should be prepared for the worst. Waterproof gear and spare sweaters are best carried in a rucksack. 'Day sacks' are available for carrying food, drink and spare clothing. A first-aid kit is a prudent addition to any backpack, not only when walking on difficult terrain but also when walking with children.

How to read the countryside
Maps provide the clues to discovering the countryside. Whatever your interests, understanding maps can enhance enjoyment. And there are maps for all occasions, whether it is plotting a long-distance route or planning an afternoon stroll. There are also specialist maps which recreate the past such as Roman Britain or Victorian London. You therefore need to choose maps to suit your needs even before you learn to decode their symbols and language.

The maps in this book will show the location of places and paths mentioned in the text. However they are not detailed enough to be used when exploring the countryside.

Which map to choose
There are several excellent map-makers in Britain but by far the most comprehensive maps are those provided by the Ordnance Survey of Great Britain—Northern Ireland has its own Ordnance Survey. In fact, the comprehensiveness of OS maps presents the first problem. How do you choose from the many series produced by the Ordnance Survey?

The difference between them is, literally, a question of *scale*. Most maps are now produced in metric scales. Take the most widely-used OS map which is drawn on the 1:50000 scale. This means that one centimetre on the map is equal to 50,000 centimetres (or half a kilometre) on the ground. A map in the 1:25000 series has one centimetre on the map representing 25,000 centimetres (or a quarter of a kilometre) on the ground; this means that it shows an area in great detail but also therefore usually covers a smaller area. Thus the larger the scale, the smaller the area covered. In order of scale, from smallest to largest, these are the OS maps available:

1. **1:625000 scale.** A frequently updated route-planning map covering the whole of Britain.
2. **1:250000 scale.** The Routemaster series which divides Britain into nine regions; useful for motorists, it also shows mountain and woodland areas.

3. **1:63360 scale.** The old one inch to the mile scale which has generally been superseded by the metric 1:50000 scale (see below) but which has been temporarily retained for some 'Tourist maps' of areas such as Exmoor, Dartmoor, the New Forest, Peak District, Lake District, North York Moors, Loch Lomond and the Trossachs, Ben Nevis and Glen Coe.
4. **1:50000 scale.** Known as the Landranger series this has become the standard OS map; it is also the one most frequently cited in this book. Great Britain is covered in 204 sheets showing footpaths and contours as well as roads. It offers admirable clarity for general touring plus considerable detail about land features, both natural and man-made. However the 1:25000 series is better for walkers.
5. **1:25000 scale.** Maps in this series are ideal for walkers because they show paths in sufficient detail to enable the correct route to be taken when paths join or diverge. Originally there were something like 1,000 sheets covering Britain but these are gradually being replaced by the double-sized Pathfinder or second series. This scale is also used for the Outdoor Leisure series which provides extra information (such as viewpoints, picnic areas, forest trails and ancient monuments) for some areas of the country.
6. **Specialist scales.** OS maps are also produced in 1:10000, 1:2500 and 1:1250 scales but these are mostly used by local authorities and planners since they show such fine detail as individual houses.

Maps in Ireland
Northern Ireland (and the Republic) have their own Ordnance Survey organisations. The 1:50000 scale is increasingly the best bet for general use, although one inch maps remain widely available.

How to read a map
Once you understand the scale of a map it will not take you too long to be able to judge real distances from what is drawn on the map. But a map can reveal much more than distances: it can suggest alternative routes which may be prettier or pass interesting viewpoints or avoid steep climbs.

The key explains the symbols used on OS maps. All standard OS maps have a clearly laid out key which identifies the features included on each map, but those features will vary according to scale.

The contour lines link places of equal height above the sea. If the lines are close together, this indicates steep slopes; if there are no contours, the land is flat. Understanding contours will enable you to translate the lines on a map into a mental picture of the countryside—where, for instance, there are valleys, cliffs or plateaus. Contour lines and heights on OS maps are now given in metres. As maps are brought up to date the gaps or vertical interval between contour lines on 1:50000 maps are being shown at ten metre intervals. However, on some older maps in this series the gap remains at 50 feet. The vertical intervals in the 1:25000 series also vary so check the map key to discover the system being used.

Grid references are a means of identifying precise locations anywhere in Britain. They are based on what is known as the national grid whereby the country is divided by a series of vertical and horizontal lines printed on all OS maps. On the border of OS maps, in the key, is a brief explanation of how to establish grid references, although the larger the scale, the more difficult it is to establish references accurately. First, look for the two grid letters which cover the part of the map for which you want the grid reference. This can be found on the key.

Secondly, take the west edge of the kilometre square in which the chosen point is located. At the top or bottom of the map you will see some large figures next to this line. Estimate the position east of this line in tenths before the next vertical line.

Thirdly, take the south edge of the same kilometre square and read the large figures on the left or right (otherwise west and east) margins. Then estimate the position north of this line, again in tenths.

You have thus established a six-figure reference number which, if preceded by the reference letters, applies to no other point in Britain. Grid references are particularly useful for walkers or people wishing to track down historic sites.

Using a compass
Most people do not need a compass to enjoy the countryside. It is only really necessary for hill walking where landmarks are fewer and the weather more likely to be hostile. For such walking the Silva compass is ideal since it has a protractor base which helps in charting routes from maps.

Safety in the hills
Most accidents occur because people have ventured beyond the limits of their own experience and equipment. This is most common in the hills or mountains where the existence of rescue units is testimony to the hazards which can be encountered. Some simple rules can minimize the risks.

The risks are always greater in winter or during bad weather. In fact, extremes of temperature—heat as well as cold—will always cause discomfort, if not danger. Many people, of course, relish the challenges posed by mountains, but novices should build up

their stamina and experience gradually. They should also seek more specialist advice than is appropriate for a general book of this kind. If in doubt, contact: The Ramblers' Association, 1/5 Wandsworth Road, London SW8 2LJ, Tel: 01-582-6878.

Ten safety rules for hill-walkers
◇ DO check the weather forecast
◇ DO tell someone where you are going and when you expect to return
◇ DO keep to your planned route if possible but...
◇ DO let your route suffer rather than yourself and turn back if conditions worsen
◇ DO take a torch and a whistle—just in case
◇ DON'T be overambitious in routes or distances
◇ DON'T travel alone in hills or split your group
◇ DON'T risk crossing swollen streams
◇ DON'T forget your map, compass, first-aid kit and high-energy food such as chocolate or dried fruit
◇ DON'T forget to let people know when you have returned

Countryside Glossary
AONB Area of Outstanding Natural Beauty. Area which is smaller than a national park but whose beauty has earned it a measure of statutory protection.
Countryside Commission The body responsible to the government for the conservation of the countryside and the promotion of outdoor recreation facilities. It is responsible for designating national parks, AONBs, long-distance footpaths and heritage coast, but also promotes country parks and picnic sites. For further information, contact:
Countryside Commission, John Dower House, Crescent Place, Cheltenham, Gloucestershire GL50 3RA.
There are separate Countryside Commissions for

Scotland and Northern Ireland: these are based in Perth and Belfast.
Forestry Commission This was created in 1919 primarily to develop new forests for timber crops. However in recent years the Commission has become much more conscious of the recreational value of their forests and has developed forest parks, trails and picnic areas in many parts of Britain. For further information contact the Forestry Commission at: 231 Corstorphine Road, Edinburgh EH12 7AT.
Long-distance footpaths A limited number of routes have been established as waymarked, long-distance public rights of way by the Countryside Commissions. All use an acorn symbol to indicate the route—or a thistle in Scotland. There are also many unofficial long-distance routes.
National parks These are the finest and largest tracts of unspoilt countryside in Britain, although the system is different in Scotland. In England and Wales nearly one-tenth of the total land area and coastline fall within the boundaries of the ten national parks. Designation as a national park brings protection to the area, although many conservationists believe the Countryside Commission lacks the teeth to be an effective watchdog.
Nature Conservancy Council A government-appointed body which operates more than 150 national nature reserves (some in conjunction with organisations such as the National Trusts).
SSSI Site of Special Scientific Interest. Several thousand sites have been designated by the Nature Conservancy Council where the flora or fauna merit some protection even though the sites may be small. The Council must be informed of any developments which would affect an SSSI but there is controversy over whether the protection is adequate.

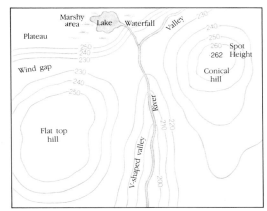

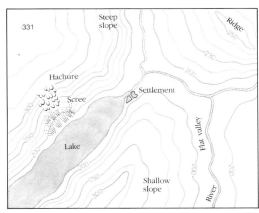

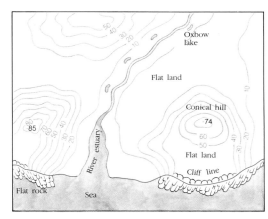

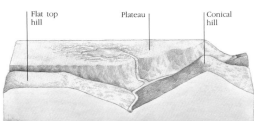

Hills and valley Evenly-spaced contours indicate uniform slopes, as in the conical hill, while a lack of contours indicates flat land as on the flat-top hill.

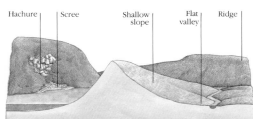

Highlands The closer the contours, the steeper the slopes. Hachures are areas too steep for contours; screes are rocky debris at the foot of steep slopes.

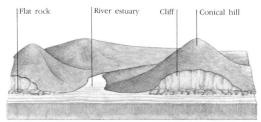

Coast Contour lines ending at the coast indicate cliffs here with flat rocks below. Where contour lines are wide apart, there are gentle slopes.

THE NATIONAL TRUST

The National Trust is one of the success stories of the 20th century. Since its modest foundation in 1895 the National Trust of England, Wales and Northern Ireland has become the largest private landowner and conservation society in Britain. Hundreds of square miles of unspoilt coastline and countryside are protected by the Trust in addition to the historic buildings and gardens with which it is popularly, if erroneously, most associated.

There are, in fact, two National Trusts since there is a separate and independent organisation in Scotland. Both Trusts have gained members as rapidly as they have acquired property. From a membership of fewer than 10,000 in 1945 the National Trust of England, Wales and Northern Ireland grew to more than a million by the 1980s; the National Trust for Scotland, founded in 1935, has a membership of around 120,000 which is broadly similar in terms of membership per head of population. Both Trusts are charities, dependent upon their members and the public for their activities; they are emphatically not government departments.

The immediate advantage of joining the Trust (beyond helping an undeniably good cause) is that it brings free entry to most Trust properties. Membership of one Trust brings reciprocal membership of the other so that members do not normally have to pay entrance fees to any Trust property. However, there are charges sometimes for specific exhibitions.

Most of the countryside and coastal properties featured in this book are by definition open space areas with free public access; in some of the more popular areas, though, charges are made for car parks during the main holiday months. Most Trust properties will be only too happy to supply information about the various categories of membership. The Trust south of the Scottish border is divided into a number of different regions which can answer questions about local attractions in more detail. Most regions also produce leaflets about properties in their areas. Look out, too, for nationally produced leaflets about nature walks and facilities designed specifically for disabled people.

The Trusts also employ a large number of wardens or rangers many of whom organize guided walks during the summer. Exploring the countryside in their expert company can open your eyes to things that otherwise you might never see, let alone appreciate. Details of guided tours can be obtained from local Trust visitor centres or regional offices. These will also provide details of opening times for the many Trust houses, gardens and historic sites. This information has been excluded from this book because the details tend to change from year to year, making it impossible to guarantee accuracy. Trust members receive a book each spring which supplies this information, but otherwise contact the Trust offices detailed on these pages or a local tourist office. Generally speaking properties such as houses tend to be open only during the summer and that—other than in Scotland—usually means from early April to late October; but, if in doubt, always check to save a wasted journey. Many houses and gardens do not open all day or even every day. In fact, it is mostly properties such as the large open tracts of the countryside featured in this book which offer year-round access.

The appropriate national or regional office for each of the 44 areas described in this book are listed below along with the telephone numbers of tourist offices and other relevant organisations. Regional and national offices tend to be closed at weekends while many smaller tourist offices shut during the winter. Every effort has been made to ensure that this information was accurate at the time of publication. **Please remember that telephone dialling codes may differ when making local calls**

NATIONAL HEADQUARTERS

The National Trust of England, Wales and Northern Ireland,
36 Queen Anne's Gate,
London SW1H 9AS
Telephone: (01) 222 9251

The National Trust for Scotland,
5 Charlotte Square,
Edinburgh EH2 4DU
Telephone: (031) 226 5922

REGIONAL OFFICES

ENGLAND

Cornwall: Lanhydrock, Bodmin, Cornwall, PL30 4DE. Telephone: Bodmin (0208) 4281.
Devon: Killerton House, Broadclyst, Exeter, EX5 3LE. Telephone: Hele (0392) 881691.
East Anglia: Blickling, Norwich, NR11 6NF. Telephone: Aylsham (026 373) 3471.
East Midlands: Clumber Park Stableyard, Worksop, Notts, S80 3BE. Telephone: Worksop (0909) 486411.
Kent & East Sussex: Scotney Castle, Lamberhurst, Kent, TN3 8JN. Telephone: Lamberhurst (0892) 890651.
Mercia: Attingham Park, Shrewsbury, Shropshire, SY4 4TP. Telephone: Upton Magna (074 377) 343 or 649.
Northumbria: Scots' Gap, Morpeth, Northumberland, NE61 4EG. Telephone: Scots' Gap (067 074) 691.
North West: Rothay Holme, Rothay Road, Ambleside, Cumbria, LA22 0EJ. Telephone: Ambleside (0966) 33883.
Severn: 34–36 Church Street, Tewkesbury, Gloucestershire, GL20 5SN. Telephone: Tewkesbury (0684) 297747, 292427 or 292919.
Southern: Polesden Lacey, Dorking, Surrey, RH5 6BD. Telephone: Bookham (0372) 53401.
Thames and Chilterns: Hughenden Manor, High Wycombe, Bucks, HP14 4LA. Telephone: High Wycombe (0494) 28051.
Wessex: Stourton, Warminster, Wiltshire, BA12 6QD. Telephone: Bourton, Dorset (0747) 840224.
Yorkshire: Goddards, 27 Tadcaster Road, Dringhouses, York, YO2 2QG. Telephone: (0904) 702021.

WALES

North Wales: Trinity Square, Llandudno, Gwynedd, LL30 2DE. Telephone: Llandudno (0492) 74421
South Wales: The King's Head, Bridge Street, Llandeilo, Dyfed, SA19 6BN. Telephone: Llandeilo (0558) 822800.

NORTHERN IRELAND

Rowallane House, Saintfield, Ballynahinch, Co. Down, BT24 7LH. Telephone: Saintfield (0238) 510721.

SCOTLAND

Glasgow: Hutchesons' Hall, 158 Ingram Street, Glasgow, G1 1EJ. Telephone: (041) 552 8391.
Grampian: Pitmedden House, Ellon, Aberdeenshire, AB4 0PD. Telephone: Udny (065 13) 2445.
Highland: Abertarff House, Church Street, Inverness, IV1 1EU. Telephone: Inverness (0463) 232034.

AREAS FEATURED IN THIS BOOK

Abbreviations
* offices that are not open throughout the year
NT National Trust
NTS National Trust for Scotland
TIC Tourist Information Centre(s)

SEASIDE

Penwith
NT region: Cornwall. TIC: Penzance (0736) 62207 or 62341. St. Ives (0736) 796297 or 797600.
Fowey
NT region: Cornwall. TIC: Fowey (072 683) 3320.
Exmoor Coast
NT region: Devon and—for Somerset—Wessex. TIC: Combe Martin* (027 188) 3319. Lynton/Lynmouth (059 85) 2225. Minehead (0643) 2624. Porlock* (0643) 862238.
Brownsea
NT region: Wessex. TIC: Poole (0202) 673322. Bournemouth (0202) 291715.
Seven Sisters
NT regions: Kent and East Sussex. TIC: Eastbourne (0323) 27474. Seaford (0323) 897426. Seven Sisters country park: Alfriston (0323) 870280.
Dale
NT region: South Wales. Pembrokeshire Coast National Park: headquarters—Haverfordwest (0437) 4591; National Park Information Centre — Broad Haven (043 783) 412.
Tywi estuary
NT region: South Wales. Pembrey country park: Burry Port (055 46) 3913. South Wales Tourism Council: Swansea (0792) 465204.
North Norfolk
NT region: East Anglia. NT wardens: Brancaster (0485) 210719. Blakeney (0263) 740480. TIC: Hunstanton (048 53) 2610. Sheringham* (0263) 824329.
Llŷn
NT region: North Wales. TIC: Pwllheli* (0758) 61 3000.
Colvend Coast
NTS Dumfries and Galloway Tourist Board: Newton Stewart (0671) 2549. TIC: Castle Douglas* (0556) 2611.
Northumberland coast
NT region: Northumbria. TIC: Berwick-upon-Tweed (0289) 307187. Alnwick* (0665) 603120 or 603129. Seahouses* (0665) 720427. Wooler* (0668) 81602.
St Abbs
NTS. St Abbs Head National Nature Reserve: Coldingham (039 03) 443. TIC: Eyemouth* (0390) 50678.
North Antrim
NT region: Northern Ireland. Northern Ireland Tourist Board: Belfast (0232) 246609. TIC: Ballycastle* (026 57) 62024. Portrush* (0265) 823333.

HILLSIDE

Black Down
NT region: Southern. No TIC is particularly near; the closest is at Petersfield (0730) 63451.
Dolaucothi
NT region: South Wales. TIC: Llandovery* (0550) 20693.
Cadair Idris
NT region: North Wales. Mid-Wales Tourism Council: Machynlleth (0654) 2654. TIC: Dolgallau* (0341) 422888.

Shropshire Hills
NT region: Mercia. TIC: Church Stretton* (0694) 722535.
Manifold Valley
NT region: East Midlands. NT information centre at Ilam Hall: Thorpe Cloud (033 529) 245. TIC: Ashbourne (0335) 43666.
Edale
NT region: East Midlands. TIC: Hope Valley (0433) 70207.
Duddon Valley
NT region: North West. TIC: Ravenglass* (065 77) 278. Coniston* (0966) 41533. National Park Information centre. Windermere (096 62) 5555. Lakeland weather forecast: Windermere (096 62) 5151.
Ben Lomond
NTS. TIC: Balloch* (0389) 53533. Balloch Castle country park: Balloch* (0389) 58216.
Ben Lawers
NTS. NTS visitor centre: Killin* (056 72) 397. TIC: Killin* (056 72) 254.
Glencoe
NTS. NTS visitor centre: Ballachulish (085 52) 307. TIC: Fort William (0397) 3781.
Torridon
NTS. TIC: Gairloch (0445) 2130. (Also NTS visitor centre in summer; no telephone).

WATERSIDE

Loe Pool
NT region: Cornwall. TIC: Helston* (032 65) 62505.
Waggoners' Wells
NT region: Southern. TIC: Farnham (048 68) 4104, ext. 554.
Henrhyd Falls
NT region: South Wales. Brecon Beacons national park information centre: Brecon (0874) 4437. TIC: Abercraf* (0639) 730284.
Upper Thames
NT region: Thames & Chilterns. TIC: Cirencester (0285) 4180.
Stratford-upon-Avon Canal
NT region: Severn. TIC: Stratford-upon-Avon (0789) 293127.
Wicken Fen
NT region: East Anglia. NT warden: Ely (0353) 720274. TIC: Ely (0353) 3311 or 2894, ext 253.
Western Lakes
NT region: North West. TIC: Whitehaven (0946) 5678. Cockermouth* (0900) 822634. Keswick (0596) 72645. National park and weather forecasts—see Duddon Valley.
Grey Mare's Tail
NTS. TIC: Moffat* (0683) 20620.
Sea Lochs of Western Scotland
NTS. NTS Countryside centre*, Morvich: Glenshiel (059 981) 219. TIC: Glenshiel (059 981) 264. Kyle of Lochalsh (0599) 4276.
Strangford Lough
NT region: Northern Ireland. Northern Ireland Tourist Board: Belfast (0232) 246609 or 231221.

WOODSIDE

Teign Valley
NT region: Devon Dartmoor national park: Bovey Tracey (0626) 832093. (There is also a Dartmoor national park information centre at Steps Bridge during the summer; no telephone).

Ebbor Gorge
NT region: Wessex. TIC: Wells* (0749) 72552. Cheddar (0934) 742769.
Ashridge
NT region: Thames & Chilterns. TIC: Berkhamsted (044 27) 4545.
Croft
NT region: Severn. TIC: Leominster (0568) 2291, ext. 212. Ludlow* (0584) 3857.
Churnet Valley
NT region: Mercia. No TIC is particularly near; the closest are at Ashbourne* (0335) 43666 and Stoke-on-Trent (0782) 281242.
Hardcastle Crags
NT region: Yorkshire. TIC: Hebden Bridge (0422) 843831. Haworth (0535) 42329.
Arnside & Silverdale
NT region: North West. NT information centre: Sizergh Castle*. Arnside TIC: Grange-over-Sands* (044 84) 4026. Silverdale TIC: Lancaster (0524) 32878.
North York Moors
NT region: Yorkshire. North York Moors national park: Helmsley (0439) 70657—weekdays only plus seasonal centres at The Moors Centre, Danby. Pickering and Sutton Bank. TIC: Helmsley (0439) 70401. Pickering (0751) 73791. Dalby Forest visitor centre*: Pickering (0751) 60295.
Allendale
NT region: Northumbria. National park visitor centre*: Bardon Mill (049 84) 396. TIC: Alston (0498) 81696. Corbridge* (043 471) 2815. Hexham (0434) 605225.
Corrieshalloch Gorge
NTS. Inverewe House (NTS): Poolewe (044 586) 229. TIC: Ullapool* (0854) 2135.

Above Signs such as this one at Ebbor Gorge indicate that you are on property protected and maintained by the National Trust.

OTHER USEFUL ORGANIZATIONS

NATIONAL TOURIST BOARDS
English Tourism, Thames Tower, Black's Road, London W6 9EL. (01) 846 9000.

Scottish Tourist Board, 23 Ravelston Terrace, Edinburgh EH4 3EU. (031) 332 2433.

Wales Tourist Board, Brunel House, 2 Fitzalan Road, Cardiff CF2 1UY. (0222) 499909.

Northern Ireland Tourist Board, River House, 48 High Street, Belfast, BT1 2DS. (0232) 231221.

REGIONAL TOURIST BOARDS
There are 12 boards within England which publish detailed leaflets about their areas; full addresses can be obtained from English Tourism or any of the local tourist information centres. Similar boards or councils exist in Wales and Scotland.
Cumbria: Windermere (096 62) 4444.
Northumbria (covering Northumberland, Cleveland, Durham, Tyne & Wear): Newcastle (0632) 817744.
North West (covering Cheshire, Greater Manchester, Lancashire. Merseyside, the High peak district of Derbyshire): Bolton (0204) 591511.
Yorkshire & Humberside (covering Humberside, North, South and West Yorkshire): York (0904) 707961.
Heart of England (covering Gloucestershire, Shropshire, Herefordshire & Worcestershire, Staffordshire, Warwickshire, West Midlands): Worcester (0905) 29511.
East Midlands (covering Derbyshire, Leicestershire, Lincolnshire, Northamptonshire, Nottinghamshire): Lincoln (0522) 31521/2/3.
Thames & Chilterns (covering Oxfordshire, Berkshire, Bedfordshire, Buckinghamshire, Hertfordshire): Abingdon (0235) 22711.
East Anglia (covering Cambridgeshire, Essex, Norfolk and Suffolk): Hadleigh (0473) 822922.
London: (01) 846 9000.
West Country (covering Avon, Cornwall, Devon, Western Dorset, Somerset, Wiltshire, Isles of Scilly): Exeter (0392) 76351.
Southern (covering Hampshire, Eastern & Northern Dorset, Isle of Wight): Eastleigh (0703) 616027.
South East (covering Kent, Surrey, East and West Sussex): Tunbridge Wells (0892) 40766.
Isle of Man: Douglas (0624) 74323 (winter) or 74328/9 (summer).
Isle of Wight: Newport (0983) 524343.

WALES
North Wales: Colwyn Bay (0492) 31731.
Mid-Wales: Machynlleth (0654) 2653.
South Wales: Swansea (0792) 465204.

SCOTLAND
In Scotland, nine regional councils operate tourist departments and a network of 36 area tourist boards. These are too numerous to list here, so we recommend that you contact the Scottish Tourist Board (address above) which will be able to give you details of the area(s) in which you are interested.

LOCAL INFORMATION CENTRES
There are more than 700 officially recognized tourist information centres in the United Kingdom. Those located nearest to the 44 areas featured in this book have been given in the appropriate section. There are also specialist information centres run by organizations such as national parks, the Forestry Commission and, of course, the two National Trusts themselves.

INDEX

ACKNOWLEDGMENTS

EDITOR'S ACKNOWLEDGMENTS

The first and greatest debt of acknowledgment must be paid to the many people who work for the National Trusts who have found time to help us compile this book. There is no space to identify all the regional information officers, wardens and rangers who answered our questions and checked the text: we hope that, in accepting our thanks, they will forgive the inevitable anonymity.

I would also like to thank the very helpful staff of the Trusts' photographic libraries in London and Edinburgh. I am particularly grateful to the late *Robin Wright* of the National Trust's London headquarters, who was ever a constructive source of advice and encouragement, and also to *Nathalie Sfakianos* and *Lawrence Rich*. *Graeme Morison* and *Peter Reekie* of the National Trust for Scotland were similarly sympathetic and perceptive to the needs of the book. The Countryside Commission, Ordnance Survey and Ramblers' Association also helped to check points of detail. If any errors eluded their scrutiny the fault lies with the book's authors rather than its diligent consultants.

A book of this kind is essentially a team product, not only involving the contributors who joined me in trekking over the countryside and whose names are listed separately, but also the people who toiled over complex layouts, intricate copy-setting and time-consuming administration. As editor of the book I would therefore like to thank *Lisa Tai* for being an imaginative art editor who, unlike some of her profession, was willing to accommodate words as well as pictures; *Isobel Greenham* for invaluable secretarial assistance in the early stages; *Vivianne Croot* for punctilious yet subtle sub-editing; and, last but certainly not least, my two editors at Octopus Books, *Nicholas Bevan* and *Linda Seward*, who managed not only to retain an overall grasp of the entire project but also to read my handwriting.

To all of them, my thanks — and the hope that they, as well as you, the reader, will enjoy exploring the countryside celebrated in this book.

Derrik Mercer. London. June 1985

CONTRIBUTORS

Paul Banham
Jim Barber
Jane Coyle
Willie Elliot
Jim Gibson
Bill Hean
Andrew Jenkinson
Lea McNally
David Mardon
Gillian Mercer
Brian Le Messurier
William Murray
Colin Shelbourn
Jean Sutton
Roger Thomas
David Tollick
Stephen Warman
Alan Whitfield
David Wilson
Geoffrey Wright

MAIN ILLUSTRATIONS

Brian Sanders 12–13, 18–19, 20–21, 24–25, 26–27, 28–29, 32–33, 34–35, 40–41, 50–51, 56–57, 78–79, 80–81, 84–85, 102–103, 104–105, 106–107, 108–109, 110–111, 112–113, 114–115, 116–117, 124–125, 140–141, 142–143, 144–145, 146–147.
Liz Moyes 14–15, 16–17, 22–23, 36–37, 38–39, 42–43, 46–47, 48–49, 58–59, 60–61, 62–63, 100–101, 118–119, 126–127, 130–131, 138–139.
Kevin Dean 30–31, 44–45, 64–65, 66–67, 76–77, 92–93, 132–133, 134–135, 148–149.
Peter Barrett 68–69, 70–71, 72–73, 74–75, 82–83, 86–87.
Martin Knowlden 94–95, 96–97, 98–99.
Sandra Fernandez 128–129.
Polly Raynes 136–137.
Hanife Hassan 8, 52, 88, 120.

SMALL ILLUSTRATIONS

Michael McGuinness

CARTOGRAPHY

Eugene Fleury except pages 7, 151.
Maggie Colwell 7.
Russell Barnett 151.
Brian Turk (reference) 151.

BOOK DESIGN

Michael McGuinness

WILDLIFE CONSULTANT

Derek Hall

PHOTOGRAPHY

Michael Alexander 9 below; Geoffrey Berry 106; John Charity 115 above and centre; Robert Estall 90 below, 149 below; Exmoor National Park 19; John Freeman 54 above, 123 left; John Gascoigne 23; S.R. Greenwood 104; John Heseltine 91 above, 122 right, 123 below; Neil Holmes 33, 35, 101, 103, 131 right and left; Images 2–3, 8–9 above, 55 above left and below, 91 below left; Douglas Lee 96, 129; Marianne Majerus 65, 67 centre and below, 68, 70 left, 135 above and below; S.&O. Matthews 24–25; Rachel McKenzie 73, 75; Lea McNally 85 above and below; Derrik Mercer 95; Colin Molyneux 9 right, 27, 28 left and right, 31, 37, 38, 39, 55 above right, 56, 59, 61, 63 above and below, 98, 99, 132; The National Trust (Alan North 49 above, below and centre, 90 above) (John Parry 41) (Ann Robinson 153) (R. Westlake 93, 124) (J. Whitaker 147 below) (Derek Widdicombe 122 left) (Mike Williams 117); The National Trust Gwynedd (Dr. N. Caldwell 8–9 below); The National Trust of Scotland 76, 113; Northern Ireland Tourist Board 116, 118; Northumbria Tourist Board 40; The Photo Source 92; Alastair Scott 79, 80, 109, 112; Roger Scruton 25, 70 right, 145; Swift Picture Library (Geoff Dore 21) (Mike Reed 15, 16, 123 right, 127); Patrick Thurston © Drive Publications 1982, from *Discovering Britain* 13; Simon Warner 137 left, 138 right, 139; West Yorkshire Tourist Information Centre 138 left; Alan Whitfield 111; Harry Williams 8, 54 below, 91 below right; Mike Williams 44, 45, 140, 142; Geoffrey Wright 47, 137 right, 149 centre. Yorkshire and Humberside Tourist Board 147 centre.

REFERENCE BOOKS

A general book such as this one inevitably draws upon many more specialist volumes. The editor and publishers would like to acknowledge the following books which were consulted on points of detail in the preparation of either the text or illustration for *The National Trust: Exploring Unspoilt Britain and Northern Ireland.*

AA Book of British Birds (AA); *The AA Book of the Countryside* (AA); *Canals Revived* by Roger W. Squires (Moonraker); *The complete guide to British Wildlife* by Norman Arlott, Richard Fitter & Alastair Fitter (Collins); *English Landscapes* by W.G. Hoskins (BBC); *Geology and Scenery in England and Wales* by A.E. Trueman (Penguin); *Geology and Scenery in Ireland* by J.B. Whittow (Penguin); *Geology and Scenery in Scotland* by J.B. Whittow (Penguin); *A Guide to British Land-* *scape* by J.R.W. Cheatle (Collins); *A Guide to the Prehistoric and Roman Monuments* by Jacquetta Hawkes (Chatto & Windus); *Illustrated Guide to Britain's Coast* (AA); *Landscapes of Britain* by Roy Milward & Adrian Robinson (David & Charles); *Literary Landscapes* by David Daiches & John Flower (Paddington Press); *Long-distance footpath guides to: Somerset and North Devon* by Clive Gunnell, *Cornwall* by Edward C. Pyatt, *Pembrokeshire* by John H. Barrett, *Cleveland Way* by Alan Falconer, *Ridgeway* by Sean Jennett, *South Downs Way* by Sean Jennett (all HMSO); *Map Skills* and *Map Practice* by Brian Turk (University Tutorial Press); *The Making of the English Countryside* by W.G. Hoskins (Penguin); *The National Trust Atlas* (George Philip); *The National Trust Guide* by Robin Fedden (Cape); *The National Trust Guide to the Coast* by Tony Soper (Webb & Bower); *The National Trust for Scotland Guide* by Robin Prentice (Cape); *One Man's* *England* by W.G. Hoskins (BBC); *Physical Geography* by Richard H. Bryant (Heinemann); *Principles of Physical Geography* by F.J. Monkhouse (Hodder & Stoughton); *The Shell Guide to the British Coast* by Adrian Robinson & Roy Milward (David & Charles); *The Shell Guide to Reading the Landscape* by Richard Muir (Michael Joseph); *The Sunday Times Book of the Countryside* by Philip Clarke, Brian Jackman & Derrik Mercer (Macdonald); *The Sunday Times Book of 1000 Days Out* by Philip Clarke, Brian Jackman & Derrik Mercer (Macdonald/Futura); *Upland Britain* by Roy Milward & Adrian Robinson (David & Charles); *A Visitor's Guide to The Peak District* by Lindsay Porter (Moorland); and many other leaflets and local guide books published by the National Trusts, tourist boards, the Forestry Commission, Countryside Commission, national parks, nature conservancy organizations, country parks and local authorities.